AN IRON GIRL
IN A VELVET GLOVE

By the same author:

Biography
Queen Coal

Health
Positive Options for Antiphospholipid Syndrome (APS)
Talking About Lupus (with Graham Hughes)
Living with Hughes Syndrome

AN IRON GIRL
IN A VELVET GLOVE

THE LIFE OF
JOAN RHODES

TRIONA HOLDEN

First published 2021

The History Press
97 St George's Place, Cheltenham,
Gloucestershire, GL50 3QB
www.thehistorypress.co.uk

British Library Cataloguing in Publication Data.
A catalogue record for this book is available from the British Library.

ISBN 978 0 7509 9679 2

Typesetting and origination by The History Press
Printed and bound in Great Britain by TJ Books Limited, Padstow, Cornwall.

Trees for LYfe

For John Cash, who made this book possible.

CONTENTS

ACKNOWLEDGEMENTS

This book has been roughly two decades in gestation. Writing it was the original purpose of meeting my beloved Joan, but my own poor health delayed things horribly. In that time a large number of people have been instrumental in making it a reality, and I'd like to thank them all. In particular, John and Pam Cash, who have gently reminded me at suitable intervals that I said I was going to write 'the Book'. John's excellent research and writing on his aunt have helped me beyond measure. Pam has also been with me all the way through with words of encouragement and sense.

My agent, Donald Winchester, kindly put up with my babble about Joan and tracked down a suitable publisher. The History Press, in the shape of their commissioning editor Simon Wright, has always been wildly enthusiastic about the project and that really inspired me. It was the team at the BBC's *The Repair Shop* programme who, while filming in 2019, woke me up to the need to get on ASAP with making sure Joan's story was not buried.

I have to mention the British Newspaper Archive in glowing terms. It is a fabulous resource and enabled me to track down long-forgotten incidents, tucked away in the pages of local news publications. I have to thank my bestie, Annette Witheridge, for introducing me to the BNA and for her endless encouragement and reassurance.

None of this would have come to pass if it wasn't for my 'A' team, namely my daughters, Tallulah and Aurora, who made this sometimes-tortuous journey with me. Their advice and patience were vital parts of the process.

Last but not least I want to thank my husband, Prof. Ian Palmer. He was the one who first introduced Joan and me, and he has been a constant support as I have struggled with the ups and downs of writing about someone so important to me. Love you Prof.

1

STRONG STUFF

This book begins with a love story. Not the boy-meets-girl kind, but an instinctive platonic love that can exist despite age differences between two people. As is so often the way with these important life events, it seemed to come out of the blue. My husband – who was working as a locum GP in Hampstead at the time – had been roped in to visit an old lady who just wanted someone to listen to her tales. I happened to be researching a book on what I regarded as 'real women', rather than the maddening chick-lit variety who infested the media. I'd been forced out of my job as a BBC correspondent and presenter due to the horribly debilitating autoimmune condition lupus, so I had been writing books instead. He realised that Joan was exactly the kind of woman I was looking for and asked her if she would be happy to talk to me. That was how I found myself at Joan Rhodes's door on a wet autumn day in 2003.

I don't really know what I was expecting as I rang the bell to the scruffy-looking garden flat in Belsize Park, north London. I was meeting a woman in her early eighties who'd once been internationally famous for her beauty and physical strength, but I knew little else other than my husband's keenness for us to come together. I should have spotted that I was in for a rollercoaster of a ride by the clues that inhabited the dingy area around her door. The rather abrupt handwritten note by the bellpush instructed me to be

The author and Joan, 2003.

patient: 'please wait it takes me time to answer the door.' Discarded giant stretcher bars, used for artist's canvases, and broken bits of once-functional detritus littered the alleyway that led to the garden.

Certainly nothing told me I was about to encounter someone who would soon become so significant to me personally, a woman I would quickly come to love and adore. Ringing that bell was a life-changing moment. Once I entered that flat, a part of me never left.

I could hear huffing and puffing coming from the other side of the door, the odd grumble, a faint complaint of pain and a gripe of discomfort. Then the commanding call for me to hang on: 'I'm coming.'

When the door eventually opened, after another interval which was filled with the jiggling of bolts, I was confronted with a bulky figure draped in a riotously colourful ensemble that would not have been out of place in the Caribbean. The visual noise was so great that it jumped out of the darkness from the depths of this intriguing home.

Two big blue eyes gave me the once-over. They were accentuated by expertly pencilled eyebrows. Joan was larger than life, both in appearance and behaviour. Her mid-length curly hair was white, but the ghost of heyday blonde still lingered. My 5ft 0in and 9st were dwarfed by her 5ft 7in and 15st. With years of practice, she hid the extra weight well, sparkling in all her finery. The showy fabric was shaped like a kaftan, held together with a huge blue paste brooch in the shape of a butterfly. It was only later that I noticed there were holes where some of the fake stones once sat. This sense of faded theatrical grandeur permeated every aspect of Joan's life.

She wasn't like any old lady I had ever met. She had the vibrancy of youth, barely contained in an ageing body. You know how you can see a much older woman and think, 'Gosh, she must have been beautiful when she was young'? Well, Joan was still beautiful. Her facial skin belied her age. Later she told me it was because she had slathered her body and face with olive oil straight out of the cooking bottle all her life. The walking frame that she clung to didn't diminish her; if anything, she used it like a podium from which to hold forth. Age had certainly not withered Joan. She had adjusted and learnt how to make it work for her.

I had managed to arrange this interview after writing a formal letter to Joan, explaining I was an ex-BBC news presenter and correspondent who wanted to write about her. An invite to lunch came by return of post. As I was ushered in, I was showered with a warm flood of welcomes and fripperies. I followed her into the depths of 37A Belsize Park Gardens and noticed how slowly she shuffled along, each step an act of willpower. She cursed her legs but laughed off the discomfort. Once again, I would come to learn that laughing in the face of pain and misery was her way of dealing with it, a lifelong trademark.

I want to say that the flat was an Aladdin's cave, or like an old curiosity shop, but neither description is adequate for the crazy jumble of oddities and dusty treasures that met my eyes. There were just too many objects to see them all at once. It was a kind of theatrical mayhem, a storyboard of a life in showbusiness. I noticed that the prized objects weren't crammed in randomly; they all had been strategically placed, having a home of their own – and from that setting none of them strayed in the coming years.

The entrance hall would have been gloomy if it weren't for the plethora of decorations. Secret spaces were guarded by floor-to-ceiling turquoise velvet curtains that were adorned with giant red swags and bows. There were lots of pots full of whatnots, plastic flowers that were disintegrating in a way that would please environmentalists and a half-mannequin decked out in a sequined basque and a straw hat with feathers sitting where a head should have been. I was glad we made slow progress as it gave me time to take it all in.

It was the same story in the living room, which would have been spacious if it hadn't been so heavily populated with fascinating memorabilia. The walls were crowded with artworks from every 'ism' you could imagine, as well as a few you couldn't because they didn't exist yet. Framed pictures of stars from yesteryear posing with Joan jostled for position on the side tables. On one long wall there were rows of old vinyl albums in their bright artistic covers sitting on tiny wooden shelves, with thousands of books on larger shelves below. It struck me that the overall effect was that of a stage set, with me as the audience, about to witness a performance about the life of a woman who had been a celebrity of her day and was still someone to be reckoned with.

All the while Joan was chattering away, giving me the guided tour of her shadow-world. I quickly became overwhelmed by the task of trying to understand this interior landscape. Acceptance was my only choice.

We sat near the French windows, facing each other across a reproduction refectory table, one end of which was obscured by grubby stacks of papers, old photographs and ancient newspaper cuttings. She had cleared a space at the other end and carefully set the scene for our lunch. There were unpleasantly crispy cotton napkins and the 'best' china cups for tea. I was left in no doubt that I was being honoured. Despite her mobility problems, Joan had painstakingly put together an open smoked salmon sandwich for each of us, decorated with lettuce and cucumber. The faux luxury was completely appropriate for this occasion. I was in my element.

Looking back, I think we were both a bit nervous. We were on our best behaviour. Me, the journalist-cum-author, and Joan, acting the cautiously willing performer preparing to tell all. As it turned out, Joan distrusted reporters; like most celebrities, she had been badly mistreated and misquoted by them over the years. She was also surprisingly shy, in her own way. Letting a stranger, an investigative journalist no less, into her precious home must have taken some courage. I was at pains to put her at her ease. I was not from the red-top tabloids and had no intention of forcing skeletons from cupboards. I was proud to have been a BBC girl for twenty years, someone who had never done the 'dirty vicar' tales. For my book, which would not, strictly speaking, be a feminist treatise but would celebrate certain forgotten women, I wanted to get to know the essence of her, her true self. I got rather more than I bargained for.

Joan had a remarkable life story that spanned almost the whole of the twentieth century. It placed her at the heart of historically significant people and places. I had thought of including her as one of a number of women in my book, but – as she warmed to telling her tales – I realised her life could not be squeezed into a chapter or two. Here was a woman who deserved to be celebrated as an icon of the female struggles of the last eighty years. She was a rebel who had subverted the male status quo of the world she inhabited. Encapsulated in this mercurial woman was a synopsis of how history had treated women and clues on how to cheat the system successfully. As the encounter progressed, we both began to relax and Joan was happily occupying centre stage, her favourite place. I made the perfect onlooker, smiling and reacting at the correct moments of the performance.

Things had gone so well that after we finished our posh luncheon, she began singing songs to me such as 'My Old Man's a Dustman' and 'The Lambeth Walk'. This was accompanied by classic theatrical movements involving arms, hands and face. (Her disobedient legs were no longer part of the act.) Her ebullience was infectious. I found myself laughing and clapping like some starstruck stalker at a stage door. I think that was when I fell in love. When Joan put on the charm, she was irresistible.

Joan regaled me with tales about some of the celebrities I had grown up knowing only from afar. She often performed with Bob Hope but didn't find him at all funny, and she wasn't that impressed by Peter Sellers when she was in one of the *Pink Panther* films. She said in real life he was 'a bit of a grump'. Most exciting were the stories about the movie star Marlene Dietrich, whom she met when they shared a stage in Amsterdam. Joan utterly worshipped her, and I think the attraction was mutual, as I'll explain later in this book. They became great friends and were in touch until Marlene died.

I had my reporter's notebook out and tried to keep up, but my shorthand was no match for the speed of her delivery or her ability to distract me. I had intended to record the interview but in all the excitement I had forgotten to get the little machine out. Maybe it was better that way, as things were not going to plan.

My journalistic instincts were buzzing but so was my heart. How could I write about this fabulous woman when it was obvious that she should be the one to put pen to paper? I knew then that I could not write a book about Joan at that time. It was her story; I felt I had no right to appropriate it.

When I eventually managed to put a more serious tone into the conversation and suggest she wrote her autobiography, her face lit up. Of course, she was planning to do just that. In fact, she had been toiling away at the project for years. Throughout her life, colleagues and fans had entreated her to share her experiences with the reading public and, in answer to the encouragement, she had sporadically jotted down great tracts of her reminiscences.

She motioned grandly to the piles of papers that occupied the nether end of the table, which she said were the bones of her book. With a sparkle in her eyes, she reached for the handwritten bundle on top of the nearest stack and asked if I wanted her to read some of it to me. In this theatrical atmosphere I couldn't help but wonder if the stage props had been set out deliberately in this way, and that I had neatly taken on my role as her biggest fan. I didn't mind – I was glad to listen. It was only polite after she had gone to so much trouble over lunch; but I was also captivated by what she had to say.

An hour or so later, she stopped for breath. I offered to make more tea and told my watch to go to hell. As I suspected, the papers were full of strong material, insightful anecdotes and glimpses of history. But she wasn't a writer; the manuscript required a lot of editing. Before I could stuff my fist in my mouth, I had volunteered to help with the project. It transpired that her only living relative, her nephew John Cash, was already greatly assisting with her endeavours. I had been cast as the besotted professional on hand to give a second opinion and possibly assist in finding a publisher.

Joan did go on to write her autobiography, which was entitled *Coming on Strong*. Her biggest help came from John, although I did chip in with suggestions here and there. It was an interesting collection of stories but the whole process from pen to publication was a complete nightmare. Once again, I'll explain in more detail later in this book. Suffice to say for now that Joan paid more than £8,000 for a run of 2,000 copies to be printed in 2007. The book sold out, but she never received a penny from the venture as the publishers went to the wall. Joan was livid. I had never seen her usually well-controlled anger before, but it burst out of her because she felt badly cheated.

When I eventually dragged myself away from 37A, after three or more hours, I was well and truly hooked. This was a seismic shift in my life. I left her home humming 'The Lambeth Walk', my mind alive with images of dancing movie stars. My world was already richer. By the time I got home, she was on the phone telling me how delighted she was with our encounter and wondering when we could do it again. This was on a Monday. I 'popped in' for tea and a chat on the following Wednesday, and so began my existence as one of Joan's confidantes.

I would be close friends with Joan for the next seven years, visiting two or three times a week, steering her through the good and bad of the NHS, helping her in and out of hospital when she became unwell. I loved her. It was not a chore – it was a pleasure to be there and to make this last passage of her life as smooth as possible.

Hers was a colourful world full of dazzling people and, through knowing Joan, I have come to understand how a woman could take on all comers and survive, no matter how hard life had been to her. Men were often threatened by her strength. After all, a woman with such a feminine figure was not supposed to be able to do what she did. Doubters plagued her all her life, verbally attacking her and trying to match what she could do. No man, or woman, ever beat her. She always won a challenge of strength. When I asked where the power came from, she told me what she did was real and driven by a deep-seated inner rage at her hugely dysfunctional early years.

You are no doubt wondering how you come to be reading the very book I said I wasn't going to write. Well, it's quite simple really. Ten years after her death I found myself appearing on camera for the first time in an age, but on this occasion it was on Joan's behalf. I was simply a part of the broader picture. In 2019, I had asked the BBC programme *The Repair Shop* if they could help rescue one of Joan's stage costumes I had inherited. It was a sexy leotard with a detachable floor-length split skirt. A similar outfit from Joan's wardrobe lives at the Victoria and Albert Museum in London and is no doubt in much better condition. Originally, my prized version would have been covered in hand-stitched metal sequins in different shades of green, but the years had taken their toll. Joan told me how she would perform at numerous theatres in one evening in London, meaning she had to unceremoniously chuck her stage outfit into a bag as she dashed from venue to venue. I suspect she had worn this costume thousands of times. No wonder it was looking rather sad; there were large bald patches and evidence of a hundred Joan-style repairs. Even the clasp on the skirt wasn't original – she had adapted a pair of paste diamante earrings to do the job. Every time I lifted the garment, more sequins wafted to the floor, leaving a sparkling trail and yet more bald patches. The crotch had been mutilated for some reason, completely cut across. Large areas of sequined fabric had faded to a grim grey and the hem was badly worn.

The programme team said they would take on the challenge. The producer loved Joan's story. And thanks to the tireless efforts of Sara Dennis, an expert with textiles, I joined the ranks of previous participants who struggled to hold back the tears when their rejuvenated, beloved object was returned.

It was during the filming at the ancient barn in West Sussex that I realised I had some unfinished business to tackle. The production crew, who were mostly aged between 20 and 30, were utterly fascinated by Joan. To my surprise, these trendy millennials seemed to have an affinity with her and, as we took various breaks in filming, they would come up and ask me more about this cool woman they'd never heard of. They were puzzled about why she had been forgotten, written out of history, or muted like so many other women. It was Sara's daughter who ultimately triggered this revisited project; she had told her mum she wanted to read the biography about Joan and was staggered to hear there wasn't one. This was a view echoed by everyone I encountered during the filming sessions. I had a lightbulb moment and realised that the time had come to bring Joan back from the dead to take her rightful place in history. Her life story demanded to be told and I was the obvious person to do it. After all, that was how I entered her world in the first place all those years ago.

So began this labour of love. I was fortunate, because thanks to the kindness of Joan's nephew John, who runs her estate, I had access to extensive archive material, her own words in her autobiography, and the mountain of research and writing he had diligently put into his own manuscript.

2

ABANDONED BABES

Young Queen Elizabeth was amused to see her husband bested by a woman in a sparkly leotard. The Duke of Edinburgh was one of the volunteers on stage for an unusual act, which involved a challenge by a beautiful artiste to match her ability to bend steel bars and six-inch nails. Being a well-built man, he would have expected to emulate any shows of strength, especially those performed by a mere woman. But try as he might, he was defeated – much to the delight of his wife and the large audience.

The occasion was the annual Grand Christmas Ball for the Royal Household at Windsor Castle. The date: 19 December 1958. Organised by the castle's social club, it was a seasonal tradition that the queen and Prince Philip would join their staff, which included off-duty footmen, housemaids, chauffeurs, cooks, officials and so on, for an evening of entertainment and dancing.

Joan Rhodes was the strongwoman in question. Built like a svelte movie star, she was a blonde bombshell capable of remarkable feats of strength that left audiences gasping in admiration. At the time, she was well known and was often described in the press as the strongest woman in the world. Joan would have been wearing one of her specially made, figure-hugging costumes that complimented her long legs and curves. There was no visible clue to the physical power she could muster.

The event was held in the opulent Waterloo Chamber, the busiest and largest room in the castle. It must have been daunting for Joan; not only was this her first appearance before the royal couple, but she was the only woman on the carefully selected bill. She would be sharing the royal stage with some of the funniest men alive, including Arthur Askey, Flanagan and Allen, and Dick Emery. But then again, Joan was good at rising to impossible odds, something reflected in her turbulent life story.

For her, appearing by command at the castle was one of her most significant achievements, a royal seal of approval. She was anxious that her performance should go smoothly but was troubled because she had no experience at such a high social level. She knew there was a protocol but hadn't a clue as to what it precisely was. As ever, she ended up busking it, which worked to a large extent although there was one sticky moment when, as a joke, she managed to cast an aspersion on Prince Philip's sexuality.

But that story can wait; we'll come back to the Christmas concert later. To understand the enormous significance of Joan's appearance at Windsor Castle, it's vital that you learn more about the remarkable journey she endured to get there.

Joan was a great one for telling stories. She was never happier than when she had everyone's attention. A receptive audience was her idea of heaven. She didn't mind talking about her painfully humble beginnings and it was clear that her experiences as a small child continued to have an impact on her throughout her long life. I remember how she would laugh at her hardships in a way that was her trademark. If Joan was in pain, emotionally or physically, her immediate reaction was to laugh. She laughed a lot in her 89 years.

Life was never going to be straightforward for Joan. The twists and turns it took are enough to make you dizzy; certainly, some of the events that dominated her development would have crushed a lesser soul.

Things looked grim right from the start. Far from being born with a silver spoon in her mouth, baby Joan found herself in a world of conflict and contradictions. It was 13 April 1921. All we know about her arrival was that her mother often complained about what a difficult birth it had been and that it took place in Lewisham Workhouse Infirmary. Just the name 'workhouse' is enough to bring to mind the horrors of the Victorian era, when these shelters for the destitute were known for the appalling conditions their inhabitants were forced to endure. The site in Lewisham was in the process of becoming a fully-fledged hospital, but there were still workhouse occupants.

Joan's immediate family, the Taylors, were deeply dysfunctional. These days it is likely the children would have been put on an at-risk register or taken into care. These were hard times for many, just after the First World War in the years running up to the Great Depression. The Taylors were poor and led a hand-to-mouth existence, frequently moving from home to home, sometimes to evade creditors to whom they owed rent.

It's likely that the war set in motion a train of events that would lead to an appalling family crisis when Joan was only 3 years old. Her father, Thomas Alfred Taylor, began his working life as a telephone wireman for Siemens Brothers. When war broke out in 1914, he was keen to share with his contemporaries what was seen as the great adventure of fighting for his country. His eagerness led him to lie about his age so he could join up. Though he was some way short of his 18th birthday, he became a soldier with the 1st Surrey Rifles.

Nothing could have prepared him for the horrors he witnessed over the next few years. He got his wish to see action, but he must have regretted that wish a thousand times when he found himself in the thick of bloody combat. According to military records, he was at several important engagements. His introduction to war was at the Battle of Loos on the Western Front in 1915. It was the first time that the British had used poison gas and it was the first mass battle for many new army units. It didn't go well for the British, who had twice the number of casualties as the Germans. Thomas Taylor got through it in one piece and went on to be involved in the Battle of Vimy Ridge. Once again, his luck held and he was subsequently promoted to sergeant. Two days later, he was thrust again into a world of bloodshed and slaughter, this time at the notorious Battle of the Somme. Almost 60,000 British troops were killed, injured or taken prisoner on the first day.

Tommy must have been a brave man to carry on, and carry on he did. The 1st Surreys were sent to rout the Germans from a 400-yard stretch of trench held between the isolated remnants of two brigades. The Surreys succeeded but at a terrible cost – 19 officers and 550 men went into the attack; an hour later, only 2 officers and 60 men survived. One of these was Sergeant T.A. Taylor.

There is no record of what shape Tommy was in after the Somme, but it's highly likely that his mental health was damaged because of all he witnessed. He was only 20 years old and had little previous life experience; to see such carnage, and to be a target of the enemy, must have been as terrifying as it gets. It's clear something was horribly wrong as he was discharged five months after the fighting on the Somme, described as permanently unfit. He had no physical injuries that we know of. In those days, soldiers with psychological injuries were said to be suffering from shell shock. Today the diagnosis would be post-traumatic stress disorder (PTSD). It is a reaction to trauma and can alter someone's personality, making them prone to flashbacks and high anxiety, which, in turn, can lead to angry outbursts, irritability and the misuse of alcohol and drugs.

He returned to his family in Lewisham, who were confronted with a very different Tommy to the one who had jumped headfirst into war. He did get on with life, though, despite what he had been through. He had an army pension, but it wasn't much, so at the end of 1918 he found a job as an aircraft examiner. He had also met 18-year-old Winifred Lowe, who was to become Joan's mum.

They couldn't have known each other long before Winifred became pregnant. A wedding was quickly organised at the Lewisham Register Office. I suspect Winifred's father, Herbert

Lowe, did not consent or even know that his only daughter was about to tie the knot as he appears on the register as 'deceased' – despite being very much alive and kicking. Already shrouded in deception, it was not to be a marriage made in heaven. Although Winifred was a strong character, it is likely that such a young woman would not have had the experience necessary to deal with such an unpredictable and traumatised man.

In the brief time the couple were together, they had four children – but Tommy ducked in and out of family life. He was around for the birth of their first child, Peggy, but then disappeared. He must have returned sometime within the next year as, twenty months later, baby number two, Joan, was born. It appears Tommy was set in a behavioural pattern. At only 21, Winifred was alone with a 2-year-old toddler and a baby of 7 months, and was pregnant with a third child, Elizabeth, who was later known as 'Blackie' for her luxuriant mane. With a meagre income, it's not hard to imagine how torrid Winifred's life must have been. It was obvious that something had to give. So, when the fourth baby, Peter, arrived, the situation reached crisis point.

In May 1924, before Tommy could do his disappearing act, Winifred confronted him and said that this time she was the one who was leaving. Piecing together the little evidence that exists, it appears that Winifred walked out, leaving the children (who were then aged 4, 3, 2, and 6 weeks) with her husband. Tommy would have panicked; he may have even convinced himself that Winifred would soon return. Whatever his thoughts, Tommy also walked out of their tiny, rented house in Catford, south London. He locked the door behind him and fled, abandoning his four helpless offspring.

Joan said that they were trapped in the house for a couple of days; but as she was only 3, it is hard to know what actually happened. In those days, much more than today, neighbours took a lively minute-by-minute interest in what was going on next door. I suspect the curtain twitchers would have spotted something was amiss in a matter of hours. It's a good job they did. The four abandoned children were in grave danger. Maybe the whole thing seemed like a game to the older ones, but the scene would have quickly degenerated as the siblings realised their parents weren't coming back. Peggy would have been able to comprehend a bit more of what had happened. Joan had her own version of events, which had no doubt been embroidered with repeated telling over eighty years. She told me that she remembered collecting rainwater for the baby. In a way, the fine detail was irrelevant to her. What mattered was that this supreme act of parental betrayal was to haunt her for the rest of her life. She said the anger she felt was what was behind her considerable strength and her later success in life. The science behind this seems sketchy at best, but she firmly believed it to be the case.

The four incarcerated Taylor children would have made quite a racket, certainly sufficient enough to alert the neighbours in this terrace of cheap houses. Eventually the alarm was raised and the police came. They had to break down the door to rescue the children. They found a scene of chaos. Joan had a cut on her head, perhaps because of a fall, and the newborn must have been giving voice to his urgent need for food and fluids. The children were taken to the nearby Lewisham Workhouse Infirmary. The eldest, Peggy, would have been old enough to give the family name and possibly the names of relatives. Joan remembered having a warm nightdress on and her head being bandaged at the hospital. She recalled how the wound itched where the hair around it had been cut and Joan said the only time the nurses were hard on her was when they slapped her hand as she tried to scratch it. Other than that, she enjoyed all the attention, a trait that would serve her well in her future in the limelight.

Joan was never one to let a crisis get her down, even at the age of 3. The workhouse team noticed that she was always laughing, and they nicknamed her after a popular character at the time, Little Audrey, who was known for her laughter in the face of adversity. This must have appealed to the toddler, who was already showing distinct signs of being a determined character. When her paternal grandmother – who was mortified that a relative of hers could be in a workhouse – came to claim her, Joan said she was told to stand on a table. Her grandmother said 'Yes, that's Joan,' but the strong-willed child, who was having a great time and wanted to stay, piped up 'No, I'm Audrey,' and refused to co-operate with the adults. Did her Grandma Ada realise this was a portent of difficulties to come?

The children were split up. Peggy went to her maternal grand-parents; Joan and Blackie to their father's parents; and baby Peter was put up for adoption. Joan and Blackie found themselves in a comfortable house called The Grange in Greenwich. Joan said she never heard much about her two other siblings at the time. She remembered repeatedly hearing she had inherited her mother's 'bad blood'. This was quite a curse for such a tiny tot, and they were words that devastated Joan. I could tell how hurt she had been when she spoke of them to me, so many decades later, as her

Joan aged about 3.

face would lose its joyous glow. It was a pain she carried throughout her life.

This time Tommy disappeared for good. As far as we know,
he never tried to find out what happened to his children. More
recent research by Joan's nephew revealed that Tommy had another
family, including a son, which may explain why he kept disappearing. Winifred, on the other hand, did show up after a few years to
reclaim her eldest, Peggy, and take her to family in Manchester.
Winifred reappeared in Joan's story much later, after her daughter
rose to fame.

Joan was a boisterous child, especially in comparison to her
younger sister, Blackie, who was much more amenable and knew
how to get what she wanted. Attempts were made to rein Joan in.
At one point the girls were sent to a convent school; but even the
strict nuns were defeated by Joan's powerful nature. She was fond
of telling the story about waking up screaming in the Catholic
boarding school because she thought there was a bear in her bed.
She must have lashed out, but in fact it was two poor nuns check-
ing she was asleep. On another occasion, she tugged off one of
the nun's veils to see if she was bald. It was all too much for the
convent, and both girls were expelled.

In the early 1930s, the family moved out of The Grange to a
smaller house, and the grandparents decided they couldn't deal
with both girls any longer. According to Joan, they decided to keep
the relatively well-behaved Blackie and hand 11-year-old Joan
over to her Aunt Lily. Joan was later told the move was to help
Lily, who had just lost her own newborn son. By this time, the
household must have been only too aware of how feisty Joan was,
so how they settled on such a crazy solution to Aunt Lily's woes
is hard to understand. Perhaps Joan's grandparents were at their
wits' end.

As might be expected, it didn't go well. Lily ran a public house
near Smithfield meat market, right in the centre of London, with
her husband, Wally Alcock. The pair met on a cruise while Lily
was mourning the death of her first husband. Wally was the wine

waiter. The pub, the Red Cow in King Street, was owned by the Courage Brewery Company; it was demolished after closing in 1938, but in its glory days it had an air of faux grandeur that set it apart.

Lily was a house-proud woman. The pub opened very early in the morning to cater for the men and women of the meat trade who had been working since the wee hours. Places like the Red Cow were often crowded: hefting around fattened carcasses built up quite a thirst and hunger. It should have been a better fit for a strapping young lass like Joan than her previous home. The pub had generous private accommodation; Joan even had her own sitting room. But trouble was in the air from the moment she arrived.

On the first day, Aunt Lily put her niece in the spotless sitting room at the back of the pub and left her there, presumably to sort out the room upstairs. Joan recalled how she was fascinated by some green and pink satin cushions and began throwing one into the air and punching it. Inevitably, the cushion burst, and Aunt Lily returned to find her precious room shrouded in feathers. Joan had earned her first smack, but the little terror simply laughed.

The family had a comfortable lifestyle for the time. It seems they had all the mod cons, including an indoor bathroom, a radio, a telephone and even a maid. Not bad for the dark days of the early 1930s. They were a family with middle-class aspirations, and so Joan was taught good table manners and how to speak properly. These were skills that would come in handy in later life.

Joan recalled that, despite the food shortages of the time, they always had plenty of meat on the table. She put this partly down to the pub's proximity to Smithfield and the fact that her Uncle Wally opened his doors so early. But she also accredited some of the good fortune to the fact that Aunt Lily was an attractive woman, much admired by the men. Joan learnt early on that, in her world, good looks were a means to an end.

One of Joan's abiding memories was watching the workers at Smithfield, particularly those known as bummarees (now called meat porters). These men were dressed in long, white rubber overalls that reached virtually to the ground and were often drenched in animal blood. They carried pig and cow carcasses, moving meat from one part of the large market to another. Other men sorted the chickens. Joan said she would watch them take the live birds, press on their chests and then throw their carcasses into a crate, dead. Although Joan loved the bustle, she felt sick at the smell of sawdust, blood and sweat. She said it put her off eating chicken for many years. Odd to think that these macabre scenes occurred in what was, to all intents and purposes, her front garden. It was a strange playground for a little girl.

Joan often wondered if her high consumption of red meat early on in life contributed to her strength. She was always a strong girl, even at the tender age of 11. One of her chores in the pub was to shift barrels of ale known as firkins, and even then she could lift one by herself, which was quite a feat when you consider a firkin is the equivalent of 86 pints of beer, nearly 8st in weight.

Some aspects of living at the Red Cow gave Joan great pleasure, in particular its location right in the midst of the fascinating streets of London. It appears that Aunt Lily gave her a surprising amount of freedom to explore. Joan loved nothing more than going walkabout.

The centre of the city was serviced by trams in those days, and she was allowed to travel on them down to the Embankment, where she often came across achingly sad scenes. It was the time of the Great Depression, a crippling downturn in the economies of the industrialised nations which followed the Wall Street Crash in 1929. In the UK, the impact of this economic disaster was most felt in the industrialised and mining areas of the north of England, where unemployment was as high as 70 per cent. Desperate men – many of whom were still recovering from their time in the war – made their way to London in the hope of getting a job, only to find themselves sleeping rough on streets that were paved with poverty.

Joan was under strict instructions not to speak to strange men who, in the words of snobby Aunt Lily, were nothing but 'dirty tramps'. Of course, this edict was ignored. Joan made a beeline for areas where men gathered and she would sit and listen to their tales of woe. Moved by their stories, she pinched food, such as cheese and ham, for them from the pub kitchen. When Aunt Lily noticed food was disappearing, she blamed the poor maid. Joan didn't see fit to put the record straight.

Although Joan's physical requirements were amply met during her time at the Red Cow, the same cannot be said about her emotional needs. I suspect being abandoned by her parents and then rejected by her grandparents taught her not to trust others, especially family. Aunt Lily appears to have tried her best to be a substitute mother, but from what Joan said, there was little love between them. In the three years she lived at the pub, Joan learnt to be self-sufficient. She said she had no friends and was quite happy on her own. She learnt about the city of her birth and felt so at home there that she was never frightened by what might be lurking in the shadows. She visited her grandparents at the weekends; Aunt Lily brought them bundles of meat and received home-grown produce in return. Joan enjoyed being reunited with her younger sister, Blackie, but the relationship certainly had its glitches.

Blackie was in a dance class run by their Aunt Violet and had been chosen to perform in the Christmas pantomime. She had a flashy red and white gingham dress and red shoes. When Joan saw them, she desperately wanted to appear in the show as well, but her Auntie Vi told her that she couldn't because she was 'too big and ugly'. This cruel phrase had a huge impact on her. A few days later, Blackie's costume was found ripped to pieces in a bin alongside the lovely shoes. The show did not go on for either girl: Joan saw to that.

Wicked jealousies aside, the important point about this incident was the way Joan handled her rejection. It stuck in her mind for the rest of her life. I don't think she ever got over being called 'big and ugly', even when she was seen by her contemporaries as not just pretty, but beautiful. Over the years I knew her she would repeat the phrase, and she attributed it to both Auntie Vi and Aunt Lily. The damage those three words did to Joan is difficult to quantify, but I suspect it is the reason that – despite her huge success in later life – she could never quite feel the truth of her beauty. Those words acted like a barrier. When she looked in the mirror she saw 'big and ugly', not elegant and stunning. Perhaps that phrase accounted for her shyness in later life. She wouldn't let most people in as they might see behind the painted façade. It is a tribute to her sheer determination that, despite being plagued by these self-doubts, she carved out an amazing career as a glamorous performer. It must have taken a great deal of courage to repeatedly appear before strangers. Like many of us, she had two personas, the public and the private.

Joan lived at the Red Cow for three years, from the age of 11 to 14. In that time, she became more conversant with London, a very different city to the one we know today. Keen to get a clearer picture of what the capital was like in those interwar years, I would often quiz Joan on the subject. Thankfully, she had a good recall for that period of her life. Her all-pervading memory was one of poverty. She felt great sympathy for the destitute men and, as we have seen, she tried her best to ameliorate their starvation, but she was only a little girl. Joan recalled the hunger marches of the 1920s, when men in the worst-hit areas of the country gathered in small groups and came to London to appeal to the government for help. She would have been aware of the most famous of these protests, the Jarrow March from Tyneside in 1936.

At Smithfield market she remembered Christmas meat auctions, where traders would sell off excess produce on Christmas Eve at huge reductions. It was one way the poorer members of the community could afford to put meat on the table for the special day. But there was no poverty for the residents of the Red Cow; Aunt Lily and Uncle Wally were kept well supplied with whatever meat they desired, including chickens and even turkeys. The payment for such favours was being able to flirt with the landlady and the offer of free pints of Courage Ale from the landlord.

Down through the decades Joan carried with her visceral memories of the scents and sounds of her birthplace that were forever rooted in her mind:

> The smells of the City were strong: beer from the breweries and pubs and the aroma of newly baked bread (no cut or wrapped loaves). On the streets there were little huts with delicious things being fried, and of course chestnut sellers. The Thames also had its own special smell, as had Billingsgate Fish Market. Covent Garden was then a fruit and vegetable market – another unique smell with 'gone off' fruit and veg, but such a friendly place. Another smell was that of the dray horses which were used for delivery or carting of coal, meat, goods from the railway stations. The horses would be left standing by the pavement with nose-bags full of feed nearly all day and the smell of horse manure was very strong on my way home from school. The sounds of the plod of their feet as they pulled their carts could be heard everywhere.

With many workers taking home meagre wages, people had to make their pennies go as far as possible and the retail world adapted to deal with this tight situation. On the high street, there was dear old Woolworths, or Woolies as it was fondly known. It sold a wide variety of goods for under sixpence. Marks and Spencer was a little more expensive and Joan said it was considered a great treat to go shopping there. M&S has clearly hung onto its cachet for being finer than the rest.

With Joan's love of roaming the city, she would buy an all-day ticket on the trams for a shilling (12*d*) and spend hours absorbed in gazing at her home turf as the tram trundled from street to street. She financed these trips by pinching silver threepenny pieces from a big jar on the mantlepiece in the pub. Joan's exploration of London was part of the fabric of her childhood and, as she acknowledged herself, she was drawn to the idea of being a performer very early on. It's almost as though she served an early

apprenticeship in the art of street performing by repeatedly witnessing what they would do and understanding how to persuade
punters to part with their pennies.

Petticoat Lane Market was a favourite spot of hers after she was
taken there by the family's Welsh maid, Nancy. Joan loved to watch
the stallholders and listen to their patter. One was a man selling
a product he called Vosverine. It came in a bottle and was supposed to keep you well while also making you as strong as a lion.
A large crowd of men would gather around the stall and hang on
every word barked out by the trader. He would select a young man
from the audience, hand him a coiled steel spring and ask him to
straighten it. Of course, the chosen punter failed miserably. Then,
with great showmanship, the seller would get the man to take a
large swig of his potion, and then – after a few minutes and lots of
banter – hey presto! It was a miracle. The man managed to pull the
spring straight with virtually no effort. This piece of salesmanship
prompted other men to clamour for a bottle of the magic elixir.
It was a performance that Joan viewed many times, and it didn't
take long for her to spot that the punter chosen out of the crowd
was always the same person. Her observations made her aware of
how gullible the public could be, and how easy it was to part a
fool from their funds, although she didn't approve of such tricks.
Instead, she held onto the belief that street entertainment could be
honest and lucrative.

Joan spent those three years living in the pub discovering the
joys and horrors of inner London. She developed a love of the
people she encountered on a daily basis, in particular the immigrant communities. Her inquiring mind liked nothing better than
seeing how the rest of the world lived. This would stand her in
good stead for her extensive travels in later life. One of the things
she adored about Petticoat Lane was its multicultural nature: the
area was home to large numbers of Jewish immigrants in the 1930s.

It's not surprising, then, that another favourite spot was the area
known as Little Italy in Clerkenwell. These days the large Italian
community, with its shops and distinctive character, has mostly

gone. Decades of slum clearances have made way for expensive real estate, pushing the immigrant communities out of the centre of the city. But Joan recalled the area in the 1930s, when it was a buzzing hive of different sights and sounds. The smell of roasting garlic and fresh lemon would hang in the air. Little Italy was regarded by the aspiring white middle classes as a dangerous place with its slums, criminals and protection rackets. Many of the shops sold foods imported from Italy, which were new to England. The local inhabitants were happy to welcome this young girl. Perhaps they sensed that she was like themselves, a displaced soul.

Aunt Lily would probably have hit the roof if she knew that her niece was visiting such a rundown area. Lily was a snob, but her niece clearly wasn't. Joan felt at home on the busy, smelly streets, often venturing there unescorted without fear. For her, the people were colourful, and she envied their way of life. She was often invited to share food, tasting ravioli and spaghetti for the first time. They were considered to be extremely exotic, 'foreign' foods in those days. When she asked her aunt why they didn't have spaghetti, she was given a fierce ticking off for being ungrateful for the effort Lily put in to feed and clothe her niece. After that, Joan never again mentioned Little Italy to her aunt, but her visits there became more frequent. Joan loved the kindness of the people, the music and the spectacle of how they lived. She found the food much tastier than the meat, vegetables and porridge she got at home.

Each July, she watched the procession of Our Lady of Mount Carmel organised by St Peter's Italian Church near Clerkenwell Road. Still going strong today, it is a focal point of the local calendar when the Italian community, dressed in all their religious finery, wave smoking balls of incense on long chains. Crowds line the streets to pay their respects and join in the celebrations.

Joan built a world in her head around her wanderings. When she was asked where she had been during the school holidays, she boasted about having been in Italy, never explaining that she meant Little Italy, a short distance from where she lived.

Joan was happiest among strangers, even though she always maintained she was shy. Her Aunt Lily had drilled into her that a lady kept herself to herself, which a much older Joan rather dryly pointed out didn't help with her later relationships with men. Despite her alleged shyness, she happily mixed with people who didn't know her so she could be a passing presence in their lives. One joy was that, unlike the inhabitants of the Red Cow, they wouldn't try and tell her what to do. Her need for independence was a powerful driving force.

One of Joan's other early passions was art. She longed to have her own paper and paints and was encouraged by her teacher at a little church school called St Sepulchre's, opposite the Old Bailey. She fondly remembered how her teacher – one Mr Munday – not only liked her but would encourage her to carry on with her 'doodles', as she called them. Her Uncle Wally agreed with Mr Munday that the girl had some innate talent, but it was not a view shared by Aunt Lily. When Joan brought works home, her aunt was dismissive and unconvinced. It must have been so discouraging. Even harder was the fact that, despite her repeated requests for art materials, she was never given the paint and paper she craved to explore her creative abilities. Joan being Joan, she found a way around this: when no one was looking, she tore the fly leaves out of the few books her aunt possessed. It took Lily some time to notice, but her niece was in serious trouble when she was eventually found out. Joan's other trick was to draw on toilet paper, which in those days was hard and shiny, so not the best material for a masterpiece. Once again, her aunt was furious. She pinned the girl down, demanding to know if she had a tummy upset because someone was using all the toilet paper. Lily had a rule that two sheets were sufficient for any job.

At the age of 13 Joan was quickly becoming a woman, even though she wasn't quite ready for it in some respects. She often told me the story of how she woke up one morning and found herself and the bed covered in blood. She was terrified and thought she must have cut herself, even though a search of her body revealed no signs of an injury. When she looked in the mirror, the face staring back was pale and worried. Joan believed she was going to die, and she had no idea why. She said she had blood on her knickers and her first instinct was to hide it. She covered up the bedsheets and tried to wash her pants. Right on cue, Aunt Lily came into her room and caught her frantically trying to hide the evidence of whatever it was that was happening to her. Joan couldn't help but think she had done something wrong, as usual, and was in a panic.

Lily disappeared and returned with a booklet entitled *Now You Are 13*. Nothing was said about this dramatic introduction to womanhood. Lily left her niece to find out some of the facts of life for herself from an impersonal leaflet which may have come from her school for precisely this purpose. No words of comfort, no reassurance that this was totally normal; just isolation, with a few printed pages spelling out what had happened. The incident left its scars. Joan felt no one understood how frightened she had been. She said she was always embarrassed about her periods. She would hide when they came and had terrible trouble asking for sanitary towels in the chemists, 'I felt ashamed and didn't know why … Stupid I was.'

Of course, Joan wasn't stupid. She was simply innocent and uninformed, perhaps surprisingly so for someone so streetwise; but then again people didn't speak of such intimate 'women's matters' in those days. It would have been a good opportunity for Joan to bond with her aunt but instead it reinforced her sense of isolation and her growing desire for independence.

The Red Cow may have provided a safe roof over her head, but the cost of comfort was becoming too high a price to pay. As with so many episodes in Joan's life, the answer to her unhappiness was laced with high drama and danger.

3

HITTING THE STREETS

The next part of Joan's story began on a chilly morning in April 1935. It was a Saturday and her 14th birthday. Joan didn't plan to run away from home, but the tensions had been building up in the years she was at the pub. Here was a free-spirited young woman, strong in every way, who was at odds with her aunt who endeavoured to control her every movement. There was no familial love to glue the cracks together, just a mutual lack of understanding and resentment. Joan was more than ready to spread her wings, even though she was still so young. The way she described that life-changing moment made it sound more like a whim than an elaborate escape plan. There was no great thought process involved.

As it was her birthday, she'd been given 8*d* to go for a swim, with enough left over for her to buy a roll as a special treat. She walked away from the Red Cow with her swimming costume, a towel and her stash of cash. She didn't look back.

Little did she expect that in launching herself into the outside world in this haphazard way, she was taking the first steps on a remarkable journey that would ultimately transport her from abject poverty on London's streets to rubbing shoulders with royalty and celebrities. But fairy tales don't just happen – in real life you have to work to make dreams come true. It was a long, tough road that few could have endured. It was survival of the fittest and strongest.

With pennies in her pocket and a hunger for adventure, Joan headed into the city. She walked into Clerkenwell, through Little Italy, all the while looking for work by studying scribbled notices in shop windows. Eventually she came to a café with a 'Waitress Wanted' sign outside. Having spent the past three years in a pub, she knew a bit about serving the public. She'd pulled pints, washed glasses and believed she had a feel for pleasing customers. She recalled the trips with her aunt to the posh Lyons Corner House, probably the one in Coventry Street in the West End, and how she wanted to become one of the serving girls, known as Nippies. They had a smart uniform of a flattering black dress, heavily starched white apron and a white headband. Like any teenager, she was attracted by the idea of dressing up. Driven by this desire to be like a Nippie, she marched into the café near Mount Pleasant and began her first public performance, acting like a much older and more experienced potential employee.

Joan claimed she was 17 and had been working in a pub that had sacked her when they found out she was under 18. Joan later boasted to me that she was a 'great little liar'; one of the more useful life lessons her aunt taught her was if she wanted to lie, she should have a good memory. The man behind the counter was convinced and told her to start work straight away.

Joan was overjoyed; she could already see herself in her neat and flattering dark dress with a little white pinafore. But at this point the encounter started to go badly wrong. She asked for her uniform and of course there wasn't one in this sleazy café. But she was given a bowl of hot soup before she started work, which she ate greedily.

Her first customers were two downtrodden men, one of whom asked for a 'Rosie Lee and two'. She probably knew what a Rosie Lee was – rhyming slang for cup of tea – but what the hell was 'two'? Joan was flummoxed. The men all laughed at her while the owner sorted out the tea and two pieces of dripping on toast. This isn't something you would see on any modern menu: a mixture of the leftover fat and juices from roast pork or beef, then spread on bread – a poor person's meal. I bet Joan hadn't had to eat many of those in her time at the pub. More ridicule came when she was told to set the tables for lunch. She was carefully putting out correct cutlery at each setting as she'd been taught at the Red Cow, but when the boss saw what she was up to he shouted at her to just leave a pile on each table. There was no room in this new world for her aunt's middle-class niceties.

Joan was banking on earning tips from the incoming stream of grubby male customers, as she was worried about finding a room for the night. She didn't get a single penny, probably due to the location of the café. It was just across the street from Rowton House, part of a chain of hostels for men who were unemployed or struggling. Though seedy, they were still superior to the dreadful lodgings available in a city such as London. In his 1933 book, *Down and Out in Paris and London,* George Orwell deemed Rowton Houses 'the best' class of hostel. In exchange for a shilling, you would:

> … get a cubicle to yourself, and the use of excellent bathrooms. You can also pay half a crown for a 'special', which is practically hotel accommodation. The Rowton Houses are splendid buildings, and the only objection to them is the strict discipline, with rules against cooking, card playing, etc.

After paying the charge for their board, and a 'Rosie Lee and two', the customers at the café would not have had a penny to spare for Joan. She ended up taking matters into her own hands when she was dismissed for the day at roughly half past three:

> I asked the owner if he could give me five shillings as I had seen an advert for a room in nearby Frederick Street and wanted to rent it. He said no – so I went upstairs to get my coat. It was raining and the café was filling up again. On a shelf were big

packets of cigarettes; I took one and hid it under my coat. I came back down and was just leaving when he called me back. 'Come early tomorrow, you can peel the spuds,' and then, 'What have you got under your coat?'

I didn't reply. There was a hush from the men as they waited for my answer. 'Nothing,' I said and on the counter was a pile of plates so I pushed them and they went crashing to the floor. In the confusion I ran out and all the way to Exmouth Market where I sold the cigarettes for six shillings; my room and a whole shilling for me.

Desperate times call for desperate measures. But Joan's first night away from home using her ill-gotten gains was a disaster. She found the house in Frederick Street and believed she was doing rather well for herself. She was about to have another harsh lesson in life, having never slept in a flea-ridden bed before. In recent years Joan had become used to a degree of comfort and care, not the first qualities you would ascribe to a hard-bitten landlady.

Joan handed over her precious 5s for a week in advance and was led up numerous flights of stairs to the top floor, where a tiny room awaited her. There was a single bed with an iron bedstead, a small table and chair, a gas meter and kettle. When the landlady got suspicious and asked where her luggage was, Joan lied that it was at the train station, and she would collect it the next day.

But the man in the café was – quite unwittingly – about to get his revenge:

I awoke in the night with a violent tummy ache and wanted the lavatory which was in the back yard down four or five flights of stairs. I knew I couldn't make it, so I thought I'd use the enamel water bucket, which had a lid, there being no running water in the room. It was diarrhoea and I just had to go – three or four times that night; it must have been the soup, I suppose.

At about 8 a.m. (I didn't have a watch) the landlady came noisily into the room saying, 'It stinks.' I tried to tell her about my upset tummy but she wasn't listening. 'Out, out!' she screamed, 'Filthy bitch!'

'Alright,' I said, 'but I want my money back.'

'No,' she said, 'That'll go for the fumigation!'

Joan's immediate reaction to this unpleasant awakening was to find comfort in one of her favourite places. She often spoke to me with great fondness about a site known simply as the Statue, a tiny piece of land near Trafalgar Square. It was, and still is, behind the National Gallery, at the bottom of Charing Cross Road. It was named after an imposing Grade II sculpture of Henry Irving that stands there. He was a great champion of performance art, having started as a humble actor in the Victorian era and worked his way up to become a leading celebrity of his day. He fulfilled numerous roles in his career, including as the manager of the Lyceum Theatre. He was also the first actor to be knighted.

Legend has it that Sir Henry owned this tiny bit of London and wanted it preserved for use by actors and strolling players to brush up their performances in front of the public. By contrast, the Irving Society says the land was donated by the City of Westminster at the turn of the twentieth century, not long after Irving died, so that statue would have a foothold in Theatreland. Whatever the case, in the 1930s it was a popular spot for street performers.

Busking was a lifeline for those who had some talent in the arts but no job during the Depression. The numbers of buskers in the city swelled dramatically as people congregated on the streets from far-flung corners of Britain. Audiences were keen to watch: during this time of great hardship and uncertainty, people wanted something jolly to cheer up a bleak world. The onlookers would have got that with an everchanging assortment of fire eaters, escapologists, singers, jugglers, dancers, strongmen and magicians, to name but a few.

The Statue was a particularly busy location as it was so near Trafalgar Square, Leicester Square and the main theatres. Night and day there were large numbers of passing crowds, tourists and locals alike. There was money to be made. People were prepared to chuck a few pennies into a pot in return for a moment or two of diversion.

It was here that young Joan discovered her true métier. She must have looked very dishevelled that Sunday and was perhaps in need of a bath after being so unwell in the night, with nowhere to wash since being chucked out of her seedy accommodation. She wouldn't have a change of clothes after running away with only a towel and swimsuit. But that didn't pose a barrier to her assimilation into the world of busking. Her escapade in the café had not gone unnoticed, and she told me how she found herself welcomed by the street performers because of it:

> Well, I still had my shilling, and fourpence left over from my original eightpence, so I went walking to the Statue. As I got there I saw one of the men from the café – it turned out to be Big Jock, one of the strongmen who was about to do his pitch. He recognised me and rushed over to tell me how much they'd laughed when I pushed the plates over, that the man had told the police and they would visit my room so not to go back there. 'If you like,' said Jock, 'you can bottle for me.'

Bottling was a very old name for going around and collecting money from the crowd of onlookers. It was illegal to busk, so performers used a leather bottle, and if the police should come along, they would claim that the bottle contained water. But the officers of the law soon caught on to this, and other receptacles began to be used, such as a hat. The practice changed but the name didn't.

By the time Joan was operating on the streets, trilby hats were used for bottling. She must have been good at persuading people to part with their cash as Jock was so pleased with the takings he gave her a 2*s* piece. This was enough to secure a bed for the night and a bit of food.

Big Jock Allen had a colourful past. He was apparently quite well known in America, where he worked in circuses as a strongman.

One part of his act was to balance a girl on top of a 20ft pole on his head. One night, things went horribly wrong and she fell to her death. He came back to England and developed a one-man street performance rather than risk more tragedy.

Being in the survival business, Jock clearly saw Joan as a good addition to his act and he wanted to look after this potential source of income. When she told him about the horrors of where she had spent the previous night, he advised her to try to get a bed at Cecil House, which was known for an acceptable level of cleanliness.

She found her way there and at the time, it must have seemed like the lap of luxury as the beds were clean and there were washing facilities. Cecil Houses were a charitable concern set up by a female journalist, Ada Chesterton, for poor or destitute women at a time when there was virtually no provision for this section of society. Ada was driven by courage and passion. She was an energetic philanthropist, who championed the plight of these women in the early twentieth century after seeing first-hand how unbearable their lives were. Several of the women had babies and no support from the fathers or their families. The male-led society would have nothing to do with them as they were regarded as beyond help.

Ada was one of the few female reporters around and she made it her job to explore the lives of those in the lowest levels of society. To get a story right, she spent time on the streets in disguise, fuelling her determination to provide help. The first Cecil House was established in 1927 and more were to open in subsequent years.

Ada knew that these women did not like answering questions and avoided shelters that had lots of strict rules. She made a point of limiting how much scrutiny they came under. The conditions for gaining entry were simple: the occupants paid a shilling a night, had to be a certain age and had to wash before getting into a clean bed. They were given tea and a slice of bread and margarine in the evening and again in the morning. Joan lied and pretended she was over 18 and settled in for a much-needed sleep.

Discovering how to get a decent bed for the night, with a bit of sustenance thrown in, was just what Joan needed. She told me that for a few weeks, the 2*s* she got from bottling was enough to deal with her most basic requirements. At this stage she wasn't looking beyond where her next meal and accommodation were coming from. Led by her innate optimism, she believed any immediate problems were solved.

But life wasn't that straightforward. One rainy day when the streets were deserted, she went to a café and 'blew a few pennies on an egg and toast' as she waited for the other street performers like Big Jock to show up. But there was no sign of any of them. This meant Joan was penniless and, consequently, homeless. That was how close to destitution she was. She didn't panic and instead wandered down to Covent Garden market. She must have looked a mess as she was soaking wet and her cheap sandals had holes in them. A trader she'd been chatting to was obviously concerned about this young girl out in such weather and told her to go home. When she replied that she didn't have a home he took pity on Joan and said she could sit in the back of his van until she dried off. He even gave her a few apples.

She said she was quite happy munching on her fruit and watching the world go by, so much so that she curled up and fell asleep. She had a rude awakening when, later in the afternoon, the trader noticed she was still hanging around and once again told her to go home. This time his pity and patience had worn thin and he forced her out of the van. Desperate for even a penny or two, Joan said she polished the remaining apple on her soggy coat and tried to sell it, but there were no takers. She wolfed it down and went in search of somewhere to sleep:

The street sweepers were clearing up the leftover rubbish and so I wandered up a back alley, a cul-de-sac. Right at the end was a barrow with imitation grass hanging from it, not quite reaching to the ground. I crawled under it – it reminded me of one of the hedges at the convent. It smelled of fruit and was dry and after a while I fell asleep.

I was woken by heavy footsteps coming down the alley. Peeping out I saw a very big policeman and I thought I must have been discovered, but I kept very still behind my 'grass' curtain. The footsteps stopped and suddenly I felt water coming through the 'grass' – the policeman was having a pee! He finished and walked solemnly away. My hiding place now smelled nasty – but I went back to sleep.

When you are homeless and desperate, smelling sweetly doesn't even make it onto the priority list.

At the time Joan was always fearful that the police were looking for her as, after all, she was a missing young girl. She imagined that Lily and Wally would be scouring the streets for her, worried whether she was dead or alive. The last thing Joan wanted was to be dragged kicking and screaming back to the Red Cow. She did her best to keep out of the way of the police or anyone who might know her; hiding where she could was part of her new daily routine.

She wasn't far from the pub in Smithfield, half a mile at the most. If her aunt had wanted to find her it wouldn't have been that difficult. I suspect there was quite a furore when Joan didn't come home that Saturday. Search parties may have been sent out but when all the fuss had died down, Lily must have decided to leave her tricky niece to her own devices. It is possible that they heard through customers and friends that she had been seen around the West End. Joan saw it as another form of abandonment. Although she didn't want to go home, this apparent lack of concern for her fate reflected how little her family cared. She felt unloved once again.

Instead, she found care, compassion and concern on the dirty streets of London. She was quickly regarded as a part of the busking fraternity and was given a degree of protection from the worst aspects of homelessness. They looked after their own.

Although Joan was fairly street savvy, she told me that she was still very naïve in many ways during this time. Possibly her ignorance of the dangers she faced was what kept her safe. She knew little about sex; I don't suppose the leaflet on periods she'd been given by her aunt went into much detail beyond an abstract reference to the birds and the bees. From how she spoke about her early homelessness, I honestly don't think it occurred to her that she might be attacked and raped as she slept down an isolated alley.

Joan portrayed herself as an innocent girl trying to find a path through hardship. But this couldn't have lasted long – perhaps just a few days – as she would have had to learn the hard facts of life

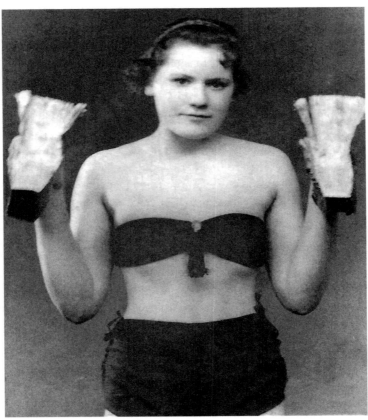

Joan, aged about 14 or 15, in a homemade costume.

very quickly to survive. There may have been a tacit code between buskers to keep an eye out for each other, but that didn't necessarily extend to the many lowlifes she would have met. She had a steep learning curve ahead of her, and not just on how to keep herself safe. Joan needed some form of income to pay for the food and shelter. Bottling may have been a way into busking, but it was not enough to guarantee a daily slice of bread and margarine, let alone a bed for the night. The crowds were unpredictable; a bit of rain or snowfall and there was little point in setting up a pitch. There was also no way of knowing if Big Jock and the others were going to show up on any particular day or time. It would have frustrated Joan to find herself once again at the mercy of people and elements beyond her control.

Joan realised there was only one way to make this situation sustainable: she had to learn the tricks of the trade. She decided to emulate those around her if she could. She had to tread the pavements with an entertaining act like the rest of the buskers. Her teachers were all around her and their tuition was gloriously free; she just had to look and learn. The most obvious person to model herself on was Big Jock:

> Bottling for Jock one day, I picked up a six-inch nail and [cloth] duster and thought I'd try to bend it like he did. I struggled and struggled, it hurt my hands and Jock laughed: 'You'll never do it!' This incensed me – 'I will!' I cried, sweat and tears running down my face. I HAD to do it – and to the surprise of Big Jock and me, I did. Every time I saw Big Jock after that he would hand me a nail and a duster and say, 'Do it again,' and I did until one day I tried to make it straight again, and succeeded. After a while I found I could break a nail. Of course my hands suffered, but I had proved something to me and to Jock.
>
> In no time I could tear a pack of cards – but cards cost money, so he suggested I try a telephone book, which would cost nothing. I took a deep breath and tried, but I couldn't shift it; but I was determined and again practised whenever I could.

An early attempt at bending a bar wearing a revealing homemade two-piece.

By now, Joan was looking towards her future. She felt she had found a skill she could adapt, namely her own surprising strength. She worked hard to emulate Jock and with that in mind, she embraced the almost exclusively male world of weightlifting. She found a highly regarded professional gym and talked her way in. The men were kind to her and showed her how to lift barbells, something she did with ease. Then they told her to sit in a corner and practise lifting weights to develop her arm strength.

Joan had made her own good fortune again. She had found a gym that would tolerate a young woman's presence, run on the importance of leading a healthy life while looking after your physique.

The gym was named after George Hackenschmidt, a famous strongman and professional wrestler at the turn of the previous century. He was known as the 'Russian Lion' and was freestyle heavyweight champion of the world. After a knee injury, he retired from wrestling in 1911. Hackenschmidt was an early proponent of weightlifting and invented a squat called 'the hack' which is still used in gyms today. He is also credited with popularising exercises such as the bench press.

But this extraordinary man didn't stop at physical achievement. It might seem unlikely, but Hackenschmidt became a well-respected philosopher. He was an educated man who could speak seven languages and counted Harry Houdini and George Bernard Shaw among his many friends. As a pioneer health fanatic, he was an icon in the world of physical culture. One of his numerous books, *The Way to Live: In Health and Physical Fitness*, is still in print today, despite first being published in 1941. Hackenschmidt would have approved of Joan as he was a great believer in developing real physical power; he had no time for conmen who pretended to have huge strength. His gym was a perfect training ground for Joan.

At about that time, Joan had been on the streets for a year or more. She was just about managing to keep body and soul going, but she was in for another upheaval. She had been working regularly with Big Jock, attempting to build her own act, when the Scotsman decided it was time to try a different part of the country. He had heard that Aintree Racecourse in Liverpool was a rich hunting ground for punters willing to part with pennies for a bit of busking. Joan was happy to go along with him. After all, he was her main means of survival. The pair hopped on a bus out of London and then began hitchhiking. In the tried and tested way, they used a simple trick to get a ride. Jock walked ahead of Joan so it looked as though she was on her own; she quickly got a lift and when the lorry caught up with Jock, she pleaded with the driver to stop and pick up 'her father'. It worked a treat.

The pair made it to Liverpool, but the plan was about to go badly wrong. Joan forgot her own lie about her age:

> On the way we met with more grafters [performers] and I chatted with a boy about my age who told me he was seventeen.
>
> 'I'll be sixteen in April,' I said.
>
> Jock shouted to me and told the others to go on. 'What do you mean?' he asked. 'You're only fifteen?'
>
> I had to confess. 'Well I'm afraid you'll have to find your own way back to London or I'll be in prison for kidnapping you. You told me you were eighteen and I believed you, but they wouldn't! Goodbye and good luck.'

Once again Joan was abandoned, this time by someone she had come to trust. Big Jock left her with nothing. No money, no change of clothes; he even took her props. Joan had never been so far from home, and she found herself more alone than she had ever been in her short life. I think most 15-year-olds would have panicked. Not Joan, though. She had her own way of dealing with disaster. Instead of crying she said she laughed and laughed like Little Audrey. She felt her only option was to get back to London, even though she had absolutely no idea how or even what direction she had to take. When she asked people for the right road, they suggested she catch a train or a bus instead. Once again Joan could only laugh at the thought. How would she afford a ticket?

She began walking in the rain. When darkness approached, she took shelter under a road bridge. Exhausted, she gathered a pile of rags and fell asleep. To give an idea of her desperation, she later told me how delighted she was to find a pair of old workman's boots.

Her cheap Woolworth sandals were shredded, so at least she now had some sturdy shoes to help carry her the many miles she had ahead, even if they were many sizes too big.

The next day, she stole a raincoat from a scarecrow in a field, as her own coat was about to give up the ghost. Her dishevelled appearance didn't stop her trying to thumb a lift, but all she got were a few pennies thrown from a driver's cab. They were enough to stop at a roadside café and buy a cuppa and a piece of dripping toast. Things seemed to look up when a driver came into the café and offered her a lift. From what Joan said he seemed nice enough, until they reached the outskirts of London. The driver stopped the lorry and demanded to know how she would pay for the ride. He made a lunge at her, but Joan grabbed his head and smashed it against the back of the seat before fleeing. Joan estimated that she must have been in Hendon. She walked until she found herself in the familiar territory of central London.

I can imagine her gritting her teeth, determined to get back to the streets she recognised as soon as she could. It was lunchtime when she found herself at Lincoln's Inn Fields. The office workers were out for their break, sitting on the grass and munching on sandwiches. Like a hungry wild animal, Joan watched them eat. She wasn't begging, but she must have looked the part:

> I saw an elderly man pick the fat bits from his ham sandwich, roll them in the paper and throw them away. I watched that crumpled paper like a cat until he moved away and I could get it. A girl removed the cheese from her sandwiches and threw the bread down on the grass behind her; just as I reached out for it she turned and saw me.
>
> I can only imagine what I looked like. I had been sleeping out in fields, my hair was all knotted and bedraggled and the raincoat I had stolen from the scare-crow, together with the boots, were all too big for me. This girl saw me reaching for the bread and hesitated. 'Here,' she said, 'would you like one of my sandwiches?'

Yes, I ached to accept one of those sandwiches, but I shrank back from her and heard myself saying, 'Keep your filthy sandwiches. I don't need your charity.' She moved away in embarrassment. From that instant I have always known how a hurt animal feels when it snarls at a friendly hand. I spent that night wrapped in my tatty raincoat under Gatti's Arches in Villiers Street and nobody disturbed me.

Joan had reached rock bottom. It was a mark of her sense of survival that the next day she began her first steps towards supporting herself. She woke with the idea that the only course of action left was do her own busking act. She went to the ironmongers where Jock got his six-inch nails, telling them that he was her dad and that he had run out of his supply. She promised to come back and pay for them later. Then she went to a local phone box and took one of the directories before making her way to the site of her first pitch near Charing Cross Station:

I laid down my props with a piece of brown paper for pennies to be thrown on and started Jock's spiel until a few people with nothing better to do stopped to watch. I handed the nails round and asked the men to bend them. They looked at me as if I was mad, so I quickly went round and bent all six nails. No money came and one or two wandered away.

'It's a fix,' someone shouted, despite the fact that I had done it (much to my surprise) before their very eyes – and my hands hurt. I got confused and picked up the phone book and said, 'And now I'm going to tear this book in half!' More people stopped to watch. The golden rule when performing is to blag them – ask for their money first. I tried, without much success, until one man said, 'It's baked!' so I offered him the book to examine. 'Yes,' he said, 'quite genuine. I'll give you a shilling.'

I slapped the book and started. For some reason, maybe I was nervous, I couldn't even start it. So I struggled on and soon got my confidence back. After all, a shilling was a lot of money and a bed for the night. What I didn't know was that the books in phone boxes are specially strengthened with metal staples to keep them together. I battled on as a red-faced man kept shouting, 'It's false pretences, that's what it is. She's a liar and a cheat. You see! Somebody call the Law, let's have a policeman!'

Suddenly the crowd went quiet and a voice said 'Strewth!' I looked down at my hands, they were running with blood where the staples had shredded my fingers, but the book was ripped across the middle and in two pieces. The first man kept his word and threw in the shilling; a few more kind persons threw in some cash and left. I scrabbled about picking up the coins and collected three shillings and eightpence for my first show. I wasn't displeased! So I now had my own act!

Looking more confident, aged about 16.

4

SURVIVAL AND STRENGTH

Joan still had a lot to learn, and she was keen to get on with it. For her there were no comfortable choices; it was simply a matter of survival. Thankfully, there were plenty of teachers on hand who were happy to help, especially if having an attractive young girl as a part of their act brought in more money.

One of her mentors was an escapologist called Big Ginger. He would tie her up in chains and put her in a large sack, people watching as she apparently struggled desperately to escape. Big Ginger would bark at the growing audience, pacing up and down cracking a menacing-looking whip in the direction of the wriggling bundle. He said he would free her if the crowd chucked a bit more money on the pavement. He must have been convincing, as the performances sometimes brought in enough for him to be able to give Joan £2 as her share. Riches indeed. The act was a trick. Big Ginger showed Joan how to tighten her muscles when the chains were being wrapped around and the bag put over her head. All she had to do was relax and the chains fell off easily. Still, it must have been entertaining to watch.

There was nothing regular about this work. Doing a successful pitch relied on numerous different elements aligning, such as good weather, the number of people on the streets and whether the performers could be bothered to turn up. Although making £2 in one day was possible, it could be many days before that happened again and, in that time, Joan would end up broke again.

In Cecil House Joan could wash, sleep in a clean bed and eat the small portions of food provided. But spending a whole shilling on staying there was a comparative luxury she couldn't often afford. To avoid sleeping on pavements, she resorted to staying in doss-houses. Among the worst were those known as a tuppenny hangover. These places would have been populated by an assortment of the most desperate members of society. For 2*d* a night the so-called guests were provided with a long bench to share, with a rope strung from one side of the room to the other. Punters would sit down and hang their heads and arms over the rope and somehow sleep. In the morning, a man, jokingly called the valet, would come and they'd be rudely awakened when he undid or cut the rope. These poor people must have ended up sprawled all over the filthy floor. It's hard to believe that places like this existed, but everything Joan says is corroborated by George Orwell in *Down and Out in Paris and London*. To research his book, he took on the role of one of the homeless, sleeping on the Embankment and staying in various doss-houses. Oddly enough, he was trying to exist on the streets of London not long before Joan ran away from home. His exposure to this existence coincided with a growing respect for the underclasses. Like Joan, he realised that most of them were there not by choice but by circumstance. He acknowledged that destitute women were treated even more badly than men.

Joan had a few regular places that she went to. One was in Islington, off the Pentonville Road, and cost just 6*d* a night. It was as squalid as you might expect but there was an upside: the chance of getting some scraps to eat. In the basement, a number of gas stoves had been installed, each one with its own meter. In the evenings it was packed with women who mostly worked in the local fruit and vegetable market. The all-pervading smell was of bacon cooking, which must have been agony for the hungry young girl. But, just like the incident where she refused the charity of a shared sandwich in Soho, Joan turned down offers to share the tasty morsels. Instead, she would hang around until the women had finished and offer to do the dishes. When they had gone, Joan would scrabble for the rinds that had been discarded and greedily eat them.

Joan likened the scene to a Victorian thieves' kitchen, bringing to mind a Dickensian London. The women wore men's flat caps and always had metal curlers in their hair as if they were preparing for an outing. But the rest of their garb belied any aspirations of going anywhere special. They wore sacking aprons, long, thick skirts and men's carpet slippers. I can imagine them shuffling around in the basement, cackling, cracking rude jokes and singing popular cockney songs from the music halls. Joan said they were a jolly bunch who seemed quite happy with their lot. They would be up at the crack of dawn to do casual portering at the Chapel Street fruit and vegetable market:

> There were no bathrooms, but four lavatories in the back yard with toilet paper which was newspaper cut into squares, threaded with string and hung on a nail; also a washing room with big sinks, hot water on a gas ring, a large wringer with a handle to turn the rollers to run your washed clothes through and bags of pegs to hang your things on the lines out in the yard, although quite often stuff would go missing from there.
>
> I didn't stay there very often as sometimes the rozzers [police] would come in and search for God knows what – nobody seemed to have any possessions and children were not allowed. I could get by because I looked much older than my years. Hard times! But I didn't care, at least I was free, and it was a good learning time.

Cinemas were Joan's other refuges. A favourite was the cine-variety theatre called the Canterbury. Here, a sixpence would keep you dry and warm for hours as you were entertained by films, newsreels and even live singers and dancers. Another bonus was that a cuppa or a bar of chocolate cost only a penny, and for tuppence you could get a filled bread roll.

Watching the movie stars glitter on the silver screen fired up Joan's ambitions. She longed to emulate them in some way, though she struggled with fears that she was too big and ugly to succeed, once again doubts sown into her psyche by her unpleasant aunts. Joan couldn't see what others could; namely that in the two years or so that she had been on the streets she had blossomed, swanlike, into an attractive young woman. Longing to be in films, Joan took to hanging out in the ABC, a café in Charing Cross Road which was popular with film extras. She would take her place on the sidelines and try to be invisible as she listened to the artistes tell their tales. She must have been shocked and delighted when she was approached by an agent offering her film work.

She'd just finished her pitch and had obviously impressed Archie Woolf, who introduced himself as an agent and asked if she'd like to be in the movies. In her situation, there was only one possible answer. Better still, in the film called *The Man in Grey*, she wasn't just going to be one of the crowd. The director, Leslie Arliss, wanted her to be in the background bending bars as two of the lead actors walked by. The stars of the movie were Phyllis Calvert, James Mason, Margaret Lockwood and a young Stewart Granger in his first big film role:

> Of course I jumped at the chance and was told to be at his office for 6 a.m. on Thursday and to get in the coach, which I did. I then noticed that a lot of the other people were ones I'd seen in the ABC. 'Good morning,' I shouted, but they didn't seem to see me. I was asked my name at what was called the wardrobe and I told them that it was Josie Terena – tearing her way through life.

Joan tried a few different stage names early on. She came up with Terena, as in tearing phone books in two. She thought it was a good joke, but it fell flat on this occasion: 'It didn't get a laugh':

> One of the assistants took me over to a rail on which there were several colourful costumes with lots of sequins on. 'This'll do, don't spoil it, it's one of our specials.'

47

The director came over to me when I had changed and asked me if I had brought my steel bars. I had been warned that I might have to use one or two so I had. He then shouted for quiet and told me to go behind a barrier and bend one and hold it up. I did, but he wasn't satisfied and told me to try again.

'We'll try for a take,' he said; there was loud music and I was behind my barrier and as Stewart Granger and Phyllis Calvert walked past me talking the director pointed to me and mimed bending the bar – but I couldn't as I now hadn't got a straight bar! Filming stopped and they took away my bent bars and brought them back straight (they had a vice). By this time the day's filming was over and we were called back for the following day. In the coach on the way back everyone was very friendly because I'd got them a second day and after that whenever I went into the ABC I was always greeted as one of them.

This was one of Joan's favourite stories of her early career. She painted a buoyant, happy-go-lucky picture of what must have been, in reality, a time of great hardship.

She said that she was paid £5 for the two days' filming work on *The Man in Grey*, so she rushed off to Woolworths to invest in new clothes. This included a skirt, mauve shirt, sandals and knickers. She went to a ladies' lavatory opposite the Statue where you could have a hot bath for 4*d*. It was a facility used by office girls so they could wash and change after leaving work and then go onto the theatre. For Joan it was a dressing room.

But, as with so many of her tales, the dates didn't add up. *The Man in Grey* was a wartime film, released in 1943. Joan would have been 22, which would mean that she had been on the streets eight years. The way she talked and wrote about her arrival on the silver screen, it would be easy to think she was still a teenager. When you watch the footage, she does look to be in her twenties. She plays one of the sideshow performers in a circus, dressed in a shiny leotard with a matching shiny bow in her hair. The sequence follows Granger and Calvert walking along chatting, then stops in front of Joan, who is central in the shot.

Joan's arrival on set came after years of battling to survive, further along her journey than she would later recall. It was a battle she was gradually winning, all the time perfecting her performing skills and finding herself increasingly able to put a roof over her head, feed herself and purchase the few items of clothing she needed. Still, there were many years of hardship ahead.

She became accustomed to mixing with the world's down and outs. When she spoke about them, she was never judgemental. Although she would often feign innocence about what they were up to, she was a canny woman who knew exactly what she was dealing with. She would have had to be to survive.

Joan was fond of talking about one reprobate called Jacobus Van Dyn, the self-styled 'Worst Man in the World'. Van Dyn would often be found on a Sunday on his soapbox preaching about prison reform at Speakers' Corner in Hyde Park. Originally from South Africa, he was famous for being covered in tattoos. Pictures show it was hard to make out the features on his bald head. He claimed to have been a gun runner for the American gangster Al Capone and to have spent time in the toughest prisons in the world, including San Quentin, Sing Sing and Dartmoor.

He was imprisoned in England after being found guilty of armed robbery, but the seven-year sentence was quashed after he successfully appealed, claiming it was a case of mistaken identity. Van Dyn said he had decided to make his features so memorable that he would never be taken for anyone else again, hence the tattoos. The popular press loved him as he knew how to play up to the public. At one point he even offered to sell his head for £5 – to be collected after his death, of course.

Thickset and mean-looking, he must have been one of the most intimidating characters in London. That didn't keep Joan away. She went to him because she was told he would be able to sort her out with a room in the house he was living in on Stephen Street, off Tottenham Court Road. It was a brothel, but when Joan told the tale she hid behind innocence, not even acknowledging that Van Dyn was clearly having very young male prostitutes come to his room:

> I was a bit scared to ask him about the room, but I did. He said yes and then asked if I could keep my mouth shut. I wondered what he meant but of course I said I could. 'You see,' he volunteered, 'I'm teaching little Johnny to wrestle and I don't want people to know.'

Her new home on Stephen Street was a huge improvement on the places she'd been staying. She was greeted by a smiling woman and taken to her third-floor room. Joan was delighted to find that it had an electric light, gas and water. All of them were on meters. There was no bedding, but she had enough money to buy sheets and a pillow from Woolies. She added the personal touch by cutting a Van Gogh picture out of a magazine and sticking it on the wall. She felt she had found a home, but it transpired that things were not as above board as they first seemed.

Joan told me she didn't realise her housemates included prostitutes and a violent paedophile. I think that may have been the case at first as she was an innocent optimist, but she must have cottoned on quite quickly. You could hardly miss the ladies on the first floor who would hang out of the windows and invite men up 'for a good time'.

Van Dyn had the room above hers and she recalled lots of 'little Johnnies' visiting, making plenty of noise and then disappearing again. Later she found out they were escapees from Borstal.

Joan's hope that she had found a more permanent address didn't last long:

> I hadn't been there very many weeks when two men knocked on my door and asked if I was comfortable, how old I was and my name. I said I was just 18 and my name was Josie Terena. They then asked me about the people in the house and I said

that the ladies on the first floor were very friendly and had lots of visitors; on the second floor was, I said, a violinist with a very bad cough and above me Van Dyn. They became very curious about him – did I hear anything that bothered me? 'No,' I said, 'but he is teaching little Johnny to wrestle.'

The men left looking very serious and official. One of the ladies rushed up and asked what they had said, so I told her exactly what I had told them. 'They've gone to get a warrant,' she said, 'you must move out at once – they'll be back. If you need money, here's a pound note to get another room.' I said that I'd manage but she insisted that I took it. A pound note was a lot of money so I did.

Once again I was homeless! I took to the doss-houses again, but before long I saw a room advertised in Dombey Street. I can't remember how much but it must have been cheap as it was the usual attic room with a lavatory in the yard and a gas ring. At least I could cook on that.

It was typical of Joan that she took delight in painting a jolly and heroic picture of life in the gutter. It was like a film script for an old movie about British stoicism in the face of adversity. I believe that she had sweetened and honed her story a million times over the years. Joan did say to me that she didn't want to leave people feeling sorry for her; she was always generous about wanting to spread happiness. Looking on the bright side was her motif. I think there was also the influence from her Aunt Lily. The more sordid aspect of Joan's existence was painted out of the picture as it would have been frowned upon by polite society. There were skeletons that would remain firmly locked up in their cupboard. But there were clues.

A window into her world is provided by a series of pictures taken by a news agency photographer in June 1938. The sequence begins with Joan leaving her digs in Dombey Street and heading off to do her pitch on Tower Hill. The young woman in the pictures looks bleak; there isn't a shadow of a smile, just sheer determination. Her

Joan, aged 16 or 17, leaving her digs in Dombey Street to ply her trade.

Setting up at Tower Hill.

Attracting a large admiring crowd.

clothes are shabby but adequate; she carries the tools of her trade in
a cheap, battered suitcase. Joan is shown setting up her pitch as the
crowds gather. There's nothing joyous about her mood. This isn't
laughing Little Audrey; this is a 17-year-old a few pennies away
from destitution.

The photographer sold the images and a story about Joan to the
Daily Express and the *Daily Mirror*. The item in the *Express* showed
her tearing a phone book. This was her first photoshoot. The payment was a full set of the pictures, which she kept for the rest of
her life. It was the beginning of Joan's publicity machine, which
would churn out the column inches by the yard in years to come.

Other pictures from these very early days show Joan in a tiny
leopard-skin two-piece that she made out of scraps of material. In
many of the originals, someone – probably Joan herself – appears
to have scribbled over the facial features. An odd act of vandalism
considering how carefully she kept mementoes of her life. In the
image, she must have recognised the big and ugly girl her aunts
spoke of.

With her tiny 22-inch waist and 5ft 7in stature, there can be no question that Joan would have been a crowd-pleaser by looks alone. Certainly, some passers-by would have been scandalised by this young girl wearing only a few scraps of cloth – you can imagine how those taking the moral high ground would have shunned her, especially other young women. Joan took no notice of their disgusted glances and tutting; they didn't know what it was like to starve.

As the years went by, she developed her street act. She carried on tearing phone books, bending bars and 6in nails but she would also lift a man in each arm and challenge punters to match her feat of strength. Men were keen to have a go, but she said none of them ever managed to emulate her.

After appearing in the national press, Joan was beginning to get noticed. There was growing interest in her, especially amongst casting agents. She was booked to appear as an extra in films and began to come in from the cold.

It was inevitable that other aspects of the exciting world of Soho would attract Joan and influence her outlook and opinions. She was particularly captivated by the group of writers and poets who, following the ancient traditions of broadsheet sellers, still managed to make a precarious living by selling their work on the streets. One such was John Singer, a now long-forgotten poet for whom she sold poems at a penny each; he would give her half of the takings. This literary group was split into two factions: the drinkers and the abstainers. What both had in common, though, was an endless capacity for putting the world to rights. Their creative use of language, vision and ideas was irresistible to Joan. So, too, was their idealism:

I became interested in politics. Some nice young men were going to Spain – the International Brigade – and so I hung around the Holborn Communist Party. They exploited me (a word they used a lot) to sell *Challenge* and the *Daily Worker*. I would go in front of any hotel and shout, 'Read tomorrow's news tonight,' until I was turned away. There was so much going on and I attended many demonstrations but I had to earn money.

Joan's flirtation with communism was brief. The idea of Joan toeing any party line is in any case quite absurd, and she continued to follow her own instinct. But the daily need to earn enough money to survive was relentless; her takings from street performing and the occasional part as a film extra were meagre and erratic. Her own words on the subject were revealing:

It never occurred to me to take a job; when I had been with my aunt people would ask what I would like to do when I grew up and I would say I'd like to be an artist – but my aunt would tell me that I had a good voice and would be a telephonist.

Both predictions turned out to be wildly inaccurate.

5

NAKED CIVIL SERVANTS

The streets Joan worked were brimming with unusual characters. She was fascinated by anyone who challenged what she regarded as the tedious norm and this led to a cherished and enduring friendship with one of the twentieth century's most remarkable figures, Quentin Crisp. Later in life he became internationally famous for his sharp wit, after writing the autobiographical book *The Naked Civil Servant*. The title is a play on the fact that he was a life model in college art classes and was therefore working for the Department of Education by posing in the nude.

Joan spotted him when she was on her way to do her routine at the statue one day. She was immediately attracted by his bright hennaed hair, garish eyeshadow, painted nails and lipstick, his Cuban-heeled boots and black suit. She followed him and saw him go into Old Compton Street, not knowing whether she was on the trail of a man or a woman. When she investigated further, she found her colourful prey in a small corner café holding forth to a large group of young students from Central St Martin's School of Art, who hung on his every word.

Joan was mesmerised but too shy to join in. She just listened and tried to make herself invisible from the back of the crowd. Quentin must have recognised her from her street performances because, when the students dispersed, he began chatting to her and asked if she wanted what he called 'a pale grey coffee'. She accepted the offer but only if it was a strong cup of tea.

Quentin was as intrigued by her as she was with him. They had a lot in common, primarily that they were two misfits who were quite happy not fitting in – in fact, both made a profession out of it. At some point the pair began discussing their work. Quentin was keen to know why Joan did what she did. It was a question with a simple answer: because she had no choice; she had to make a living somehow. Joan no doubt explained her fragile circumstances and she would have had a sympathetic hearing.

Like his new friend, Quentin knew what hardship felt like. In his early days he did whatever was required to survive. As a teenager this included working on the streets to sell his body. He was always happy to talk about being a 'rent boy'; for him it was simply part of the fabric of his life. He did what he needed. Quentin was thirteen years older than Joan and by the time they became friends, he was much more experienced than her, having explored most of the darkest corners of London.

He had been targeted because of his sexuality from an early age. He was verbally and physically attacked on a daily basis for his unusual appearance, but it didn't stop him dressing as he wished. The homophobes would beat him to the floor, but he would always get up, wipe away the blood, be polite and hobble away. His courage to stand up for his rights as an individual made him a true gay icon, one of the very first. Many would try to emulate him in generations to come, but Quentin was unique.

Quentin decided to mentor Joan; he would be a self-appointed guide to survival. Telling Joan that her looks were perfect for being an artist's model, he convinced her to give it a try, saying it was easy work and the pay was good. It was clearly something that had not entered her head. I think that when she first heard the job title, she didn't quite realise the degree of exposure required.

Quentin mapped out how she should go about getting the work. Firstly, she should head to one of the art schools and ask for the life-art master. Then she would have to lie about having posed for a number of well-known artists. Joan followed his directions and was taken on to do two days a week from 10 a.m. until 4 p.m., over thirteen weeks. She was ecstatic as she was paid 18*s* a day.

Joan only realised what the work entailed once she had been offered the job and asked Quentin what to expect. He explained that she would have to take all her clothes off behind a screen, sit on a dais and strike a pose for as long as the master said. Joan hadn't anticipated that she would have to even take her knickers off and

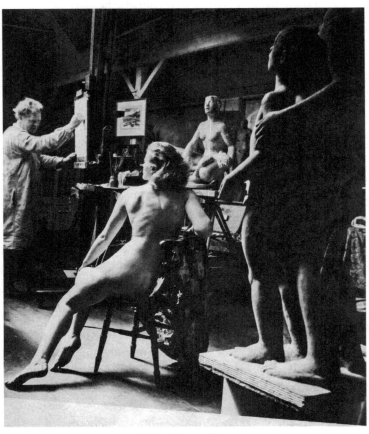

Joan modelling for an unknown artist.

felt intimidated by the idea. Then again, although she wasn't keen on stripping completely, a guaranteed daily income was worth a bit of discomfort and blushes.

Her first session went just as Quentin had said. Joan took to the platform and found herself surrounded by more than thirty art students hugging their easels or painting benches. It must have been daunting. To make matters worse, there were some rulebreakers like herself. She recalled that one student was a certain Lucian Freud, who winked and then started flicking modelling clay at her. In later years, after they had become friends, Freud told her he remembered the occasion as he had never seen a life model blush all over.

The total nudity must have bothered Joan as she went to great lengths to cover up even just a little:

> I managed to solve the knickers problem – I used to buy men's posing slips from Robert Gross stores, which are rather like the thongs girls wear today, only smaller. The Robert Gross shop was near Great Portland Street Underground station and I used to say the slips were for my brother who was a bodybuilder. They asked me to bring in a photograph of him and I said he wouldn't give me one – a white lie.

Joan went down well as a life model. She got plenty of work and found herself posing for some great artists. At one point she was booked for a term at the Chelsea School of Art which was then based at Manresa Road. There was one artist in particular who liked to use her. At the time, Henry Moore was working as an art teacher at the college. Joan said she had no idea who he was other than being a rather demanding customer, but she appreciated his work:

> After a day of various different poses from 10 a.m. to 4 p.m. he would ask me to stay on and pay me an extra ten shillings to pose for him. It wasn't easy – I had to stay on my side on one hip and one elbow. The hip hurt a little. He placed a vase between

The kind of pose Joan struck for Henry Moore.

my knees to keep them apart – tiring, but he was very kindly and I had a rest every fifteen minutes. He didn't talk but drew all the time. I wanted to see some of the drawings but I never asked. Later I saw some of his shelter drawings (scenes in the air raid shelters during the war) and recognised my pose. I hadn't realised that he was such a famous artist.

Quentin was also an artists' model and continued to make a living from this work for three decades. He would tell Joan how he took pride in distorting himself into impossible poses and holding them for as long as he could. It was so extreme that even the art students studying his body were uncomfortable. His early life experiences were encapsulated in his literary triumph, *The Naked Civil Servant*, which was followed by numerous other books, the proceeds of which helped keep him solvent.

Quentin was a near-constant figure in Joan's life. When she got home from her work around the country or abroad, one of the first things she did was track down her friend, invariably finding him in a Soho café sipping pale grey coffee and mesmerising an audience of admirers. Their friendship lasted right up until his death, even after he moved permanently to New York in 1981. The pair kept up a lively correspondence; in fact, one of Quentin's last letters was to Joan. More about him later.

After initial struggles with her middle-class morals, Joan grew in confidence about stripping off for a room full of aspirant artists. Perhaps she felt she could wrap herself in an invisible cloak of respectability in that she was working for a noble cause: the greater good of the art world. She must have become quite inured to such a set up as she began also appearing nude in a completely different environment.

In the early 1930s, the Windmill Theatre in Soho was in its death throes when it was rescued by the risqué. Its fortunes changed dramatically when the owner, the eccentric socialite Laura Henderson, brought in the talented impresario Vivian Van Damm. The censor, the Lord Chamberlain, was responsible for enforcing the obscenity law that forbade the display of nudity on theatrical stages. This legislation was not going to stop Van Damm. He went to the censor and argued that if the performers were to stand still they would resemble a naked statue, like a work of art. How could art be seen as morally unacceptable? Amazingly his arguments won the day and so *tableaux vivants* arrived in London's Theatreland, and the legend of the Windmill Girls began. At some point a very young Joan became one of the naked statues. This was probably the first time she appeared on a proper theatrical stage.

She never acknowledged this major step in later life. She wouldn't have wanted people to think she was prepared to earn a crust by titillating dirty old men. The information comes to light through looking at her considerable archive. It's not hard to guess that she would have approached this change in direction with some trepidation, but then again she had become accustomed to the art students staring closely at every inch of her unclothed body.

In the theatre, at least there was a stage to separate her from the ogling audience, and the bright lights would have prevented her from seeing them clearly.

Joan loved to tell a tale. I don't want to say she was a good liar – although she admitted this much to me – but it was more than being economical with the truth. Rather, she was creative: a true storyteller. Why relate a bland incident when you can embroider it with lots of excitement and drama? She was careful to create her own narrative over the years and she wanted to give her life a beauty and majesty that perhaps didn't match up with the truth. With these events happening so long ago, it is hard to get to the bottom of most of her stories, but my research did uncover a perfect example of how Joan chose to twist the facts to fit her desired image. She was always at great pains to paint a heroic picture of life on the streets, but the truth caught up with her when I tracked down some old newspaper cuttings from August 1938.

One of Joan's favourite stories was about how she was arrested after physically picking a man up in the street. In Joan's version, it was daytime. Two men were following her, taunting her about whether she was as strong as she claimed. Exasperated by their persistence, she eventually began to lift one of them, but as his feet left the ground a policeman came along and assumed she was up to no good and attacking an innocent bystander. Joan lost her balance and grabbed the nearest means of support, which just happened to be the policeman's whistle chain. It snapped instantly. She was arrested, charged with assault and appeared in Bow Street Magistrates' Court the next day with a gang of her friends cheering her on from the public gallery. She said the case was dismissed.

The court reports in several newspapers tell a different story. Here's the version told by the *Daily Herald* on 12 August, under the headline 'Strong Girl Gives Pavement Show':

A girl wrestler and weightlifter, who gave the name of Joan Terena, aged 19, was placed on probation at Bow Street for obstructing the pavement by giving a weight-lifting exhibition.

A charge of assaulting a policeman who arrested her by kicking him in the leg was dismissed. The girl's real name was said by the police to be Taylor and her age 17. P.C. Hague said just before midnight the girl and five men were indulging in horseplay. She lifted and carried two men and passers-by had to walk off the pavement. He had to use some violence as she was exceptionally strong.

Miss Terena said that she went in for weight-lifting and was being paid while learning wrestling. On the night of her arrest some men acquaintances made a bet with her that she would not lift one of them. She lifted one and then another – a power-fully built man.

When the constable arrested her she seized his whistle chain to prevent her from falling but did not kick him.

This piece was accompanied by a picture of Joan bending a bar on her neck and tearing a telephone book in two. It was taken just outside the court. Joan was never one to pass up publicity, good or bad.

6

A WEDDING AND A WAR

One of the strangest pieces of the jigsaw puzzle of Joan's life was the question of matrimony. She was fond of telling me, and anyone else who would listen, that she would have loved to have been married but no man had ever asked her. She would roll her eyes at this point and shake her head in a mock attitude of dejected sadness. But there was always a smile and a cheeky sparkle in her eyes. Being passed over by men because of her Herculean strength was a trope she always used in her act. She made out that men ran away from her in fear that she might hurt them. Here was a gorgeous, statuesque, blonde bombshell who could literally pick men up, and yet she claimed that she couldn't get a boyfriend as men were too scared of her.

As we have seen, Joan was certainly not wedded to the truth. Yet it was still a shock to discover after her death that she had consistently been dishonest about a significant event that impacted her profoundly. I suspect certain aspects of her life became inconvenient truths and had to be carefully concealed so they could be left behind. Joan had spent the best part of sixty years hiding from the truth. It had never occurred to me to question where the name Rhodes came from: like everyone else, I assumed it was for the stage, just as 'Josie Terena' was. I wish I had tried to pin her down on this as it might have prompted her to share her long-hidden secret with me. It was a bit of a bombshell when I found out that this was in fact her real name. You see, she did marry — a few months after the Second World War broke out.

Her husband's name was Arthur Leonard Rhodes and he was a 23-year-old carpenter from Bow. The two met at the Serpentine in Hyde Park, where Joan and a friend would go swimming. Joan mentioned Arthur dismissively in her memoir. She said he was simply a friend who would walk her home from Soho at night. He would get her to the doorstep, give her a chaste kiss and then carry on walking to his home in the East End. Joan would have just turned 18. He was clearly a respectful young man who was serious about having a relationship with her. There's a picture of the pair looking fresh faced and in love. Arthur was a handsome young man, with gentle eyes and a movie-star jawline.

Inevitably, facts about Joan's life as Mrs Rhodes are rather sketchy, but there are a few scraps of evidence that show they were often apart for long periods of time. Arthur was in the RAF and away from home. He did accompany Joan to a family wedding in 1941 in Nottingham. By this time the three Taylor sisters — Peggy, Joan and Blackie — had been reunited. It was Peggy, the instigator of bringing the girls back together, who was getting married.

Why did Joan bury her marriage? Was she ashamed? Was her reason for becoming Mrs Rhodes not a romantic one? It was a time of great upheaval, with the arrival of another earth-shattering conflict. A lot of young people grabbed hold of what happiness they could at the time. With the horrors of the First World War still fresh in many minds, the prospect of more slaughter on the battlefields must have been terrifying. Perhaps Joan decided 'what the hell' and agreed to Arthur's repeated proposals. It was probably the first time in her tumultuous life that she hoped she could rely on another human being. In her memoir, Arthur was demoted to

Joan with her new husband, Arthur Rhodes, on their wedding day, 18 November 1940.

the role of boyfriend or chaperone. Perhaps the fact that she was worrying about being able to pay the rent on a flat influenced her to accept his hand:

'I'll help you,' he said, 'I'll move in with you – will you marry me?' I gave no answer. He was very handsome, 6'2" in height and athletic; a great swimmer. And so it was; the war had just started and after a few weeks he was called up and went into the Air Force. I never saw him again.

Joan's marriage only came to light thanks to the diligence of her nephew John. During his tenacious researching, he unearthed a wedding certificate, issued at Kensington Register Office, that stated that on Saturday 18 November 1939, Joan Louisa Ada Taylor and Arthur Leonard Rhodes were married.

They began their life together in a rented flat, 53 Elgin Crescent in Notting Hill, long before the area became home to the ultra-wealthy; in those days it was full of grotty, cheap accommodation. Arthur carried on working as a carpenter until he was called up and joined the RAF. It's clear from documents that Joan was pursuing her stage career at the time, which was beginning to look promising.

She had worked as an extra in films but was overjoyed, no doubt, when she received a much more exciting proposition from the British Broadcasting Corporation's new television service. This was cutting-edge entertainment, and all the performances were live. The corporation had started doing a magazine programme called *Picture Page*, transmitted from Alexandra Palace. In 1939, the BBC was being seen in almost 20,000 homes up and down the country. It might not sound like a large number by today's standards, but television was still a novelty in those days. It was a huge achievement for Joan to get onto the small screen. No recordings survive, but she must have impressed as she was asked back for two further performances. She was well paid, 6 guineas (£6 6s) for the first occasion, 9 guineas for the next two. At this point she was still using the name Josie Terena and gave her postal address as care of the Windmill Theatre.

The war broke out only days afterwards, and TV broadcasts ceased as the government feared that the VHF transmissions would have acted as a beacon for enemy aircraft flying over London. Furthermore, the technicians and engineers were needed for the war effort, especially in the development of sophisticated radar systems.

Joan had a strange relationship with the war. In her version of this time of death and destruction, she said she managed to mostly ignore what was going on; she even claimed to enjoy the war. She asserted that, from the first moment a siren sounded in 1939, she was a 'conchie' – a conscientious objector – but that political stance seems to have had quite a lot to do with her heart and not her head:

> I would go down to Soho and swear that no way was I going to join in. Boys had joined the International Brigade and gone to Spain to join in the Civil War – men came back and were promptly conscripted; if they objected they were told 'If you can fight in one war you can fight for Britain.' Many were on the run.

It's not clear what year she was referring to but it must have been the early 1940s. She was part of a Soho group of conchies and said that was where she fell in 'love at first sight' with a man called Bert. Of course, this doesn't sit very tidily with the fact that she was a relatively new bride. As ever, her recollections of events seemed to be a convenient muddle:

> I first met Bert at Tony's [café], he was surrounded by Soho intelligentsia and everyone was chattering away, all talking at once as usual. He was just sitting back listening and then when they all suddenly stopped he capped the lot and ended the debate in one sentence. They all slowly left; I stayed. He was tall, slim and fair and wore a trilby hat at the back of his head, and after a while he smiled at me and I noticed his beautiful teeth. I was captured!

It's difficult to pin down this new love of Joan's life. In terms of official records, he is virtually invisible. What is traceable is his birth certificate that shows his full name was Herbert Sanders and he was born in 1916 in County Durham. That's all that has been found in the way of hard facts.

Those who knew Bert spoke warmly of him. His accent belied his northern origins. One of the attributes that attracted Joan was his quiet intelligence; he was well read and had a wisdom beyond his years. Like her, he would sit quietly on the sidelines and listen to the rest of the group argue. The difference was he would bide his time and then chip in with a single observation that had the effect of confounding the others and shutting them up. She loved watching this performance and saw in Bert a kindred spirit. He was obviously better suited to Joan than Arthur, who was by this time stationed away from home with the RAF.

Bert had no papers and therefore no ration book. It's likely he was a deserter, on the run from the authorities. He obviously felt comfortable with others who were in the same position as him and that was how he found his way to Tony's, the cheap café in Soho. It seems this was another whirlwind romance for Joan, once again with the war in full fury and the ever-present spectre of being killed in a bombing raid. People didn't waste time. Bert, who was probably of no fixed abode, moved in with Joan at the first chance he got. He clearly knew when he was on to a good thing. And it was a relationship that did work for a long time; the years they spent together is evidence of that:

He walked me back to Elgin Crescent and in all innocence I asked him in for coffee or something. 'Something,' he said and he never left. In those days you couldn't live in what was called 'sin' so I told my neighbours that he was my cousin. We stayed together for about sixteen years and I never really heard his full story. He had been in the Merchant Navy and had been involved in some gun battle and never went back to sea.

The neighbours would have been aware that Joan was married to Arthur, who had been living there with her. Curtain-twitching was actively encouraged during the war; the government wanted people to be observant. It went from being a tiresome hobby to a question of national security. Seeing another young man living with her would have raised eyebrows and no doubt resulted in some vicious gossip. They would have guessed that Bert was a deserter and that would not have gone down well, especially as Arthur was off serving the war effort with the RAF. The canny locals would not have been fooled by the 'cousin' story; they would have been adept at adding two and two and getting twenty, and in this case they would have been correct. In her memoir, Joan carefully skirted around the fact that she was a married woman. She was a rule breaker who wanted to wrap herself in a shroud of decency, but was not so bothered with meeting the social mores of the time that she denied herself a life with a man who was her soulmate. With this knowledge it's possible to see why she wanted to erase her marriage.

Elgin Crescent and the surrounding area was heavily bombed during the war. Joan certainly had cause to feel under attack, but she insisted that it didn't bother her. I did try and tease out her wartime stories, but she never engaged in the horror narrative that most people would have cleaved to. Instead, she painted fanciful pictures that reflected a dogged determination to see the bright side of life:

> I enjoyed the blackout and used to walk around without shoes and if anyone mentioned it I would say I hadn't any clothes coupons, everything was rationed but I never felt poor or needy. I kept busy. I used to walk down by Hyde Park to Notting Hill Gate and sometimes there would be incendiary bombs raining down like fireworks. I never once went to a shelter and thought it fun to be the only person out during an air raid. I would pass bombed houses and think nothing of it – as I've often said, I wasn't very bright!

She portrayed herself as the epitome of the 'Keep Calm and Carry On' motto. From her own account she was having a great time, a busy social life where she and Bert would go out and eat for a few pence. Bert would magic up eggs and meat; he had contacts in the black market. They would hang out with their conchie crowd, mostly at Tony's, where they were welcome to stay until the wee hours of the morning and no one seemed to bother them.

But the bombs did make their mark on Joan's consciousness eventually. There was one night when Joan came across a house that had been destroyed. She witnessed a woman being pulled from the rubble – alive, but only just. This horrific scene was burnt into her mind; she was haunted by it. It was an encounter that could not be turned into a pleasant anecdote for her admiring audiences. She wrote a poem that encapsulated her feelings at the time:

> A bomb had fallen and a house blown down
> And a woman lay in the street in a tattered nightgown
> She cried for her man and two sons
> Who'd been murdered by German guns
> A lady came along and covered her up
> And gave her hot tea in an old chipped cup
> She looked up at me and nodded her head
> A few moments later I knew she was dead.

Joan said that after this she didn't go out much. She had no stomach for light-hearted socialising: it felt wrong. Witnessing such an appalling scene would have driven home to her how fragile life was. When you see someone die up close in such horrific circumstances you can carry away a survivor's guilt – 'Why her and not me?' To get through that feeling she went into a form of denial: she decided to ignore the war as best she could. A tall order when you were living in the heart of a favourite target for the German Luftwaffe.

Always on the lookout for employment, Joan was quick to abandon her conchie credentials in exchange for a meal on the table or getting the rent paid. Someone suggested to her that she should audition for the Entertainments National Service Association (ENSA). ENSA was an organisation set up in 1939 to entertain British armed forces during the Second World War. The government recognised the importance of keeping up morale among the troops by putting on shows for them. It was an opportunity for the famous to do their bit for the war effort; the illustrious list of performers included Noël Coward, George Formby and Vera Lynn. ENSA was also a useful training ground for launching a career in showbusiness; it nurtured the likes of Peter Sellers, Terry-Thomas and Kenneth Connor. Needless to say, it was an unlikely role for someone who was pledged to pacifism, but that didn't deter Joan.

She quickly put together an act of sorts, basically doing an eccentric dance to whatever music they chose, a bit of bending and stretching followed by tearing up a phone book. She kept it minimal as getting hold of bars and nails to bend was problematic with a war on. Her application was successful, and she took on a three-month tour of various factories producing items for the war, starting at an airfield near Catterick Camp in the North Riding of Yorkshire. Towards the end of the tour the troupe were at the aircraft factory at Filton near Bristol when, after the performance, the city was bombed. Joan related how the other girl in the show, who shared a room with her, was utterly beside herself with terror, screaming that they would all be killed. As for Joan, who would come to be known as the 'Mighty Mannequin', she just pulled the blanket up around her head and drifted off to sleep.

7

CARRYING ON

The war didn't stop Joan's nascent career; in fact, it did quite the opposite. When people feel like their world has been turned on its head, they look to entertainment for some respite. During the war, there was great succour in sitting cocooned in theatres that felt detached from what was going on in the real world. Audiences found themselves enveloped in a fug of cigarette smoke tinged with the smell of disinfectant, but there was nothing unusual about this and there was comfort in familiarity. For them, going to see a show was like the days before the conflict broke out. It was a brief intermission from the privations and dangers of a world they no longer recognised. This was great news for variety shows brave enough to keep their doors open. Business was brisk and performers like Joan were more than happy to fulfil this need for distraction.

It was a landmark day for Joan when she was approached by the theatrical agent Pearl Beresford to take part in a show in north London. This was in 1940, and the role involved nudity, but once again the tableaux would be static to slip under the radar of the obscenity laws. It was all to be enacted with as much dignity as possible, which probably was a tough call as dirty old men heckled from the stalls. This was something Joan was familiar with from her time at the Windmill Theatre. She'd also had several years posing in the buff for art colleges. It's unlikely she would have had any qualms about going down this road. Variety theatre in the 1930s and 1940s was extremely popular and seen as a much more socially acceptable entertainment than music hall, its highly risqué predecessor.

For Joan, being approached was a big break, and, all down to the astute instincts of Pearl Beresford. Another powerful woman and an actress and singer herself, Pearl was in tune with the world of variety – she knew what the producers and punters wanted to see and where to find the right people to deliver the goods. Pearl was an excellent talent spotter. Her office was in Charing Cross Road and she saw Joan doing her street performances nearby. She calculated, correctly, that a beautiful young woman who could bend bars and tear up phone books would go down well with audiences. This was the beginning of a fruitful long-term partnership.

The bill for the show read 'Personal Appearance of Miss Britain, the World's Most Beautiful and Strongest Girl':

> She booked me for Collins Music Hall in Islington as 'Miss Britain' doing nude poses ('Don't move!') described by the compère and then in the second half of the show (in costume!) tearing a telephone book and bending a bar. The poses were quite modest: one 'In a monastery garden' kneeling and with a piece of silk hiding most of me and then the 'Young Javelin Champion' with my back to the audience – 'Turn 'er rahnd!' shouted a loud Cockney voice. I picked up £10 for the week and then back I went to Charing Cross Road. I suppose it all helped the war effort.

The rest of the show was made up of mediocre acrobats, dancers and comedians – but imagine what a change it was for Joan to be working away from the vagaries of the weather and have a paying audience. They might have been rough, ready and rude but their reliable presence meant she didn't have to worry about where her next few pennies were coming from. There was also some prestige in appearing at Collins' Music Hall, which was steeped in history having been open since 1863. All that is left now is a blue plaque and its façade after the hall was destroyed by fire in 1958. However, all is not lost for the music hall; at the time of writing, there are plans to redevelop the site back into a theatre.

As for Joan, her brief spell in Islington ended and she was forced back to the streets, but only for a relatively short time. She was beginning to make her mark. It might not have felt like it as she went through her daily street routine, but being spotted by those further up the ladder meant her career was heading in the right direction.

During the war, the film industry was embraced by the government as a means of keeping up the national spirit. With official approval came the funding needed to keep the cameras rolling. Joan had been a huge fan since her years spent on the breadline, when she would duck into one of the myriad of cinemas in the West End as a refuge. She would tuck herself into a cheap seat and spend hours gorging on the flickering images, watching the stars glitter on the silver screen. She saw some films so often she knew the dialogue by heart. It's no wonder that it became her ambition to emulate the glamorous actresses who populated this emerging field of entertainment.

Another step on the ladder was being contracted to appear in a touring show called *Scandals and Scanties*. As the name suggests, it was far from a high-class venture. Once again, Joan was called upon to strike a naked pose. It was a long way from rubbing shoulders with movie stars but it was an income, and Joan had been forced to do worse in the past.

According to the theatre newspaper *The Stage*, the show began touring in December 1942. The lead act was Hal Moss and his Mayfair Swingtette. Moss, a talented violinist, was well known for his work on radio. Also on the bill was a 'Sensational and Daring Nude Cuban Dancer', a woman described as the top Australian comedienne with the bizarre name of Louise Crotch, and a motley crew of long-forgotten singers and dancers.

Joan was billed under her early stage name: 'Gorgeous Terena Rhodes and her lovely ladies presents her Art Tableaux of Living Statues.' This fits in with her contract, which identified her as 'Joan Terena Rhodes, known as Terena Rhodes or any other given name' and states that she will appear, as required, as 'Posing Act, Tableaux, Show-Lady, Nude Dancer, Spectacular Act, Sensational Dancer'. It stated that she would be paid £8 a week plus a bonus not exceeding £3, should her performance 'satisfy Management in every way' – whatever that means. There was an additional note typed in red stating that the agreement was 'always subject to war conditions and emergencies'.

The war plagued the production as Hal Moss saw his musicians called up one by one. He did his best to find replacements but inevitably most of them had no previous experience in the theatre. It didn't bode well for the tour. *Scandals and Scanties* lasted a few months, closing after it had finished at the Theatre Royal in Castleford.

Once again, Joan headed back to the streets of central London to earn a crust. But the woman who came home from the north was finding her feet and the courage she needed to take back full control of her life. While on the road, she decided the time had come to sort out a glaring error from the recent past. She wrote to Arthur and told him never to come home again and that she wanted to end the marriage. It seems that this came as something of a shock to Arthur, who wrote back begging her to change her mind. Perhaps he didn't realise that she was already living with another man. When Arthur did come home on leave at Easter, Joan refused to let him through the door. No doubt if he did manage to push past her, he would quickly see that someone had taken his place. There's no evidence of Arthur making any further attempts at reconciliation. It appears he finished his leave and went back to his work for the RAF.

The next we hear of Arthur is when the divorce papers came through, years after Joan had closed the door in his face. She received a copy of Arthur's petition for divorce on the grounds of her desertion of him for a period of three years or more. The marriage was formally dissolved on 2 May 1947. Arthur was never mentioned again and the only keepsake she retained from her ill-fated union was the name Rhodes. She decided to keep the whole episode a closely guarded secret for the rest of her life. Stepping back and looking at her life at the time, it is possible to see why she adopted this course of action. In those days, living in sin was bad enough but cheating on a husband who was serving his country with a probable deserter pushed the set-up into the realms of unpatriotic. As a woman with high ambitions to be a famous performer, she knew that a scandal like this could ruin her.

As ever, Joan did things her way. She wouldn't let anyone else dictate how she should live her life; she didn't bow to social conventions. If she wanted something, she took it and figured out later how to make it work. She showed great courage for one so young at a time when women were supposed to be quietly obedient. Context is important here. Imagine you have just been through six years of living in a world overshadowed by Hitler and his bombing raids. For young people, it was a time to take back some of the life they had been forced to give up. The mood was one of relief but also one of 'living for the day'. If you add that to the Joan cocktail, you can see why she must have thought, 'To hell with it; I'll do it my way.' After all, she was already strongly inclined to do what she wanted. Appearing in the nude was regarded as scandalous but that didn't stop her, and it's clear that Bert didn't attempt to keep her covered up in public.

Joan carried on doing nude appearances after the end of the war. Among her huge collection of keepsakes is a poster from April 1946 for the Catterick Camp Officers' Club, an army base in Yorkshire that had its own Gaiety Theatre for entertaining the troops.

OFFICERS CLUB
CATTERICK CAMP.

SPECIAL ATTRACTION

SATURDAY, 6TH APRIL, 1946
FLOOR SHOW
at 10-30 p.m.

Britain's Strongest Girl
Miss JOAN RHODES
The Beautiful Model who is giving
1. NUDE STUDIES.
2. EXHIBITION OF STRENGTH.
AT THE GAIETY THEATRE, THIS WEEK
will give an
EXHIBITION OF STRENGTH
at THE CLUB

BEAUTY AND STRENGTH

ARE WOMEN THE WEAKER SEX?
Come and See for Yourself.

Spencers, Printers, Richmond.   Phone 2107.

The bill from a show for the Officers' Club at Catterick in 1946, part of entertaining the troops.

The notice reads: 'Britain's Strongest Girl Miss Joan Rhodes – The Beautiful Model who is giving (1) NUDE STUDIES (2) EXHIBITION OF STRENGTH ... ARE WOMEN THE WEAKER SEX? Come and See for Yourself.'

In the same year, Joan ventured briefly into the world of fashion, appearing in the spring collection of the designer Simon Massey. She was a natural in front of the camera. The pictures of her modelling show a refined-looking young woman with a tiny waist wearing a self-possessed expression. She was physically in great shape, tall and trim, though not stick-thin. In those days, bones sticking out meant destitution, not beauty.

The role of mannequin didn't last. Joan continued to work the streets while a steady and growing stream of contractual work came in. Pearl Beresford engaged her to appear on a float as an athlete in the Lord Mayor's Show. This was, and still is, a highly prestigious annual event in London's calendar. It's been held for over 800 years and brings the city to a standstill. Joan told me that she remembers her float going past thousands of cheering onlookers but all she was concerned about was how cold she was in her skimpy outfit. As she told me this tale Joan went off into her bedroom and came back with the actual garment. She showed me her teeny tiny shorts, which looked small enough to fit a 10-year-old. They were a great hit on the big day.

As ever, Joan attracted odd characters. One of them was Mickey Wood, whose Mayfair gym she joined to learn judo. She hadn't anticipated that Mickey would take an interest. He was described in the *Sunday Mirror* in 1947 as a former lightweight wrestling champion who had survived a tough life. He had brain surgery as a child, served in the First World War and was a lieutenant-instructor to the Commandos during the Second World War. He'd originally taken up body building because he was so frail. Having been through so much, he was a tough man to impress, and he had a particular dislike of fraudsters. When he met Joan his first instinct was to deride her and accuse her of being a fake. This did not go down well with Joan, who quickly taught him a lesson:

'Why do you want to learn judo?' he asked me, 'Want to go throwing your weight about?'

I told him that I didn't need judo for that and that I was already stronger than I wanted to be and could bend nails and tear up phone books. He sneered. 'Yes, I know – phone books – it's an old trick. They bake 'em in an oven.'

'Is that phone-book over there baked?' I asked him, and went across the room and tore it into quarters. I banged his punch-ball right off its leather straps, picked up a heavy looking barbell and heaved it straight from the ground.

Mickey Wood said, in a far away voice, 'That barbell weighs 360 pounds. You've probably just made a world record. Who did you say you were?'

I told him: 'Joan Rhodes.'

'Never heard of you,' he said, 'but we'll make people hear of you, believe me! Bring a pair of shorts with you tomorrow morning.'

When I got there he had a crowd of press photographers and we took pictures for the next couple of weeks.

Pictures from the sessions led to some great publicity for both of them. The *Daily Mirror* ran a piece in February 1947 showing Joan throwing Mickey over her shoulder. Then the *London Illustrated News* ran a two-page spread with the words: 'A girl with her strength and figure (height 5 ft. 8 in.; bust 34 in.; waist 24 in.; hips 36 in.; shoes and gloves 7) and her physical faculties, ought to be a big hit.'

This triggered similar articles in magazines around the world. The media loved filling column inches with pictures of Joan; a skimpily clad strongwoman was good for sales. Joan didn't learn much judo, but she benefited from Mickey's knack for publicity.

With the war over, BBC TV was allowed back on air. This was great news for Joan as the programme she'd appeared on, *Picture Page*, was revived and its makers wanted her back in the studio. She was also in a show called *New to You*. Pearl dealt with the contract and managed to squeeze a bit more money out of the corporation this time: 10 guineas (£10 10s) per performance.

As the world settled into a new post-war normal, Joan found herself seeing more of it than she had anticipated. She was off to sunny Spain in charge of a ragtag group of showgirls.

8

¡VIVA ESPAÑA!

Joan had always been fascinated by different cultures and so when Pearl asked her if she would like to go on tour to Spain, her first trip abroad, the answer was never in doubt. Not only was the job location appealing, but the wages were irresistible: she would be paid £14 a week, minus Pearl's 10 per cent. All she had to do was persuade those managing the tour that she was right for the job.

She'd be one of ten dancers. Pearl advised her not to mention tearing phone books and bending bars; this engagement called for a showgirl and dancer, not a strongwoman. The fact that Joan had no training in dancing didn't pose an obstacle in her mind. She would have assumed she had mastered the art of throwing herself around the stage in what approximated to a dance routine during her performances for the troops. Or so she thought. For the interview she was told to wear her prettiest dress and only a hint of make-up, just lipstick and powder.

She was seen by Joe Collins, father of the actress Joan and the author Jackie. He became one of the most influential talent agents in the world, promoting the likes of the Beatles, Peter Sellers and Shirley Bassey. Joan bounced into the room and proudly displayed some publicity shots of herself in the nude. She had hoped they would clinch the deal, but Joe was disapproving. Although he liked what he saw, he warned her to ditch the naughty images.

This was a very high-class show. Still, he was impressed enough to give her the job.

Despite what Joe had to say, the troupe of ten girls who gathered at Victoria Station at the start of the tour were far from classy. Most of them couldn't dance; only a few had dancing experience. Their clothes were mostly ragged as rationing was still in place in 1948.

At 26, Joan was the eldest of the group. This didn't stop her tinkering with the truth when it came to applying for a passport. She shaved off five years to make herself almost as young as the other girls. She wasn't worried about falsifying official documents; she always regarded adjusting her age to suit a situation as her prerogative. It was a habit of a lifetime. The risk of being found out was slight. This was long before computers took over the world and people could be checked in a matter of seconds. Pearl, who'd known her for years, knew the truth and judged that her seniority qualified her as the best person to put in charge. She sent Joan a lengthy letter that she was to carry with her during the trip. It was a cross between a teacher laying down the law and a mother hen clucking about letting her brood loose on an unsuspecting Spain. Some of the issues Pearl tackled cast an intriguing light on how Britons viewed 'foreign climes' so soon after the war:

20th January, 1948.

Dear Joan Rhodes

First and foremost you are going abroad and you are going to a country, Spain, which is a Fascist country. Now that means that they have different political and religious views from those that we hold here in Britain. I would suggest, without knowing your political views, that you do not express any opinion about politics or religion and certainly do not convey in any way a feeling of comparing their country to our country unfavourably. For one thing they would not like it any more than we would like it here if the position were reversed and secondly it will keep you out of a lot of trouble.

I would like you each to remember that many Spanish people will be meeting you as a representative of Britain and it may be that you are the only British person they have met. Therefore, please remember that you are an ambassadrice for Britain and so please let them see British girls are well mannered, well behaved and kindly, but I would really like to impress on you again, because this is really important, not to compare their system of life to ours and not to tell them how better we British people are to them (although, of course, we really do know it).

The tone speaks volumes. In those days, Spain was regarded with suspicion. Pearl's words of advice were charmingly prim and proper, even when she dealt with the tricky matter of sex:

Surely, I do not need to tell you not to listen to tales from tall dark handsome strangers even though those strangers may go out of their way to cultivate your friendship over a period of time. You are all picked for being attractive girls, an attractive girl in show business is the rule, not the exception and although Spain may seem a very romantic country it is possible that if you do not let your good sense guide you, what may seem very romantic will afterwards appear very sordid, very tawdry and disillusioning.

She even strongly urged the troupe to write home, avoid alcohol and make friends with Spanish families if they could:

Remember to write to your parents every week because they are bound to be concerned about you. Don't drink alcoholics please. Remember the Spanish people look upon women who smoke in public as being of a very low type, so please watch this for your own sake. Whenever possible make friends with families so that you can get to know the family side, the nice side, of life over in Spain and so that you can come back with happy memories and friends.

I wonder what a modern theatrical agent would make of these instructions. Of course, Pearl didn't want to find herself on the receiving end of an international incident, but she does appear to have had genuine concern for her girls, perhaps because she came from the same background. For instance, she had them all signed up safely on an Equity/Variety Artistes' Federation standard contract for Europe. The tour was to run for twenty-six weeks with fourteen performances a week. Would her little lambs obey her strictures? Of course not.

Inevitably, Joan was given the nickname of Head Girl, and in that role she quickly felt the weight of responsibility. As they travelled to Madrid by train, their two compartments were invaded by a horde of Spanish labourers whose behaviour was hardly going to endear the girls to the local population. They ended up crammed into one carriage with their coats over the window to block out the view of the men shouting obscenities and making lewd gestures. Their suitcases were piled up to stop any of the ruffians getting in. A scary start to the adventure.

The next hurdle came when they got to their seedy accommodation, the Pension Delicias. They were told rehearsals began the next day at noon and they must be dressed for the occasion. No one had told them to bring rehearsal gear. Being a bit racy, Joan had brought some slacks, although she paid a price for being trendy as women wearing trousers in Spain were thought to be prostitutes at that time. When she went out, a group of aggressive young men crowded around and heckled her. She was ready for a fight but decided escape was her best course of action in a foreign country. But that was nothing compared with the next headache.

The following day in the rehearsal rooms, the British girls came face to face with the sobering reality of their shabbiness. They were confronted by ten petite and smartly turned-out Frenchwomen. Dressed in leotards and the correct shoes for rehearsing, they looked every inch like professional hoofers. Joan's team were in a shambolic mixture of outfits as Lee, one of the girls, describes:

We were attired in a strange assortment of garments … dirndl skirts, threadbare slacks – Joan, alias 'Rhodes el Capitan', was sporting a navy and white striped sweater, navy slacks and white plimsoles; just ready for Cowes. Terry [was] in a pair of black celanese pyjamas, while Rosemary wore white shorts, white spiky court shoes, a faraway expression and a very revealing off the shoulder blouse … Merle had already danced with a show in Italy, Pearl and Maureen had both been in revue and I had done my stint at the Cabaret Club so, as I remember it, we were the only four who could, in fact, dance.

The French girls, all highly experienced dancers, were known as 'Les Ballets de Paris' and were sharing the bill with the gang from Blighty. Their disdain for the motley crew from across the Channel was visible in their pretty faces. The trouble was that not only were most of Joan's girls ignorant of basic dance steps, but there had been no time for any of them to even try dancing together. The British girls must have been mortified as the choreographer put the French girls through their paces. The contrast could not have been more glaring. Joan tried to explain the limitations of her troupe but the woman was having none of it. She had the French girls demonstrate how it should be done and wanted the British girls to reciprocate by showing what they could do. It was a disaster, of course. I imagine the choreographer clucking like an angry hen as it dawned on her that she had her work cut out if she was going to get this lot in shape.

Fortunately, she didn't stomp out of the rehearsal room in a histrionic rage. She calmed herself and told the girls they would be called 'Ballet Taub from London' and that they had one month to learn ten dances. Then they would be appearing at the Grand Via Theatre. Joan said she vividly recalls thinking there was no way they were going to pull this off. But the choreographer was determined, and according to Joan she drilled the girls morning, noon and night like a sergeant major. It would be nice to report that the hard work paid off, but this wasn't Hollywood. Despite their best efforts, they ended up needing an extra month before they were deemed good enough to go before the public.

One of the toughest aspects of the show was the requirement for quick costume changes as there were so many routines. The outfits were tailored for each girl, but that didn't make the process any easier. The costumes were very complicated with body padding, clip-on moustaches and bowler hats. One act required them to wear plastic printed with flowers, which was a thin transparent material that would tear easily. By the end of the tour the girls found themselves mainly clad in sticky tape.

With a beatific look, Joan told me how she would quietly go back to her hotel room after a performance and genteelly read a book as the others hit the town. Having said that, she wasn't quite Snow White. On one occasion she made herself an itsy bitsy sunbathing bikini out of a scarf, but it was so small that a local policeman decided it was obscene. He covered her up and made her move on, much to the disappointment of an admiring crowd of men. There was also the occasion when she decided to make the train journey to Lisbon more exciting by climbing out of the carriage and travelling on the roof. Hardly the actions of a saint, more a naughty schoolgirl. But she avoided the temptations of local men, unlike some of her charges. Despite the exhortations from Pearl, by the end of the six-month tour there were only three English girls left in the troupe; the others had found their tall, dark strangers.

Joan arrived home armed with precious new skills. One of the first people she wanted to see was Quentin, something that became habitual in the coming years when she was on the road. He was her mentor and friend, so she wanted to share with him the ups as well as the downs. She tracked him to one of his usual cafes and over pale grey coffee and builder's tea, she regaled him with tales of her adventure, sharing how through hard work and determination she had learnt professional stagecraft. Her apprenticeship as a strongwoman working the streets was over; she had graduated. And she needed to keep the money coming in, as she and Bert were in debt. It's not clear how Joan's weekly wages had been spent while she was on the road, but the most likely culprit was the almost derelict flat in Belsize Park where the pair were living. Although Bert provided the labour, money was needed to make it liveable.

37A Belsize Park Gardens was in a dreadful state when they moved in. The deal was that Joan and Bert could rent it for only £90 a year if they repaired it. There had been a German bomb land in the road outside and the damage in 37A was extensive but not irreparable. The ceilings were down, floorboards were missing and glass was broken. Only one room was liveable but that was enough for the young couple, who passed themselves off as married. According to Joan, Bert certainly pulled his weight. He got mates in to help clear the place, then set to work making it habitable. Although he found most of his materials on the black market, the project would have been costly. Bert's situation hadn't changed financially as he still had no ID card or National Insurance number. All he could do to earn a crust was casual work and there wasn't much of that around. Joan was the breadwinner, a state of affairs that continued throughout their time together. It was tough but it was the way Joan preferred things to be, with herself firmly in control.

She got home to a more presentable flat patched up by Bert and his gang. There was a new large sofa, but what overjoyed Joan the most was that they'd built her a wardrobe in her bedroom. However, this wasn't a time to sit back and admire their handiwork; there were bills to pay and mouths to feed. Joan was a committed female hunter-gatherer.

She wouldn't have known it at the time, but Joan was in the process of putting down strong roots after a life constantly on the run. She lived at 37A for the rest of her life, sixty-two years. The large garden flat was a mirror of her life, stuffed with relics and mementoes, as I found when I met her there for the first time decades later.

She began her search for work by visiting some of her old haunts in Soho and the Chelsea Arts Club, a well-known hang-out for artists, actors and luvvies in general. She found her sister Blackie here with their mutual friend Alec Clunes, father of the actor Martin. Joan would often talk about how Alec flirted with her but that she always resisted his charms. It looked as though it was a wasted trip to the club as no one had any useful leads on possible work. But as she was leaving, she snaffled a copy of *The Stage* and took it to a café where she could study the listings of shows on the hunt for performers.

There were a number of ads looking for dancers and then a strange entry which read 'Freaks wanted for new show – Would You Believe It.'

Joan opted for familiar turf and went to several dance auditions but as she watched the competition go through their paces, she realised she just wasn't good enough despite her months on tour. She then went for a job as a showgirl. This involved putting on high heels, being able to wriggle and walk at the same time while looking sexy. She fared better here and was told to go to a dressing room with one other girl called Daphne; they had clearly passed the test. But then the woman in charge of the selection came in and said quite simply, 'Tops down.' Daphne had no qualms, but Joan was having none of it. Her time on tour in Spain had changed her. She had decided that the days of flaunting her naked body were over; her aunt would have been delighted. Despite desperately needing the work, she refused to go topless, and, inevitably, she was shown the door; Daphne got the job instead.

Thankfully, this new Joan was not averse to the weird and wonderful, or she and Bert might have starved. She revisited the ads in *The Stage* and decided to audition for the freak show. This form of entertainment had boomed in the Victorian and Edwardian eras, when exhibiting people with physical abnormalities on stage or in circuses was considered quite acceptable; even Queen Victoria found them amusing. Dwarfs, giants, conjoined twins, those with sexual anomalies, women with beards and so on were in demand. One of the most famous people on display was Joseph Merrick, known as the 'Elephant Man'.

You could not stage a freak show today. Parading people with disabilities would be rightly abhorrent to the public. Not that we

prurient humans aren't still fascinated by those we regard as different to the rest. You just have to look at TV programmes that deal
with physical and mental difference to confirm our hunger hasn't
abated; it has just been packaged differently.

For Joan, stepping into this strange arena was a career-changing
decision that was to mark the rest of her life. Pete Collins, the
theatre impresario, was putting the show together and Joan easily
got an interview. However, the session didn't have a promising
start, as Pete could see nothing strange about Joan.

Joan found herself in a packed waiting room. She later described
the scene:

> It was crowded out with midgets and a couple of very tall men,
> a man with no arms and a couple of very ugly people. I sat there
> until my name was called and then went into the inner office
> where a chubby man was sitting at a desk with a girl beside him
> taking notes.
>
> 'Well,' he said, 'you don't look very freakish to me.'
>
> 'I'm very strong,' I said.
>
> 'What's the good of that?' he replied. 'Well, I can make an Act.
> I tear telephone books into quarters and break six-inch nails,
> I've just been in Spain in a show for nearly a year.'
>
> 'What weight can you lift?' he asked.
>
> I said: 'I've lifted 360 pounds in Mickey Wood's gym, I could
> probably lift more. I can lift two men – one in each arm – or
> support a platform with six men on it. I can lift you.' – I reck-
> oned he was about 15 stone.
>
> 'Try,' he said.
>
> So I did, and walked round his small office as he laughed. 'All
> right – you can have a contract – what's your name?'
>
> 'The Mighty Mannequin,' I said.
>
> 'No, your real name,' he said and I told him it was Joan Rhodes.
>
> 'Right,' he said, 'you start at the Nottingham Empire in two
> weeks' time and I expect you to have your costume and music

ready by then. £17 per week – your costume will be a leopard-skin leotard I suppose.'

'Oh no,' I said, 'I wear an evening gown.'

'Now that's freakish!' said Pete Collins. 'Come in tomorrow and sign the contract.'

Success! Now all she had to do was come up with a convincing act, with a costume and music. It was a bit of a tall order to sort this in just two weeks, but Joan was driven by necessity and gritty determination that had got her this far. As it turned out, the sewing lessons enforced on her by her aunt when she was younger came in handy. She bought some shiny material at Portobello Market to make a skirt that cost her only sixpence. It was the rest of the outfit that ate up her limited funds. She bought a sexy black basque and made it come alive in the light after stitching multicoloured sequins all over it. Then she stuck some sequins on her shoes – and, hey presto, she had her costume.

She turned to an old friend, Frank Richardson, for the nuts and bolts of her act. He ran rehearsal rooms in Gerard Street. He gave her a pile of phone books and helped select the right music. Not the 'March of the Gladiators', as you might expect for a strong-woman act, but the much more demure 'Sweet and Lovely', with drum rolls at the appropriate moments. She couldn't risk perform-ing on the streets now as someone from Pete Collins's office might spot her and she'd been careful to hide her lowly past.

It was an anxious train ride to Nottingham. When Joan was confronted with the rest of the cast at the station, her heart sank. Some of the group she'd come across at Pete Collins's office were there, including a couple of giants, a dwarf and a man with no arms. She admitted that she wondered what on earth she was let-ting herself in for, but she had gone too far to back out at this point. She'd signed a twelve-month contract and the pay would be welcome. The other nagging worry as they headed north was how her cobbled-together act was going to go down. She'd never had

The cast of Would You Believe It, *1949. Joan is fourth from the left in the back row.*

the chance to do a run-through in public so she had no idea what an audience would think.

Her first show at the Nottingham Empire was a matinee, and she was to open the second half. Worried, but professional, Joan went through her new 'Mighty Mannequin' act, tearing phone books, bending nails and glittering for all she was worth. She went over her allotted seven minutes, but the enthusiastic applause confirmed she was on the right track. She was told she could run to nine minutes in future. From then on, her confidence began to build and she started enjoying herself.

One of the headline acts was billed as 'The Greatest Heavyweight Contest Ever Staged: The Battle of the Giants – combined weight sixty-three stone'. The two men were real giants but not over 9ft tall, as the publicity for the show cheekily claimed. The promoters used every trick they could to make the men seem taller. One was Belgian-born Fernand Bachelard, who reached a full height of 7ft 4½in. His adversary was Ted Evans, Britain's tallest man at 7ft 8½in.

In a circus-style twist, the referee of the fight was called 'Pippi the Famous Midget', said to be 34in high. He would weave in and out of the giants' legs, making a nuisance of himself but also putting his life in danger, much to the delight of the audience.

Another performer was Elroy, the 'Armless Wonder'. He had been born without arms but could do everything he needed to with his legs and feet. He could draw and paint, thread a needle, shoot a gun and eat and drink using his feet. Once, he even made a crafty attempt at touching up Joan. He said, 'You're a pretty thing,' and put one of his legs around her waist, giving her a squeeze. I don't think his attempt to molest the Mighty Mannequin went down too well, but she wouldn't have had much trouble repelling Elroy.

Joan had a particular soft spot for 'a very sad lion' called Mushie. A young woman called Ellen Harvey who said she had grown up with him would put on a bathing costume, wrestle with the creature and then lie back and let Mushie eat a steak off her forehead.

To add to the excitement, Ellen claimed that the animal was far from tame and had attacked at least twenty-four people, including herself. Joan wasn't convinced that 'gentle old' Mushie, who she only saw let out of his cage 'for that few minutes of the show', was a danger to anyone other than the musicians in the orchestra pit:

> During the show they would wheel his cage on and a chain which was attached to him would be hooked onto a metal ring in the centre of the stage. Mushie would saunter out and urinate against the backcloth and Harvey would say, 'That's what he thinks of Nottingham' – or whatever town we were in. One evening Mushie was feeling a bit off and pee'd into the orchestra pit onto the band leader, who was wearing a wig which fell off. The audience loved it but it only happened once in the year I was with the show!

As the show travelled to the top variety theatres up and down the country, Joan was finding herself more and more in the limelight.

All the local newspapers clamoured for pictures of this gorgeous girl bending bars and picking up hefty men. At one venue an agent wanted to sign her up but only if she stopped using 'a silly voice that sounded like the bleedin' Queen'. He had obviously missed the point of Joan's act.

Joan came under a lot of pressure from Pete Collins to lift weights on stage but she was having none of it. As far as she was concerned, she did not want the bulging muscles of the average all-in-wrestler. She would have hated looking big and manly. The warm reception she received from the public assured her that she was right to insist on being glamorous and feminine.

Her act prompted many column inches of publicity. It soon became routine that after the first night at a new venue, a photographer and reporter would ask to take pictures of Joan picking up the tallest of the giants, Ted Evans.

In reality, Ted was quite fragile. A complication of gigantism is weakness in many parts of the body. At first, he was scared that Joan would drop him, but gradually he came to trust her grip. In fact, he complained that her grip was too firm and that she had bruised him. Joan wasn't convinced and thought he was complaining for the sake of it, but Ted was probably telling the truth. People with Ted's condition are more at risk of premature death, and he died about nine years after doing the show. He was just 34 years old.

Joan would agree to drop celebrities on purpose if it meant good publicity, something she did to the famous cricket commentator and broadcaster Brian 'Johnners' Johnston. She was performing at the Shepherd's Bush Empire during one of his live shows, known as *Let's Go Somewhere*. He asked if she could lift all 14st of him, and she promptly obliged. Small change from his pockets went everywhere, which he was probably expecting. He was unaware Joan had been primed by the producer to let go of him so he fell to the floor. He was shocked to find himself landing on the stage with a bump. It made such an impression on Johnners that he mentioned the incident in his autobiography many years later.

As her time with the show was coming to an end, the tensions between Joan and Pete Collins mounted. He wouldn't release her from her contract early so she could take up an offer to perform at Boswell's Circus in South Africa. This infuriated Joan, who, as we know, didn't take well to being told what to do. He did try and persuade her to stay on his books, offering her £20 a week if she promised not to tell the other performers. But Joan was not open to negotiation; she was bloody minded and headstrong when faced with someone trying to make her do things she didn't want to. She was so angry with Pete that she would rather face unemployment than tie herself to him for any longer. She refused to have anything more to do with the Collins menagerie. It was a huge risk, familiar territory for Miss Rhodes.

She quickly cobbled together a cunning plan. Instead of doing endless auditions or going from office to office, she went along to the Empire Billiards Club in Frith Street, Soho, where most of the theatrical agents hung out at lunchtime to play snooker. She got herself a ginger ale and sat in the club, quietly waiting to see if anyone would take the bait. It wasn't long before one of the most famous agents in town, Solly Black, approached her:

'Tell me,' he said, 'we're all in show business here, we've enjoyed your act, it's a very fine act. But what my friends and I want to ask you' – he nodded towards the bar where several other agents stood watching – 'is what is the trick in your act? I mean to say, a slip of a girl like you – you're hardly half my size. How can you lift giants and tear phone books and stuff like that? If it's a conjuring trick it's a very clever one, but you can't expect us to book an act without explaining how it's done.'

I said: 'You think it's a fake?'

He laughed. 'Come on, we know it's a fake.'

So I lifted him up into the air and carried him round the billiards tables with my arms stretched over my head. It was a very dignified club and for a moment there was a shocked silence.

Then everybody started roaring with laughter and I knew I had won.

Solly Black promptly gave me a contract and from then on I had no trouble with theatrical agents.

It was an excellent result. Joan had risked it all and won. Solly was one of the best in the business and he was her agent until his death in 1959. He had influence at home and abroad. He was also linked by marriage to the Winogradsky brothers, better known as Lew and Leslie Grade, and Bernard Delfont, basically British showbiz royalty at that time. A sparkling future beckoned as Solly was the perfect agent to build on Joan's growing popularity and celebrity.

9

BABY BLUES

The 1950s had arrived and with the new decade came exciting new opportunities thanks to Solly Black. The former wrestler-turned-theatrical agent was a bit like a rotund fairy godfather. He looked after his acts, nurturing them and doing his best to guide them to some kind of financial order. Just like Pearl Beresford, he took a parental interest in this unlikely strongwoman. He encouraged her to keep a record of her earnings, to pay her National Insurance and to always be honest with the taxman. As a result, she became an inveterate hoarder, never throwing away anything which might help her with the annual chore of filling in tax returns. He also urged her to keep a scrapbook of press cuttings and, in a rare display of obedience, she did just that by registering with the International Press Cuttings Bureau. When her fame became global, she was getting cuttings mentioning her from weird and wonderful venues all over the world. It became something of an obsession and, thankfully for her biographer, she kept every single snippet.

Joan's first out-of-London stage appearance for Solly took her to the Palace Theatre in Mansfield, Nottinghamshire. She wasn't happy. She hated the theatre and the shoddy accommodation that had been organised for her. This prompted an angry letter to her new agent and an early power struggle. She put in a plea for better digs but also for more future bookings to be in London. At least on her home turf she could control her surroundings better.

Below is Solly's characteristically witty reply (which also includes evidence that his secretary wasn't the best of the bunch):

SOLLY BLACK LTD.
15th February 1950
Dear Joan,
Many thanks for your letter enclosing commission for Television, for which I enclose receipt.

I am very sorry to hear about the bad accomodations [*sic*] at the Palace Mansfield, but you can only blame yourself, I do remember your mother saying please Joan don't go on the stage, but the glory and the glamour of the footlights attracted you so much, that you could not resist it, I am sure that you are sorry now.

Fooling apart, I am trying all I can to fix you something before you start with the show, but unfortunatly [*sic*] I cant promise London, anyway if I do get an offer I will phone you immediatly [sic].

Your Television was definitly [*sic*] a big succes [*sic*], and everybody liked it. Kind regards,
Yours sincerely. Solly Black

Poor spelling notwithstanding, it was a clever letter that would have appealed to Joan's sense of humour while disguising the harsher message: basically 'shut up and get on with it'. Solly must have won this first round as Joan continued to work for him, no flouncing out. Thank goodness she did control her fiery nature as he had great plans for his new act. The first part of her career development involved ensuring she was seen as far and wide as possible. For Joan, this meant clocking up lots of road miles. She didn't mind too much as she had indulged in an extravagant purchase – she'd somehow got her hands on a brand-new, maroon-coloured Morris Minor soft top. It came with the registration BEE 853, which made her love it even more.

Looking at records of the bookings, it is possible to reconstruct Solly's thinking. His initial aim was to target established theatres up and down the country. Big, small, buzzing or staid – he didn't mind, so long as it furthered Joan's fame. Then he would fill in

With acrobats at the Finsbury Park Empire.

any gaps with appearances in night clubs. Her act was perfect for cabaret as the audience participation played well in these more intimate environments. By this point, Joan had settled on how her act should go. She could tweak it here and there and she was confident enough to adjust her time on stage and adapt content to better suit the audience. Theatre bookings would normally be for a week, sometimes extended to two, whereas cabaret tended to be shorter runs and 'one-offs' – their attraction for Joan was that they were most likely to be in London.

In fact, Solly found her a cabaret booking in London immediately after Mansfield, before sending her to theatres in Crayford and Sheerness in Kent followed by Tonypandy and Queens Park. Thereafter she hardly drew breath, with every week booked up. April: Oldham, Middlesborough, Gateshead, Bishop Auckland. May: York, Workington, Doncaster, Rochdale (two weeks). June: Hull, Eastbourne, Bolton, Cambridge. July: Wood Green (Essex), Southport, and then an eight-week summer season in Skegness.

It was a good time for live performers in variety theatres and cabaret clubs. With unemployment at less than 2 per cent and manufacturing and heavy industries working at capacity, every town of medium size and upwards could support a theatre and find the audiences to fill it. Of course, television was beginning to take off, but there was still a way to go before most working people could afford one, so the glittering stalls and balconies were still packed with those who wanted to indulge in a bit of light-hearted escapism.

It was also still in fashion to hit Britain's beaches in the summer. Package holidays abroad weren't in the realms of possibility; flying anywhere was considered to be something exotic and the province of the wealthier middle classes. Seaside resorts were popular and gladly braced themselves for the annual invasion that brought financial riches with it. Wakes Week, a traditional holiday period, was in full swing for many mill workers, especially in Blackpool, Lancashire, which was the beating heart of the beach holiday scene.

It would have been a heady atmosphere for performers like Joan as everyone was simply out to have a good time. One year in the early 1950s, she did an eight-week season in Skegness, a favourite destination for the miners of the Derbyshire, Nottinghamshire and South Yorkshire coalfields. By the beginning of September that year, Joan had been doing a six-day week for a total of thirty-two weeks. Gruelling, perhaps, but this slog provided a much-needed income.

By this time, Joan was a seasoned performer and her act was worked out precisely. She said she became a different person when on stage. She was strong, sexy and very glamorous. Her voice was crystal clear with a carefully acquired regal accent. Under her direction she would have two spotlights searching the stage and when they found her, she would start to sing. She wrote the words herself and one of the phrases inspired the title of this book:

> To look at me it's hard to see I live my life without love –
> The romance ends when the balcony bends;
> I'm an iron girl in a velvet glove.
> I meet a man, I shake his hand, and my impression lingers –
> He screams in pain –
> I've done it again –
> Look! No fingers!
> When the tyre goes flat on a moonlit hill
> he should have a jack, but has he?
> I'm used as a jack, instead of a Jill –
> I have to lift the chassis!

Joan would ask for four strong men to come onto the stage so they could inspect her props to confirm they were not fake. She called them her 'committee'. There were plenty of volunteers and an usherette would let the chosen ones through. After confirming the veracity of the tools of Joan's trade, she would bend a ⅝-inch steel bar around her neck. She made it look easy but when she asked the four men to have a go at unbending the bar, they all failed miserably:

Next I would hand each man a six-inch nail and say, 'In a moment I'll tell you what to do with it' – that always got a laugh; I often wondered why! So I'd ask them to bend the nails – very rarely one might kink it – I'd then proceed to bend three of their nails for them and the last one I would break in two by bending and straightening it rapidly until it snapped. Of course it got very hot and I used a yellow duster to protect my hands, but after I'd broken it I would hand it back and the man would usually drop it because of the heat! This would get modest applause, although it was actually the hardest thing I did, often getting blisters on my hands in spite of the duster. It hurt even more if I had a second show that night.

Joan would then bend another steel bar but this time it was flat: she would put it in her mouth and appear to bend it with her teeth. In fact, the strength came from her neck and arms but it looked good and it was a crowd pleaser:

Joan flexes her muscles.

Job done.

After that I'd ask the men if we could have a tug of war. I'd produce two ropes with stirrup-like handles which I held in one hand and asked two men to pull on one side and two on the other; to pull when I said 'Pull' and not to jerk, and to stop when I said 'Stop'. They didn't always stop when I told them and sometimes one would jerk, in which case I'd say, 'One of you is a bit of a jerk,' which also got a laugh and the Jerk would be red-faced.

The finale of her act was ripping up a phone book. We don't have these chunky directories today, but in the mid-twentieth century they could be found in everyone's home in numerous alphabetical volumes. They ran to thousands of pages and were about 2–3in thick. Her 'committee' would be asked to inspect the phone book to ensure it wasn't rigged in some way and then she would wave it around, give it a few slaps and proceed to rip it in two. She said that if she was feeling in the mood, she would then go on to rip it into quarters:

> I would thank the men and give them a small photograph and say, 'I'm not married – I was engaged once but I broke it off!' All through the act I had little gags. Sometimes if I got someone on stage being a bit stroppy I would say, 'Keep it up and you'll soon be a strong woman!' I didn't change the act much once it was established as it ran well and I could always pad it out if they wanted more time.

Testament to the success of Joan's act and Solly's careful management, she continued to be popular with the same performance across the world for more than twenty-five years. She certainly was no one-hit wonder; it was extremely rare for a speciality act like hers to survive for any great length of time. She had found a winning formula in her unique act and the audiences continued to lap it up for a quarter of a century. I think she was surprised and delighted with her continued success; she certainly worked hard to keep her name in lights.

But before we get out the party hats and balloons to celebrate, there is a painful twist in her tale at this point. Life wasn't about to give Joan a free ticket to happiness. Research by her nephew John revealed that in early 1950, Joan discovered she was pregnant. It was the kiss of death for a performer who relied on her looks. She would have been devastated: here she was on the verge of something and she was facing her worst nightmare. Having children of her own was not part of her plan. She would have been sick with worry. At that time abortion was illegal; it did not become available for women until a change in the law in 1967, and even then, there were strict criteria to be met before a woman could qualify for a termination. It is hard to imagine how trapped she must have felt. This was also ten years before the contraceptive pill was available so if a young, unmarried woman wanted to have sex, she was always taking a huge risk. Condoms were available but they weren't as effective as they are today. If you happened to be poor and pregnant, your options were cruelly limited. Many women turned to backstreet abortionists where they were often putting their lives at risk or, like Joan, they took their lives into their own hands.

Her diary from the time indicates that she was due to do a cabaret and then a television appearance, but scribbled on the pages is simply the word 'ill'. This covered a four-week period. According to John, half a century later his aunt admitted to a friend that she had once been pregnant and had subjected her body to a self-administered abortion. It worked, but clearly the price to her own health was high – a whole month off work was a perilously long time when there was no money coming in. She must have been very unwell.

Joan would not have trusted anyone else to take such a risk with her body. As we know, her life was governed by an all-consuming desire to stay in control. The last thing she would have wanted was to put herself in the hands of a charlatan who might kill her in the process. In keeping with her desire to look after herself, it is unlikely that Bert, whom she was living with at the time and was probably the father, would have had anything to do with this episode. Men in the mid-twentieth century kept well away from 'women's issues'. She probably didn't tell anyone else that she was 'in trouble'. The fewer people who knew the better.

This conjures up a chillingly lonely scene for Joan as she did what she could to sort out the crisis. She would have felt shame about being pregnant and unmarried, but I suspect one key driving force behind her actions was dread at the prospect of becoming a mother. Her experience of 'family' was hugely negative after being abandoned at the age of 3, and then finding herself with an aunt who appeared to have no love for her. She would have viewed the idea of becoming a mother herself as horrific, perhaps going some way to explain the drastic action she took.

Once again, her powerful will to survive pulled her through and after four weeks, she went straight back on the stage. But dark fate hadn't finished with her. The following June, she got home from a show in Hull only to discover she had been burgled.

Thieves had broken into the flat and stolen all her clothes, including treasured costumes, and her jewellery. Another violation, but this time the event was turned to Joan's advantage. She was clearly becoming quite a celebrity because news of the break-in spread like wildfire and was widely reported in the British press. And it didn't stop there. As the story gained momentum and the facts were embellished, the speculation about what strongwoman Joan would do to the thieves if she caught them spiralled out of recognition. The piece even appeared in Australia, where the *Sydney Sun* decided to illustrate Joan taking her revenge. Through the cuttings agency, she saw the cartoon which portrayed a large musclebound, masculine-looking woman. Joan was mortified and wrote to the editor, enclosing a real picture that made the most of her stunning figure. Not to be put off, the paper ran a follow-up piece:

Joan Rhodes, London's self-styled Mighty Mannequin, is mightily amused at a *Sun* artist's idea of what a strong girl looks like.

On June 15, *The Sun* reported a burglary in 27-year-old Joan's London flat while the Mighty Mannequin was executing feats of strength in a vaudeville act. The sketch accompanying the story depicted a beefy Amazon knocking stars out of the burglar.

Today, *The Sun* received a letter from Joan, with [this] photograph, revealing as much of her physique as a Bikini swimsuit allows.

'I must say I was most amused at the artist's idea of how a strong woman should look and have enclosed a photograph of the way I really look,' wrote Joan.

'Incidentally, I am writing a book called Men I have Picked Up. It does not include the burglar,' she added.

The Sun apologises for picking up the idea that beefiness goes with mightiness.

Sorry, Joan.

Then, as if dogged by a horrible curse, another drama of the non-theatrical kind came into Joan's life. She was back on the road from 11 September, travelling to East Ham, Luton, Jersey, Kings Lynn and Liverpool, but the touring came to another abrupt halt and she had to take three weeks off for something described as 'an operation'.

There is precious little information available about what this operation was, but three weeks is a lengthy time in hospital. Considering that she had carried out a self-abortion earlier in the year and may have done some damage to her body in the process, it is likely there was a gynaecological reason. It would also explain why the actual type of operation was kept quiet, although no secret was made of her stay in hospital.

Joan could ill afford to sit around recovering in a hospital bed. She was keen to get back on the boards and earn a crust. She persuaded Solly to book her for cabaret at the Savoy for two weeks from 13 November. She completed the engagement but had misjudged her healing abilities; she was forced to take another two weeks off to undo the post-operative damage she had done. Most people might have given in at this point, especially as she'd had a punishing year all in all. But that wasn't Joan's way of doing things. She was determined that nothing was going to get in the way of her career. She ended the rollercoaster of a year working in Aylesbury gritting her teeth and bracing herself for whatever else life was going to chuck in her direction.

10

HORNY HOLLYWOOD CALLING

Joan embraced hard work, so she was delighted to find her act fully booked up. It was a bit of a treadmill, with at least two shows a day, six days a week, for the foreseeable future. But this was just what she was aspiring to. She was a perfect story for the media with her blonde bombshell appearance and her humble beginnings. Wherever she went she had the local and national press knocking on her dressing-room door demanding she picked up something (or someone) heavy. She was more than happy to oblige. At last, Joan was becoming famous both at home and abroad for her looks and her quirky act. It was a young starlet's dream.

To top it all, she was approached by a group of movie moguls from a place she had always dreamed of conquering: Hollywood. This consortium of businessmen had decided that Joan was perfect for the role of Tarzanna, the female answer to Johnny Weissmuller's hugely successful portrayal in the *Tarzan* films.

Not only did Joan look like a movie star but it must have felt to her that she was en route to being one for real. After all she had been through, Joan must have been beside herself with joy and

Joan takes on the world.

A glamour shot.

excitement at having such a glittering future ahead of her. You can sense it in how she wrote about these events years later:

> I was photographed climbing trees and trying to look glamorous. A brochure was made up which I never saw finished. I was then introduced by phone to a Mr Wildberg who would offer me a contract for Hollywood where I would be groomed to star in a film written specially for me and I would become Tarzan-na! They would start by depositing a vast (by my standards) sum of money in a bank before even filming, but first I had to meet a man at the Savoy Hotel and he would explain it in detail.

Joan would have gone to the plush Savoy Hotel in all innocence; although she was streetwise, she was still surprisingly naïve. She put on her best frock, a restrained smattering of make-up and headed for her glittering future. It never occurred to her that anything unsavoury was going on:

> I went along to the Savoy and asked at reception for the man I was supposed to meet. A pageboy took me up to the room, knocked on the door and left me. The door opened and there stood a fat, elderly man with a hairy chest wearing boxer shorts – and nothing else. I would have liked to have run away, but he grabbed my hand and pulled me into the room – it was a suite and I could see his wife lying on the bed in one room.
>
> 'We were resting,' he said, 'and now give me a hug and show me how strong you really are.'
>
> 'I'd rather not,' I whispered.
>
> 'Oh well,' he said, gripping my hands and trying to place them on his body – I'll leave you to guess where.
>
> I pulled away and said, 'I'm sorry, I can't stay.'
>
> 'You do want to be in films?' he countered.
>
> 'No thanks,' I said and made for the door, muttering to myself, 'not if it entails that!' – I hadn't heard of the casting couch in those days. I was blushing as I left the Savoy.

I remember in the later period of the twentieth century how the mention of a casting couch would be treated as something of a joke, certainly in the journalistic circles that I mixed in. Jealous men would say that a woman had been promoted ahead of them because she had slept with the boss.

The phrase originated in Hollywood where it was used in a jokey but damning way to imply that actors were prepared to do anything to land a part. But it was far from a joke: the abuse was rife. For decades the reality was concealed by actors too scared of ruining their career chances if they spoke out. It meant some movie moguls came to feel it was their God-given right to take advantage of them. A warped perk of the job.

It was the case of film producer Harvey Weinstein in the twenty-first century that threw the spotlight on the criminal nature of Hollywood's exploitative underbelly. For thirty years he took advantage of his power over those struggling to 'make it in the movies'. It took great courage for his victims to come forward and this united effort, sitting under the banner #MeToo, stopped the sexual predator in his tracks. In 2020, he was found guilty of criminal sexual assault in the first degree and of rape in the third degree and was sentenced to twenty-three years in prison.

Almost seventy years before Weinstein was brought to justice, Joan was a victim of the casting couch. The fact that this man was expecting her to go along with a threesome shook Joan right to the core. This was clearly nothing unusual for this revolting sex abuser. From hearing Joan's first-hand account, I got the feeling that she wasn't just shocked by this encounter, she was actually scared.

By now Joan was in her thirties. She was confident and had the beginnings of a good career. Despite those attributes, she felt she couldn't tell anyone about what had happened at the time. She wasn't the kind of person who was ground down by the vagaries of life, as we have already seen, but this incident eroded some of her precious emotional reserves. It tarnished her trust and cruelly crushed her dream of being a movie star in Hollywood.

Imagine how difficult an encounter like this must have been for others in less fortunate circumstances. It was a stark choice – the casting couch and fame, or the Hollywood doors slamming firmly shut in your face.

In this instance, it was Joan who slammed the door shut. The following day, her phone rang constantly. She ignored it, but then relented. John Wildberg was anxious to know how the encounter at the Savoy had gone, but he was in for a bit of a shock, as Joan had made her mind up:

> I said I wasn't interested in doing films and I didn't want to leave England. He responded that I had verbally agreed and I couldn't get out of it, six people were sponsoring me, etc., etc. I still couldn't tell him what had happened and felt a fool. I told him I had an engagement in Scotland so wouldn't be in touch and put down the phone. He wrote to me pleading with me to reconsider, saying, 'There may be things you are not at liberty to tell me, but for your sake as well as mine, won't you please reconsider this once and for all?' Had he guessed what had happened, I wonder?

John Wildberg was no exemplar of morality. He started as an American copyright attorney and then became a theatre producer. The fourth of his five marriages, to novelist Ursula Parrott in 1934, ended in June 1938 on the grounds of his 'intolerable cruelty'. His fifth wife died after overdosing on sedatives in 1950. He was in bed with her but seemingly failed to notice in time to try and save her. There isn't much written about him other than those basic details and the fact that he was behind a series of Broadway musicals, including *Porgy and Bess*. This deal would have meant a huge financial and professional boost for him as it got him involved in big-time Hollywood.

The surviving letters he sent Joan, including contract proposals, show him trying to persuade her to go ahead with Tarzanna. At first, he appears puzzled by Joan's sudden change of mind after the encounter at the Savoy. Before, negotiations had been going well. But later his approach to her softened, indicating that he may have investigated matters and realised what had transpired. But he was wasting his time; there was no way that Joan was going to sit on anyone's casting couch. She was mentally scarred by the assault but once again, she adapted to the new situation and got on with her career as a strongwoman.

Joan never identified the fat, old abuser, and she didn't look for help or support from those around her either. She must have felt it was pointless to expose him as he was so powerful that no one would believe her voice against his. This sounds sadly familiar. She suffered the shame of a victim, thinking that somehow it was her fault, and I think a part of that unjust emotion stayed with her for the rest of her life. I wonder if she thought that making a revelation would harm her career, even at a later stage. With her sharp memory for names, she would certainly have been able to tell the police exactly who he was. What we do know is that for the next seven decades, untold numbers of actors suffered and faced the same turmoil and secret anguish. We can only hope that the Weinstein conviction has stopped some of the abuse. In TV journalism there is a cliché ending often used in reports: 'Only time will tell.'

The Tarzanna incident certainly put Joan off reaching the bright lights of Hollywood, but it did not get in the way of her burgeoning desire to be a film star. She had always been attracted to broadcasting in one form or other. She talked of working as an extra and stuntwoman from time to time in the very early days, but the details are, unfortunately, vague. There is a mention of her on the Internet Movie Database (IMDb) website working as an uncredited stunt performer in the 1944 film *Man of Evil*, but it wasn't something she ever mentioned to me. When her act became a bit more polished, she attracted the attention of directors looking for colour and visual interest in their background shots, something she provided in the 1943 film, *The Man in Grey*.

Her first noticeable appearance on the big screen was in a British B-movie called *Johnny, You're Wanted*, which was released in 1956. The director, Vernon Sewell, was well established in the UK and took quite a shine to Joan and her performances. So much so that he chose to weave her act into the plot.

Johnny, played by character actor John Slater, is a long-distance lorry driver who finds himself caught up in a murder hunt. The police suspect him of killing a young woman who hitches a ride with him. She disappears when he goes into a roadside café for a cuppa. Her body is found further down the road. The police find out he had given her a lift so began a manhunt. As they are getting closer, he dodges into the nearest building, which just so happens to be a theatre. He finds himself on the stage, where Joan is in the middle of her act. She thinks he is a volunteer and uses him in her tug of war against four men. Before Johnny can wander off, she persuades him to join her in tearing up phone books. Of course, he is a miserable failure, which is followed by laughter from the audience after she shakes his hand to thank him, and he clutches it as though he's in pain.

It really looked as though Joan had broken through to films as the credits said, in large writing, 'Introducing Joan Rhodes' and an image of her picking up a man was included in the publicity posters. She got an impressive chunk of screen time, two and a half minutes in total. The scene was filmed at the Palace Theatre in Reading. She was about 34 at the time and looked every inch a star in her sequined basque and fishnets. She used dialogue from her real act which she delivered in the carefully crafted posh accent that had become one of her trademarks. The sequence made good cinema. She popped up in the film again, this time briefly giving evidence to the police. And the motif of tearing phone books was revisited several times, including right at the end of the film. It wasn't a hit movie, but the final product was regarded as a relative success.

Poster for the film Johnny, You're Wanted *(1956), featuring Joan.*

Less successful was the next film she appeared in. It was called *Il Mondo di Notte numero 2* (*The World by Night No. 2*). Her act was filmed in Italy in 1961; it was three minutes long and was included in what was basically a long montage of performances in night clubs across the globe. One critic described it as being 'a duller than dirt travelogue'. I don't think Joan would be amused if she could see that today her credit on IMDb is below a name check for Rita Renoir, billed as a 'caged stripper'.

As we will see later, Joan kept plugging away at her film career right up until the 1980s. Her career on television was much more constant.

In true Churchillian fashion, Joan just kept on going, no matter what degree of hell she was wading through. She got on with the day-to-day business of earning a crust and making the world sit up and take notice of her. She was still acclimatising to being a star when she did a stint at the glamorous Cirque Medrano in Paris. It was hugely famous for inspiring some of the world's greatest painters including Degas, Renoir and Toulouse-Lautrec. The Medrano was a cultural landmark, and it was quite a coup to be on the bill.

Joan said that when she got the booking, she had no idea that it was a real circus. There was a bit of a shock waiting for her, although she did love the smell of horses and straw. The newspapers often said she had started in circuses but Joan was at pains later in life to say this wasn't the case. She preferred to be seen as a performer who started on the mean streets of London, working her way up to variety theatres and stardom.

As she headed for the Medrano in Montmartre, she said that once again she didn't really have a clue what she was getting herself into. It was a case of jumping in and seeing what happened. The first hurdle she faced was feeling rather scruffy alongside those in such the fabulous costumes. Her homemade outfit was still something cobbled together out of a black bra and removable black skirt with a slit right up one leg. But as rehearsals got underway, she felt more accepted as the other performers were interested in her act and wanted to examine her props. Joan knew a smattering of French, which she threw into her performances for good measure. While she was there, the American actor Buster Keaton did an odd show that Joan said involved his wife, a bed and lots of booze. She never elaborated what shape this bizarre-sounding act took.

Bracing herself, Joan went into the sawdust ring on her first night and hoped for the best. Her act went down well, the French audience smitten by her elegance, beauty and unusual skills. But nothing prepared her for what she found when she got into her dressing room the following morning. It was 'filled with flowers and newspapers':

The press had taken me to be the star! I was amazed! One write-up said: '*Une pin-up qui résiste à quatre hommes est la vedette du Cirque Medrano!*' [a pin-up who resists four men is the star of the show]. Another: '*Force et Beauté à Medrano*'. *Ce Soir* published a large picture and said: '*Cette jeune (et forte) Anglaise a etonné les Parisiens*' [this young (and strong) Englishwoman astonished the Parisians].

I was besieged by photographers and fans. It didn't go to my head but I did start to learn French. *Radar* did a whole-page picture and *Marie France* did a couple of pages. I was still unable to communicate with people and so in my free time I used to wander about Paris, always alone. I loved the Sacré Cœur. I stayed in a small hotel on the Bvd. Clichy – room with a bath, quite cheap, which I believe later became a brothel – in my time it was mostly used by artistes from the strip-joint a few doors away from the Moulin Rouge (which I later played).

Reviews like this helped kindle what became a lifelong love of working abroad for Joan. She often felt that foreign audiences appreciated her more than those at home. After her stint in Paris, she was booked to appear on Spanish TV. This was such a big success that she began getting more and more bookings across Europe. She felt that she was regarded as simply a freakish variety performer in Britain, whereas she was admired for her fitness and natural strength in Germanic and Scandinavian countries, and in southern Europe she was seen as an elegant, glamourous and sexy young woman.

That didn't stop her being continually challenged by those who felt she couldn't be as strong as she claimed. One encounter particularly amused Joan:

> I was in Vienna when a solemn deputation representing the Olympic Games Athletes of Vienna requested me to accept a challenge of strength from their two gold medallists, the weightlifters Willi Pankl and Fritz Flenner. I was told that it was to be in a café. I consulted the cabaret manager, hoping that he would say 'no way,' but he, no doubt thinking about publicity, said that I should accept the challenge.
>
> I thought that maybe not too many people would be there in a small café; I didn't know that in Vienna a 'café' is a vast beer garden and that this one held about 3,000 people and it was packed! Herr Pankl handed me a 10-inch nail, saying, 'let's see if you can bend this.'
>
> Feeling something was strange, perhaps it had been hardened, I quickly replied, 'Oh no! After you.' He tried but he couldn't bend it, so I thought I might as well have go. To my great surprise it bent almost as easily as my six-inch nails and so I went on and broke it in two. They all smiled and became very cheerful and friendly – it seems that they had all thought me a fake and now they couldn't do enough for me. We then sat at a table and they drank frothy beer and banged their glasses on the table. I always had a strong escort when I was in Vienna – it's a golden memory!

Being repeatedly challenged was an occupational hazard and, to some extent, part of the act. To sell yourself as the 'Strongest Girl in the World', you had to be ready to prove it and there were always plenty of people, mostly men, who were ready to step up and put her to the test. Joan believed that a lot of those who did this felt their manhood was somehow being put in doubt by the very existence of a woman like her, which would be funny if it wasn't rather sad. Joan saw herself as a performer, not as an opponent.

Some venues used this quirk of human nature to attract bigger audiences. One nightclub in Lisbon, Portugal, ran an advert offering a handsome cash prize if anyone could replicate just one of Joan's feats of strength. Nobody took up the challenge until the last night, when a large, strong-looking man from the audience lumbered forward. She handed him a nail and a duster to protect his hands from the heat created if he managed to bend it. But the man refused it and instead pulled another six-inch nail from his pocket which he said he had bent himself earlier. Joan wasn't fooled for a moment; she realised he was a trickster. She could tell that it was one of her own nails which she had bent at an earlier show. Sending him up, Joan took the half-bent nail and snapped it in two, much to the delight of the audience, who also recognised the man as a fraud. Not only did he fail to qualify for the cash prize, but he never saw the end of the show as he was escorted from the premises.

Sometimes, the reaction to Joan's act went too far. When she was appearing at the Medrano in Paris, one man appears to have become obsessed by her to such an extent that he became her stalker. He would follow her around the city shouting abuse, showering her with insults. Joan wasn't scared by him; by all accounts he was a diminutive local who obviously felt intimidated and belittled by this remarkably strong woman. The abuse went on for days and was really beginning to annoy Joan. It took a lot to make her angry, but this silly man was hitting the spot. He should have realised that upsetting the 'Strongest Woman in the World' was foolish and potentially dangerous.

As Joan only had a limited supply of bars, she would take them to a backstreet garage to borrow a vice so she could straighten them between acts. The stalker followed her, no doubt ranting as per usual, and her patience wore out. In a rage, she got one of the straightened bars and bent it around his neck like a hefty collar. Furious and unrepentant she left him there, trapped in a steel necklace. It took two of the mechanics some time and a great deal of effort to free him. Joan was not bothered by her Parisian stalker again.

11

FREAKY FANS

Joan's sexy strong act appealed to people right across the fandom spectrum, from the sane to the complex. As with so many documents that charted her life, Joan kept most, if not all, of the fan letters she received over her many years in showbusiness. Going through the mountain of faded stationery, I found they were mostly from young men desperate to meet her or be picked up by her, both literally and in any other sense of the phrase. I think because her act was about female physical strength it sparked an interest in some unusual quarters. Genuine health and fitness fanatics would write to her and continued to stay in touch for the rest of her life. Joan is still celebrated today by organisations set up to promote a healthy lifestyle. But there was a darker side to the following she attracted. Perhaps because she was seen by some as a bit of a freak, there were those devotees who had more perverse intentions towards her.

One of her most disturbing fans was the notorious fascist James Larratt Battersby, who described himself as 'Hitler's missionary'. He believed the foul dictator was the new Christ. Although he claimed to be sane, he was without doubt seriously deranged and dangerous.

Battersby was born in Stockport, Greater Manchester, to a family of hatmakers – but millinery was of no interest to this extreme

As she lifts an anvil, you can see Joan's powerful arm muscles.

Nazi supporter. He dreamed of a world where Adolf Hitler was worshipped as a god. At one stage, he was a district leader for Oswald Mosley's British Union of Fascists. Unbelievable as it may sound, he was also instrumental in establishing an institution dedicated to Hitler in Petworth, West Sussex, in late 1945. It was a matter of months after the end of the war and at a time when revelations about the Nazi death camps were still coming to light. It is staggering to think that Battersby and a few other rabid fascists were able to create the League of Christian Reformers in Britain, a so-called religion dedicated to worshipping Hitler.

British fascist James Larratt Battersby, who stalked Joan. (Public Domain)

Joan was appearing in a show in Southport in 1953 when Battersby forced himself into her consciousness. Having seen her perform he began to haunt the stage door, day after day, night after night. She had no idea who he was but immediately noticed his resemblance to a Nazi stormtrooper. She described him as being over 6ft tall, with a shaven head, wearing a long leather coat and jackboots. Joan instinctively knew that this was a man to avoid like the plague. She didn't like the look of him. On the first occasion, she went in through the stage door, completely ignoring him on her way to her dressing room. Later, she asked the doorman who he was and learnt that he was claiming to be a journalist.

Battersby, having established his target, was not to be brushed off. He was tenacious. He began to send in messages for Joan via the stage door. Dangerously ignorant of whom she was dealing with, Joan seems to have softened as the week wore on. He must have come across as cultured and clever, disguising the revolting truth. Joan took up the story:

> The next day there was a note saying his name was James Battersby, he was a writer and he wanted to meet me. I didn't respond. This went on for the whole week. On the Saturday, instead of going to the stage door I went to the front of house and there he was, talking to the manager. He said how much he enjoyed my work and would I spare him a little time and have coffee with him. Well it was Saturday and I'd be moving on that night so I saw no harm in it; he was obviously an educated man and seemed pleasant enough.
>
> So I walked with him along Lord Street and I noticed one or two people staring at us. I realised we had walked past most of the coffee shops so I asked him where we were going. 'Oh,' he said, 'My housekeeper makes far better coffee than any of these places and I can show you some of my work.' It seemed OK – he had a housekeeper! – so I went along with it. We stopped at a very ordinary little house, he rang the doorbell and an elderly woman opened the door and showed us into a sitting room. 'I've promised Miss Rhodes some of your very excellent coffee,' he said and she hustled out of the room.

There's no question that Joan was taking a terrible risk in ignoring her first instinctive dislike of Battersby but I think she had persuaded herself that even though he was big, it was the middle of the day and she was stronger than him so he couldn't hurt her. She might also have focused on his claim to be a reporter. She knew the power of good publicity so it is possible that she thought he might be able to help her make some headlines. How wrong she was. Within seconds of the housekeeper leaving the room to make coffee, he went into action:

> The moment she left he threw himself down on his knees and said, 'God has sent you at last! You do know who God is?' I just

stared at him and wondered what was coming next. He went to a bookcase and took out a small book and showed it to me. Inside was a picture of Hitler. I was in shock. 'God has chosen you to be the mother of my son, who will be the strongest man on Earth.'

Joan didn't hang around for any further deluded declarations; she fled to the safety of her hotel. But that wasn't the end of his attempts to persuade her to join him in his madness. He tracked her down a few weeks later, when she was working in a different part of the country. He sent a letter to the theatre demanding that she come back to Southport immediately so they could continue God's work. Joan ignored the letter, and it seems Battersby gave up.

If Joan had kept an eye on the local newspapers, she would have seen that her suitor had attracted some of his own headlines not that long ago. In November 1952, he was at the Cenotaph in London for the Remembrance Day ceremony. Just as Big Ben finished chiming the eleventh hour, he disrupted the traditional two-minute silence, shouting, 'This is the day of English judgement. I speak the truth. English children must be saved. Trust God and the eternal Christ. Heil Hitler.' He then gave the Nazi salute. The crowd around him went mad; they were infuriated and there were shouts of 'cut his throat' and 'string him up'. The police later said they arrested him as much for his own safety as anything else.

It transpired that he had got married in 1935 and had four children. The next time he turned up in the press was three years after the incident at the Cenotaph, when his horribly mutilated, headless corpse was found on Formby Beach. He had thrown himself off the Mersey Ferry and his body became entangled in the propellers. Before he killed himself, he sent a note to a newspaper saying, 'My work here is complete. I follow the Fuehrer to glory and eternity. Through the sacrifice of the Aryan martyrs our world victory is assured. Heil Hitler.'

By this time Joan was hugely popular across Europe. She was hopping on and off planes and learning to enjoy her celebrity status. Her act went down particularly well in upmarket casinos and flashy nightclubs. France was one of her favourite countries to work in; she liked going to Paris and Lyon and then down to the Riviera. Although she had her favourite places, she simply loved the different cultures of countries such as Italy, Spain and Portugal. She was also in demand in more northerly climes such as Denmark, Sweden, Norway and Finland. In each venue she did her best to learn enough of the language to be able to communicate with audiences even if it was at only a very basic level. She would collar a waiter or guest who spoke English and learn a few phrases in the local tongue such as 'Good evening', 'Four gentlemen please to help me', 'bend the nail' and 'pull the rope'. It was a clever move as audiences loved the fact that she had made the effort to try and communicate with them in their own language.

Inevitably, Joan found herself performing for some of the wealthiest people in the world, particularly on the French Riviera and in Italy. Invitations to join the various glamorous groups for drinks after her show became the norm. Joan did agree to some of the requests – sipping good champagne was no hardship. She must have been fascinated by their lavish lifestyles as she visited yachts owned by these big hitters. But there was no part of her that felt at home with these enormously wealthy people; she regarded mixing with them when she wasn't on stage as part of the job. If you wanted to be a top international celebrity, you had to be known and admired by the world's cognoscenti. You also had to be seen to be mixing with them, so getting snapped with the super-rich by press photographers was an important part of this courtly dance. Getting publicity is no different today, although the stories and images are delivered in a myriad of new ways. Then and now, it all matters to those who want to embrace celebrity and make a living out of being a star.

There were some strange inhabitants in the land where money was no object, especially among those with royal blood. Joan's first encounter with royalty came from the former Egyptian king, Farouk I.

She'd been contracted to appear in a film in Italy, the follow-up to *The World by Night*. After that she was booked to do a month at the trendy Casina delle Rose in Rome. Situated in a park near the Via Veneto, it was a popular watering hole for the rich and famous. Since the war, Rome had earned the sobriquet 'Hollywood on the Tiber' because so many US film companies were using the city for blockbusters like *Quo Vadis*. The arrival of movie stars like Robert Taylor and Deborah Kerr created a feeding frenzy among the media, which in turn led to the phenomenon we now know as the paparazzi.

The first Joan knew about catching the attention of the former king of Egypt was finding huge baskets of flowers stacked outside her dressing room following her initial appearance. On the second night, she got into her room to find yet more bouquets, this time crammed into the small space. Not only was she annoyed that she couldn't get on with preparing for her act, but she couldn't stand the smell of the bouquets of tiger lilies. She asked a waiter to put them all outside but he wasn't keen:

> The manager came, looking very serious and I explained that I couldn't dress in the room with them and asked, 'Do you want me or the flowers to have the dressing room?' He brightened up a bit and said, 'You, of course', but that the flowers must be hidden as they were from one of his favourite clients, ex-King Farouk (of Egypt), who had enjoyed my show so much that he had ordered them to be sent every night!

It's typical of Joan that she wasn't particularly impressed by being pursued by royalty; she was more annoyed than bowled over by attention. Farouk was not exactly a pleasing prospect. Reports say he weighed in at over 20st and was described by one acquaintance as being so gluttonous that he was nothing more than a head with a stomach.

Farouk was living in exile after being forced to abdicate in 1952 following a military coup. He was notorious for his lavish lifestyle. He had a particular penchant for large-busted, statuesque blondes and kept a number of partners who were put in a pecking order. He clearly had his eyes on Joan; perhaps he was even planning to make her one of his mistresses. Who knows, if she had behaved herself she might even have bagged the number one slot. But Joan wasn't good at doing as she was told:

The next night Farouk and his party came again and the manager told me that King Farouk would like to try some of my nails – the ones I broke – but we would have to go to the manager's office as Farouk was sensitive and didn't like to try it in public. He was said to be 20 stone in weight although he didn't look it – I was around 10 stone then. I went to the manager's office, taking four or five 6-inch nails with me and a couple of yellow dusters and was greeted by a smiling Farouk who shook my hand with a strong grip. I handed him a duster and a nail. 'No,' he said, 'you wrap it up for me.' I did and handed it back to him, fearing the worst. He struggled and struggled, the sweat running down his cheeks – in the meantime I broke mine and handed the pieces to the manager, who glared at me and promptly dropped them because they were so hot! I explained that was why I used the dusters, so as not to burn my hands.

Farouk took it well and later asked for a signed photograph and my nail – I signed it: 'It was a noble effort.' The next night he came again and the manager came to me to say that the King would like me to join him at his table, so I did. I had hardly sat down when Farouk stood up and said, 'We go now. I will have the pleasure to drive you to your hotel.'

Now I wasn't booked into a hotel but was staying in a private flat, so I told him I was with friends and they would be in bed already. He said, 'I have 29 beds, would you like to break one for me?' and to my horror I replied without thinking, 'Not tonight, Josephine.'

He appeared not to notice and we went out to a huge limousine and on the back seat were two heavy gentlemen. 'Who are they?' I asked.

'They are my bodyguards,' he replied.

'Oh,' I said, 'you won't need them!'

As good as gold, Farouk dropped Joan off unmolested at the flat and promised to be at the casino the next evening. And sure enough, there he was. Joan did her performance, changed and was ushered to the ex-king's table where a chair had been positioned for her next to him. You don't get more top table than that. He ordered her champagne and fresh orange juice for himself. Soon, Joan realised that there was someone trying to get her attention, despite the fact that she was clearly rather occupied. Standing behind her was a young American who must have found his way into the VIP area. He asked her to dance despite the presence of the heavyweight royal competitor for her attention, not forgetting his collection of musclebound bodyguards. Joan politely declined and carried on trying to entertain Farouk.

But the young man was not to be put off. It was later in the evening when he came back for another attempt to get her on the dancefloor and this time was rewarded with more success. When Joan spoke about the incident, she had decided that he must have been a cheeky journalist looking for a headline. If she was right, then he did his job well, because her actions caused an international scandal:

Now I knew nothing of protocol and didn't really know much about mixing with the aristocracy. The American returned and said, in a hushed voice, that he admired me so much and once round the floor would be OK and then he could tell his friends that he had danced with the strongest girl in the world – so I fell for it! I excused myself and had hardly reached the dance floor when the whole of Farouk's party got up to leave.

The next day the newspapers were full of it, saying that I had snubbed Farouk. It was just that I didn't know; I then suspected the American was a journalist. I've never trusted them since! I thought a lot of people would ignore my show and was worried that my contract might be terminated, but no, the place was packed every night with people who were curious about the girl who had snubbed a king – but no one offered to take me sightseeing and I was always alone.

Farouk continued his playboy lifestyle up to his death in 1965, at the age of 45. He died as he lived, gorging himself in a restaurant accompanied by a gorgeous woman. He was in the Île de France restaurant in Rome when he collapsed. There was no post-mortem, so the cause of death remains a mystery. Some reports say he suffered from a heart attack. There are those who believe he was poisoned by the Egyptian secret service but there is no firm evidence to support this.

Ex-King Farouk had a vast circle of friends and acquaintances, and he wasn't the only one of them to develop an interest in Joan, an intriguing woman who looked like a movie star and could lift two men. Joan caught the attention of two familiar faces among the elite at that time – the infamous Dockers. Sir Bernard Docker was an industrialist from Birmingham and one of the wealthiest men in Britain. He was the chairman of the Daimler Motor Company and other high-profile companies like BSA, the Birmingham Small Arms Company. He was amused by the media interest he attracted as he always seemed to be grinning enigmatically in press photographs. But it was his second wife, Norah, who was the real star. With her undoubted talent for grabbing headlines and provoking public interest, she made 'the Dockers' into pure media gold. They were like pioneer media celebrities, long before the likes of the Beckhams. If the internet had existed, the couple's antics would have attracted millions of followers from around the world and no doubt they would be reality TV megastars.

Norah adored nothing more than hitting the headlines for her extravagances. She flaunted her wealth at every opportunity, thereby making the public either love or hate her. She filled the gossip pages for at least two decades and, from what the acidic columnists wrote about her, it looks as though she became more a subject of ridicule and hate than one of love and admiration. Showing off one's glittering wealth so soon after the devastating war, when so many were struggling to feed their families, was hardly going to endear her to the masses.

Despite her arrival on the public stage as a fabulously wealthy woman who loved throwing her riches and title around at every opportunity, Norah's early life had more in common with Joan's experience. Born in 1906 to a working-class family, Norah told the media her arrival was in a tiny flat above a butcher's shop in Derby. Her father, who worked hard and eventually had shares in a car showroom, died by suicide when she was just 16, and the family fell into poverty. She went to London to seek her fortune and worked as a paid dance hostess at the exclusive Café de Paris where she charged £1 per dance, a lot more than the other girls. She quickly landed her first millionaire husband, Clement Callingham, the head of Henekeys wine and spirit merchants, but he died seven years later. The following year, Norah got her hands on a title, bagging Sir William Collins, the boss of Fortnum and Mason and Cerebros Salt Co. Ltd. She openly admitted that her second marriage was simply for the money and prestige. Two years later he was dead and she was on the hunt for her third millionaire. Step forward Sir Bernard Docker and the madness began in earnest.

Sir Bernard had a yacht made for Norah, the *Shemara*. It was sumptuous, no expense spared, with thirteen guest rooms. In the early 1950s, Joan got to know the luxury yacht and its inhabitants intimately. Most summers she was contracted to work in the south of France, in particular Nice, Cannes, Juan-les-Pins and Monte

Carlo. Being a sun worshipper, she loved these resorts, swimming and getting a tan when she wasn't working. It was while she was in Cannes that she first came across the Dockers. She had just finished her performance at the Palm Beach Casino when she was invited to join Sir Bernard and Norah for champagne. She sat with them for a while but she was tired and not in the mood to drink so she soon said her goodnights. What she wasn't expecting was a furious outburst from Norah who berated her for leaving. Lady Docker was known for being a bit of a loudmouth, especially when she'd had champagne and that was quite often.

But the Dockers were determined to make Joan one of their crowd. They went back to the casino a few days later armed with a bouquet of flowers and an invitation to stay with them on their sumptuous yacht. Joan couldn't resist such an adventure.

The *Shemara* was luxurious. A steel-hulled motor yacht, 212ft in length, with a crew of thirty to look after the lucky guests. Joan was particularly impressed by her en suite bathroom. Almost as soon as she was on board, she was told to change into her bikini so she could join in the fun and games. Guests on *Shemara* earned their keep, and Joan was expected to water ski with the Dockers' son, Lance. Although she was a strong swimmer, she had never tried water skiing. What ensued certainly entertained the rest of the party but left our strongwoman feeling a bit weak at the knees:

> Lance helped me on with the skis and I was given a rope and was suddenly being pulled out to sea. I panicked and poor Lance, who was swimming beside me, tried to calm me, shouting, 'Straighten your arms!' which I tried, but the skis came up in the water above my head. I grabbed at Lance and pulled his head under the water, realised what I was doing, let his head up, apologised, and then did it again! The driver of the boat saw what was happening and stopped; I swam back to the *Shemara* thoroughly ashamed of myself. Everybody was laughing and I was given a large drink which I gulped down – horror! It was gin! I rushed to my cabin and threw up.

The next day I tried again and everyone was much happier, but I don't think they enjoyed me as much as on the previous day!

Not only was Norah fond of drinking but she had a magpie nature. She'd taken a shine to Joan's teeny-weeny leopard-skin bikini and seemed keen on having one until she heard it was from C&A. To her, this was a down-market clothing store. She shuddered at the thought of what the media would say if they caught her wearing something from such a shop:

> Another day I was wearing some sandals which I had bought in Monoprix [a French Woolworths-type shop]; they were also leopard print and had a toe-post. She asked to try one on and had the same size foot as me (and Garbo). After the C&A bikini I didn't like to tell her they came from Monoprix so I said that she could have them as I had two pairs – she accepted them at once. That evening when I went to my cabin there were six pairs of hand-made sandals lined up.
> 'Have them all,' said Norah, 'they're made for me in Bond Street.'

Joan painted a relatively modest picture of Norah but she was notorious for getting drunk on pink champagne and behaving badly. The press loved her because she was known to slap waiters and abuse club owners and fellow socialites.

There was a Pathé newsreel report in 1954 of Norah and Bernard entertaining thirty-three miners from Leeds on board *Shemara* as a thank-you for an invitation to their pit. The banquet was vast, with every imaginable kind of luxury food available. It must have shocked most of those who saw the footage, as the country was only just coming out of rationing. It must have stuck in the miners' throats as they sipped the champagne, ate the fine foods and pretended to be having a ball. At one point a much 'imbibed' Norah was on the poop deck doing the 'Sailor's

Hornpipe' as the embarrassed miners clapped and tried not to seem too uncomfortable.

The Dockers came to a sad end. All their spendthrift ways led to Sir Bernard being forced out of his various companies, and gradually the many houses and treasures were sold as the money ran out. They fled to the tax haven of Jersey where Norah continued to be too vocal for her own good. It was reported that she said the inhabitants were 'the most frightfully boring, dreadful people that had ever been born'. Not a good way to endear yourself to the locals.

Sir Bernard died in 1978. Norah was discovered dead in her bed in 1983 by a maid at the Great Western Royal Hotel in Paddington.

12

THE ARTIST AND THE ARTISTE

Despite her nautical antics and royal company, Joan would not
have described herself as a party animal. After shows abroad she
would often just return to her hotel, eat a simple high-protein meal
and settle down to write letters home or read a book, one of her
favourite pastimes. Surprising for someone who sought stardom,
perhaps, but a lot of performers say the same. Appearing on a stage,
a safe distance from the audience, was bearable as the structure of
the encounter with other people was highly controlled; there was
space both mentally and physically for detachment. Like most of
us, Joan had two faces, one for the public and another for her private life, which she guarded assiduously. I understand her reticence
to let people in once the 'show' was over. Having another persona
to embody is a way of getting through and making a living in
tough professions where forward women were, and still are, treated
with suspicion.

The likes of Farouk and the Dockers were entertaining per-
sonalities, and their lifestyles would have fascinated Joan's creative
mind. But they were still seen as 'work' in Joan's mind. She would
never regard them as friends. They were part of her job; they
might be able to help her with achieving stardom and success.
Those she chose to be with in the shadows of her busy life were
the special ones, the true friends. They were lucky enough to be

Joan was a healthy cocktail of brains and beauty.

regarded by Joan as interesting people who were worth the effort. These fortunate few would be rewarded with endless kindness and fierce loyalty.

The renowned artist Dame Laura Knight was in this tight circle. The pair were close for a large chunk of their lives, until Laura's death in July 1970. Joan adored her.

Dame Laura, as well as being a hugely talented artist, was a trailblazer for female equality. She stood out in the twentieth century as an example of what a 'mere' female could achieve in a world dominated by men. She worked across the artistic mediums, producing watercolours, oils, etchings and drypoint. She was known for her figurative painting in the theatrical world, especially circuses, but also for embracing English Impressionism. Not only was she a champion of her gender, but Dame Laura worked to help marginalised and painfully poor groups, such as the Traveller community, by exposing their plight.

She was made an official war artist, one of the very few women to fill that role. In 1946, when she was almost 70, she asked to be given the job of witnessing and painting the gruelling Nuremberg trials where Nazi perpetrators were brought to justice. It meant days and days of listening to evidence of their extreme brutality. When you consider what she had to listen to, it reflects her strength of character and courage. Not only could she work through hours of nightmare submissions, but in the process manage to produce brilliant work that summed up this historic occasion for posterity.

The man with the task of ensuring she was as comfortable and safe as possible during the trials was Major Peter Casson, who had the unwieldy title of Deputy Assistant Adjutant-General with the British War Crimes Executive. Canadian-born, he was a charming, cultured man who loved the arts. It must have been a joy for him to act as escort to a woman who was regarded as the greatest female artist of her time. He remained friends with Dame Laura after the trials. He knew she was always looking for the perfect model for her portraiture and when he met and became firm friends with Joan when she was appearing in Vienna in the early 1950s, it occurred to him that the two women should meet. He invited them both to a party in London and they were duly introduced. He lit the touchpaper and stood well back to see what would happen. There wasn't an explosion as such, more a coming together. For both women it was an encounter that was to have an impact on the rest of their lives:

> Peter Casson, whom I had met in Austria and who had taken me to meet the strongmen, phoned to invite me to a party and introduced me to Laura Knight, the painter. I heard her say, 'Who is the golden girl?' He took me over to her – I was in awe – such a famous artist – I'd always admired her paintings of dancers, clowns and the circus. We chatted and after a short while we were friends.
>
> 'Would you consider letting me paint you?' she asked.

'Yes please!' I said.

'We could start next week,' she said, 'Peter will give you the address and telephone number of my studio. It's in St John's Wood.'

'Very near me in Belsize Park,' I answered, 'I'll be honoured.'

What ensued were numerous sittings in Dame Laura's purpose-built studio in her garden. Joan's description of these sessions gives a fascinating insight into how this celebrated artist went about her trade:

As I entered another lady came to greet me – she was Ally Bert, whom Laura had painted with Ally's husband who was a clown, I have a print of it. Laura liked the jumper I was wearing; it had a wide neckline, but not wide enough for Laura who came over and tugged at it until it hung loosely around my shoulders.

'That's better,' she said and then stared long and hard at me. 'What do you do?' she asked.

I think that Peter had clued her, so I told her I'd been called 'the strongest girl in the world' but I thought there must be stronger women, and that I was making my money as a cabaret act.

She went quiet and started drawing on the canvas. After a while she said 'Yes' to Ally and put down her brush. This, I found out, meant we needed coffee. Ally bustled around in the tiny kitchen and came out with three mugs of coffee and a copy of *The Times* and then wound up the gramophone and put on a record – some ballet music, I seem to remember. Laura danced around, smiling, to it and then after we had downed the coffee she became serious again and Ally signalled for me to take up the pose. Ally started calling out clues for the crossword. All was quiet except for the deep sighs of Laura and the scratching of the paintbrush.

After two hours we had finished the crossword and Ally took out the mugs and came back with her coat on. Laura said thank you to me and it was time to go – I wanted to peep at the painting but I didn't dare! I seem to remember that the sittings went on for about twelve times. By then I had got used to the routine, but we didn't always finish the crossword!

A few days after the last sitting, Laura phoned me and asked me to come to the studio to view the finished painting. I was astonished: it was a beautiful painting – flattering, I thought. She then asked me to come for a further sitting. I wondered why but

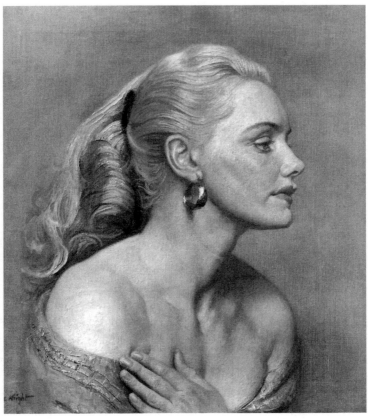

Dame Laura Knight's portrait of Joan, 1955.

I went, and found she wanted to give me, as a sitting fee, a drawing of myself. In fact she gave me two framed ones which have hung in my flat ever since.

In the next spring Laura invited me to the Royal Academy private viewing in which the picture was on display. Everyone who saw it loved it and a man from somewhere in the north of England bought it and so far as I was concerned, that was that, but a few years later Laura invited me to another private viewing at the Grosvenor Gallery and there it proudly hung. It was there that Laura introduced me to L.S. Lowry, a very shy man but I did manage to get him to chat for a while – I admired him and his work very much.

Dame Laura was a formidable name in the art world by the mid-twentieth century. She was a pioneer for women artists who were often dismissed as not being as talented as their male counterparts. Most of them were simply ignored. A powerful character like Laura, who was bursting with talent, was not prepared to make do with obscurity. Like Joan, she was a grafter. She gradually worked her way to the top; she talked about the smell of burning in the process as she destroyed any work which she deemed not good enough. Only her best work would do if she was to demonstrate that gender had nothing to do with art and artistic excellence.

Laura reaped the benefits of hard work. In 1929, she received a damehood for her work in the field of the arts. Then, in 1936, she was the first woman to be elected to full membership of the Royal Academy. Her glittering success stands as a testament to her skill and determination. Dame Laura was a key figure in the fight for equality. It was her very existence that opened up new opportunities for female artists, then and now.

There was quite an age gap between the two women; the artist was forty-four years older than the strongwoman, easily old enough to be her mother, which might explain why this relationship became so important to Joan. Here was someone she heartily

Christmas greeting from Dame Laura, 1964.

admired and loved from the first meeting. Someone she could be proud to be associated with, unlike the woman who abandoned her and her siblings. Dame Laura was a gracious, kind woman who was happy to sit and listen. If Joan could have committed to paper what she desired in a maternal figure and close friend, then Dame Laura fitted the bill perfectly. This relationship reminded me of how I came into Joan's life and how she was to me both a mother figure and a beloved friend, almost as though she was passing the baton on.

In the early days, Joan was at pains to impress. As the sittings continued, the pair got to know each other and, in the process, Joan painted her own self-portrait, not using brushes but words. Dame Laura was known for her love of the circus and she had spent time behind the scenes sketching and painting the people behind the acts. She got to know many performers personally. When she asked Joan about how she got into the business of being a strongwoman, Joan adapted her story to fit her audience. She dissembled and said she began her career in the circus at the age of 15, working high in the air of the big top on the trapeze. In telling this version of her life, she performed one of her special tricks; she massaged the facts in a truly convincing way that relied a bit on truth but also on weaving a fabric of colourful and engaging fantasy. I think she probably just wanted to please Dame Laura, who wrote about Joan in her autobiography, *The Magic of a Line* (1965):

> This beautiful young woman turned out to be Joan Rhodes, the world-renowned professional strong woman. Although she could tear a telephone book in half by the turn of the wrist, and throw a man weighing sixteen stone over her head, she had no bulgy muscles. Her slim form was perfection: as for her head, it was superbly sculptural.
>
> Joan was a grand woman, with intelligence far above the ordinary; she well deserves the fame she has earned today, both on the stage and on television. I never enjoyed painting anything more than herself, and through the exhibition of that work at the Royal Academy, I got a number of commissions.

Joan didn't need to embellish her story to impress Dame Laura – the truth was heroic enough, as she no doubt realised quite quickly. Embroidering her history was a positive coping mechanism, a way of controlling the situation and ensuring she would not be rejected after what had happened to her as a child.

The portrait was a huge success when it was shown at the Royal Academy in London in 1955. Its journey is worth charting. It was bought by a Midlands businessman for £300 and fell out of sight for years, occasionally popping up on loan for a few exhibitions. Then in 1991, Joan's sister Blackie spotted it for sale in a catalogue for an auction in Leeds. The sale was that very day. In a panic, Joan phoned the auctioneers just as the picture was coming under the hammer. She was allowed to bid on the phone, desperate to possess this important slice of her history at any cost. In true Joan style she was successful, but the final hammer

had come down at an eyewatering £3,464.25, ten times more
expensive than when the oils were fresh. The purchase cleaned
out Joan's savings but she never regretted it. The work sat in pride
of place in the flat for the rest of her life; it was always a comfort
and inspiration to her. She said it was worth every penny. She
wanted it to go to The National Portrait Gallery on her death,
but the institution foolishly rejected it. Things probably worked
out for the best, as it is now one of the prized pieces in the Royal
Academy collection. Funnily enough, it has ended up where it
began. Joan would have approved.

The last time Joan saw Dame Laura was in 1970, when she was
invited to visit her at home in St John's Wood. It was April so it
must have been a treat for Joan's birthday. As a gift she was offered
her choice of one of the paintings on show in her studio:

> I was shown into the large studio which was full of her paint-
> ings. Laura and I sat on two huge chairs – she looked quite frail.
> Her housekeeper came in with a tray of tea and a cream birth-
> day cake. Laura saw me looking at a huge painting called 'The
> Larch Tree' and she asked me if I would like to choose a painting
> as a present. I was speechless – I couldn't! I would, and should,
> have picked 'The Larch Tree' but instead I just said I couldn't
> make up my mind. 'Well,' she said, 'next time.'

Afterwards, Joan rued her decision to pass on the generous offer.
But it simply wasn't in character for her to take such an enormous
gift from a friend. Sadly, Dame Laura died three months later at the
age of 92. At the funeral Joan found she could not laugh in the face
of such a devastating loss; Dame Laura had meant the world to her
and she grieved. For once, the tears came; she often said it was the
first and only time that she cried. The grief lived with her for years,
but she didn't indulge in gloomy thoughts. That really wasn't how
Joan operated. Instead, she would celebrate Dame Laura's life and
achievements, sharing her fabulous memories and stories about
this iconic woman.

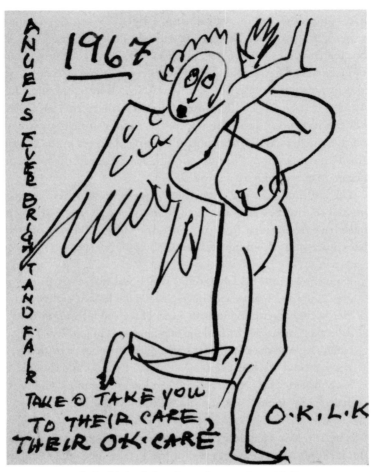

A playful sketch from Dame Laura to Joan, 1967.

13

BUSY, BUSY, BUSY

Joan had made it – she was a star. Despite the enormous odds against her, the 1950s found her at the pinnacle of her career. She had climbed so far from the gutter; it must have felt incredible to have achieved her dream. She was in demand everywhere. She found herself flying across the world for stage and TV appearances, all across Europe and America. Her diaries from those years are packed with engagements. This was her golden era, and she was appearing with some of the biggest names in the business. From the pictures you can see that she looked every inch like the glamourous people with whom she was sharing a stage.

But there was no time to sit back and savour her success. Her bookings covered a vast area, and she was on the road 24/7. In the UK, Joan appeared in venues like the London Palladium but she also travelled the length and breadth of the country, performing in cabarets and nightclubs as well as theatres. Her work abroad took her from Brussels and Paris to Cannes and Reykjavík. Meanwhile, she had an eye on cracking the American market.

At the beginning of April 1955, she flew to New York to appear on a hugely popular Sunday night television show called *Toast of the Town*, later renamed *The Ed Sullivan Show*. The programme had become a part of the intrinsic culture of the United States; it was a tradition for millions of families to settle down on the sofa at the

Joan single-handedly beats one of her 'committees' of strong young men.

end of the weekend and be entertained. At its peak in the 1960s, it attracted up to 80 per cent of the audience share. To be invited to appear on it was considered a great honour, and for many performers from outside the USA it was a brilliant opportunity to get exposure. The show, while embracing new talent, also made room for less modish variety acts. It was a lifeline to vaudeville, which would have come to its demise sooner without this show. Sullivan was a great champion of female and African American performers. He regularly fought with producers to ensure these acts were promoted. He was particularly fond of the Supremes, whom he simply called 'the girls'.

It was this influential show that introduced the Beatles to the United States in the 1960s; their music was already topping the charts, but the American audience hadn't seen the boys live. It was a hugely historic event that is said to have changed American popular music forever. It triggered off the cultural phenomenon known as the British Invasion, where anything from the UK was seen as the ultimate in trendiness or cool. Later, this led to a counterculture between the two nations in the decades to come. The first

"—and she can tear a telephone directory in half, too!"

Newspaper cartoonists loved Joan.

appearance by the lads from Liverpool attracted a record audience at the time of 73 million viewers.

Given a platform like this, Joan was right to anticipate that her appearance would rocket her to stardom across the pond. Even better was that she was going to take a top slot which involved opening and closing the show. But things didn't go exactly to plan.

Joan was buoyant when she got off the plane and performed for the pack of press photographers, picking up a 14st reporter and tucking him under her arm before being driven to meet the producers. She must have thought she was on top of the world as she came face to face with them. But after studying footage of her work, they decided her costumes were indecent and she needed to cover up for family audiences. It seems like a bizarre decision as wearing a basque and removable slit skirt was standard costume for variety everywhere else in the world. It must have been a real slap in the face and sent her into a panic. But Joan didn't have time to remonstrate; instead she dashed off to Saks Fifth Avenue and bought a more demure blue, cotton dress.

Joan wasn't the only one to fall foul of the prudish censorship of the programme's controllers. Elvis Presley, who appeared on the show three times the following year, was told he was not to gyrate and shake his hips in the suggestive way he did when he was dancing and singing. The straightlaced moneymen decided that what he did was obscene and somehow immoral as it sent young girls into an uncontrollable frenzy. Even Ed Sullivan was reported to have taken a dislike to the man who would be The King. But there was no denying his ability to smash the TV ratings, so the programme felt it had to give in to popular demand and allow this wild rock-and-roller to do his thing, within strict limits. Their thinking was to use clever camera work to avoid the wriggles that sent the girls so crazy. The singer was asked to tone down his performances: 'less crotch-work, please' was the message. But they didn't trust him so most of the time during his live performances the camera shot him from the waist up.

Watching the footage, you can tell from the screams of the audience that Elvis was jiggling his hips every which way. Inevitably the story was leaked to the press, probably by Elvis's manager Colonel Tom Parker. It was a great headline grabber; here was this up-and-coming superstar being told not to be so sexy as he was driving young girls mad. Elvis was reported to be upset by all the fuss. But, as they say, any publicity is good publicity.

One of the programmes he appeared on captured a reported record-breaking 82 per cent of the American viewing audience. And in the end, Sullivan appeared to have changed his mind and shook hands with Elvis. He gave his guest a ringing endorsement, saying, 'This is a real decent, fine boy. We've never had a pleasanter experience on our show with a big name than we've had with you. You're thoroughly all right.'

As Joan's show was broadcast live from a theatre on Broadway, the timings were vital. The idea was that the programme would open with her bending a steel bar in her mouth, and that bit was OK. The other performers would do their turns and then at the end Joan would come back to do the rest of her act. On the bill were Fred Astaire and the Will Mastin Trio, whose youngest member, a certain Sammy Davis Jr., stole the show. Whether on purpose or not, the trio substantially overran their ten-minute slot, forcing the director to cut Joan's reappearance. She had been squeezed out of the show. She was livid; so much so that fifty years later we would be sitting having a cuppa and a chat when she'd get on the subject of Sammy Davis Jr. and start complaining bitterly about what he did on her big night. I don't think she ever forgave him, although she went on to work with him occasionally.

Joan was invited back to appear on the Ed Sullivan Show later that year. This time she arrived fully armed with a modest frock and was ready to do battle for her slot. She needn't have worried. It all went well and she was considered to be a great success.

This was the big time; she was rubbing sequined shoulders with the elites of the showbiz world. She found herself performing on the same stage as some of the biggest names in the business, one of them being the English-born comedian, film star and singer Bob Hope. Little did Joan know that her performance with him would jettison her into global headlines and earn her a place in the annals of entertainment history.

Joan's pacifist days were long over and she was happy to entertain American troops, just as she had performed for ENSA. She'd done a month at a large cinema in Reykjavík, two shows a day. Once she got used to the cold and the smell of sulphur from the hot springs around her accommodation, the Borg Hotel, she was quite happy. She was glad to do a return visit over Christmas. This time she was sharing the bill with Joy Webster, a British actress who had appeared in *The Avengers*, and Yana, a glamorous singer who was rarely out of the charts. But most significant of all in the line-up was one of the biggest names of the day – Bob Hope.

Joan wasn't impressed by him. As with so many comedians, once he was off stage he came across as humourless. But the two of them appear to have had a good working relationship right up to the point where Joan managed to drop Bob on his head in front of a packed auditorium of laughing US airmen:

Bob Hope was a surprise. I didn't find him funny as a person. He wasn't interested in me – I think it was Yana he was interested in. She was beautiful, had an interesting voice and was outgoing, whereas I was shy and felt, once again, big and ugly in comparison. As I got to know her I liked her and she wasn't a bit like the impression I had of her at first.

Well, we flew to Reykjavik [*sic*] and were shown around the National Theatre which as I remember was very nice; then we were taken back to the airport to be flown by helicopter to Keflavik where we were to perform before the USAAF. We had a hasty lunch – fishy, I remember – and then to some dressing rooms to get ready for three shows. Each show was packed with American airmen who were delighted with Bob Hope and Yana and then me. At the end of the first show it was the loudest applause I'd ever heard. After a small snack and a drink we were on for the second show, by this time quite tired and Bob flagging a bit. Another short rest and the third show – I was exhausted; we'd been at the airport in London in the early hours of the morning! I braced myself for the third show.

Bob did a little song with me: 'Embrace me, my sweet embraceable you,' and I would sing the line, 'Come to mama, come to mama do,' and then lift Bob and put him on my shoulder and walk off stage. It had gone very well in the first two shows so I had no fear, but I think we were both tired. I couldn't believe it when he took a flying leap at me – one of my four-inch heels broke and he went right over my shoulder and I fell on top of him.

He lay there stunned and I signalled the stage manager to close the curtains, which he did, and then such a commotion! Someone came to me and asked what Bob's first words were; all I could think of was, 'I really fell for you, Joan.' He thanked me afterwards for putting the words into his mouth and on the plane back next morning we drank champagne together.

Of course the press all over the world made it sound much more serious than it really was, but a little later a cablegram arrived which read: 'It should have happened earlier and harder' – signed Bing Crosby!

Watching the video of this on YouTube there was certainly no sign of Hope taking a run at Joan, but he did seem nervous. This was partly in jest but there was also a flavour of real anxiety as Joan squeezed him around the waist and picked him up briefly a few times. He joked about knowing what a tube of Pepsodent toothpaste felt like. Then she lifted him safely in her arms like a very large besuited baby. She did it with ease, as though he was as light as a feather and then she went for the big lift over her head. He stretched out and the pair overbalanced with Hope crashing to the floor; he landed on his head and Joan fell on top of him. You can see that he must have taken quite a blow to the cranium – the brief glimpse of him on the ground shows him lying there stunned.

It transpired that Hope was fine, just a little bruised, but that could have just been his ego taking a knock. No man, especially one who thought so highly of himself, likes being dropped by a woman. The pair rode out the media storm that ensued and, like true professionals, made the most of the publicity.

Joan said that Hope suggested she should stay in the States as her act would go down well. She was offered a six-month contract in the US and a further six months in Australia, but she turned these offers down. She freely admitted that she was too scared to say yes. She couldn't countenance being away from her beloved London for a whole year. Joan adored her garden flat in Belsize Park. She felt safe there and this was an important factor in her life after all

Joan picks up Bob Hope and doesn't drop him this time.

that had happened in the past. It was the home she had constructed for herself. Bert was still sharing the place; by this time their relationship was more a friendship, but she still valued it. Any stability was to be prized.

Dropping Hope on his head was one of those crazy quirks of theatre history that lived on long after the event. Years later, in 1970, Joan was invited to make a surprise guest TV appearance on the British version of *This is Your Life*, hosted by Eamonn Andrews. It was Hope's turn for the programme to honour him, reviewing

Picking up Bob Hope during his This Is Your Life *special with Eamonn Andrews, 1970. (From Joan's personal archive; original picture from Thames Television)*

major events in his life. Joan did pick him up but was careful not to lift him too high. Joan said that after the show Hope was genial but distant – they did manage to laugh about what had happened, but clearly there was no bond between them.

Other than the time she spent in front of an audience, Joan saw herself as an observer of those who had achieved stardom, mostly through their own hard slog and unquestionable talent. She purposefully kept to the perimeter, always watching, always drinking in the details; not necessarily to relate events to others, not to pass on first-hand showbiz gossip, but to feed her own curiosity. She wanted to know about them and their lives without having to confront them with questions. As with Quentin Crisp, she preferred to keep to the sidelines, safely anonymous. Quite a contrast to her professional persona. Joan was a woman of contradictions but also of great discretion and honour. She would never betray the trust of those around her, especially those who she allowed into her own inner circle.

As we have seen with Dame Laura, Joan was fiercely loyal and supportive of those she gave her love to and on rare occasions, this amnesty was given to people she came across in theatres and clubs around the world. Among this select few was one of the biggest movie stars to ever grace the silver screen.

14

MEETING MARLENE

Back in the 1920s and 1930s, the world didn't have the endless means of broadcast entertainment available today. There was no TV, radio was in its infancy and the internet would have been mis-interpreted as something you put over your rollers to keep them in overnight. Newspapers, magazines, books and theatre were mainstays of those hungry to escape their humdrum existence. The arrival of the cinema was a huge change to the viewing landscape.

It's amazing to think that the whole movie machine came to life and began its global domination only about a hundred years ago. At the vanguard of this phenomenon were the beguiling figures who inhabited the screen. But it is long enough ago for the major-ity of those under a certain age, say 40 or 50, not to know who these people were or comprehend their contributions to motion pictures. Queen of the pack was the German-American actor and singer Marlene Dietrich. For those who don't know who she was, I would suggest thinking of her as a heady mix of the femininity of Madonna, Monroe and Mirren with lashings of Depp's quirkiness and Pitt's chiselled features.

We don't really have comparable big names these days; they don't make movie stars like they used to. We do have lots of celebrities but often it is hard to know what they actually do, and by the time you find out, they have disappeared to make way

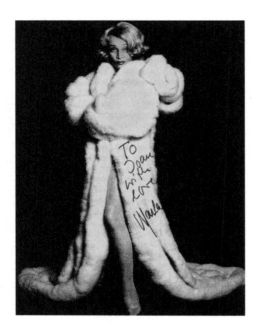

A much-cherished momento from Marlene, Copenhagen.

for the next wannabes. Marlene was a performer of historical importance. The films she worked on were groundbreaking. She was a pioneer. Not just because she was starring in the early talking movies but because she took her image seriously. She painstakingly choreographed every shot that she was in, deliberately working to convey her message, whether it was her beauty, intelligence or acting ability. What set her even further apart was her apparent delight in playing with sexual identity. Marlene was known for her fluid gender expression, dressing as whatever gender she wanted to, whenever she wanted to. She was happy to express her bisexuality at a time when most people wouldn't have had a clue what that meant and, if they did, they would strongly disapprove. In her performances she was at home appearing as a stockinged singer in a sleazy Berlin bar, showing lots of divine leg and titillating the largely male audiences. But she was equally happy to don a top hat, trousers and tails and break the confines of acceptable behaviour by flirting with gorgeous young women who shared the screen. Marlene wasn't scared to challenge sexual stereotypes. It was a role that incurred fierce criticism from those who liked to inhabit what they saw as the moral Christian high ground. Marlene was happy to do battle with the holier-than-thou censors and refused to change a thing. She was horrified when she arrived in Hollywood to find how puritanical everyone was, especially after being brought up in Berlin, where sexuality was as fluid and vast as the Atlantic Ocean. Today she is lauded as an LGBTQ+ champion; she stood for the right of people to choose.

Dietrich was the star of one of the first German talkie films in 1930, *The Blue Angel*. That year, she caused a scandal by kissing a woman on the lips in Josef von Sternberg's film *Morocco*. It's thought that this is the first kiss between two women on commercial camera. Marlene and her director, who was also her lover, stood firm when the heads of the studio tried to have the scene pulled.

Critics at the time said that Marlene was not a woman nor a man; she had a gender all of her own. Her policy seemed to be that if you fancied someone, you slept with them, and she had many lovers. Not that you would think so to read her autobiography, *My Life*, published in 1987. Here she paints a picture of a fabulous lifestyle in Hollywood where she had lots of famous friends but was also a doting mother and loving wife. She was known for her insistence on privacy. Another portrait of Marlene's life came to light when her only child, Maria Riva, filled in a lot of the more sordid details in her tell-all biography in 1992, shortly after Marlene's death. There were an impressive number of famous names on the list. These included Yul Brynner, Mercedes de Acosta, Edith Piaf and Frank Sinatra. Maria said that from an early age, she got a full report from Marlene about her encounters.

One of the more shocking aspects of Maria's side of the story was her contention that at the age of 15, she was forced to live with a woman who raped her for eighteen months. In 1993, she recorded a TV interview with the American broadcaster Diane Sawyer to promote her book. She said her mother moved her into an apartment near hers with the PA of one of her lovers. Maria said she believed this was a deliberate attempt to ensure she became a lesbian so she wouldn't marry a man. This would have meant Maria leaving the mother who had refused to let her go to school or to have friends, always keeping her by her side, even during filming in the studio.

Joan wouldn't have known about most of this when she encountered Marlene in 1965. She would have been aware of the star's bisexuality but not the broader picture. Joan wasn't one to listen to the ferocious gossiping that went on behind the scenes in showbusiness. She didn't even realise that she was about to work with one of her screen idols until she arrived at Copenhagen airport for her second booking in the city. As she went through airport arrivals, she was shocked when she spotted a large poster with Marlene Dietrich emblazoned on it, advertising the show at the Tivoli Gardens – with Joan's name sharing the bill. She sped up her pace as she wanted to get to the venue as quickly as she could to not miss a minute of seeing the legendary movie star:

> Marlene was on stage discussing lighting; she directed every part of her show and I sat in the stalls taking it all in. Even in rehearsal she was very beautiful and polite, but she knew what she wanted, and got it! The technicians went out of their way to follow her instructions. Then she left the stage, but was back in a few minutes with her music, and she and her pianist Burt Bacharach went through all her numbers not once or twice, but many times until for her it was perfect.

Joan and the rest of the performers just sat and watched in admiration until they were herded away to see their dressing rooms and the green room where refreshments were laid on. No one expected the great lady to join them. And yet:

Marlene came in and sat with us. She looked very relaxed, dressed in white slacks, brown shirt and a white raincoat. She didn't do the 'Big Star' act at all – she was one of us and we loved her for it. Twice she asked us all to a Saturday dinner at a nearby hotel – always generous.

We settled in and when we opened on the first night it was to a packed house. I closed the first half and noticed Marlene standing in the wings and applauding me – she was a very generous lady! When I went to my dressing room there were flowers and champagne from her. She followed the interval and did the whole of the second half of the show. Sometimes she would insist on having the stage washed during the interval, and after her show she would search it for any sequins which had dropped from her dress and sew them on again herself – she didn't care for having a dresser.

In Joan's archive, I found a small pocket diary from 1965. At first there seemed to be nothing much written in it, but as I was about to put it back in the storage box, I noticed some entries about Copenhagen and her time with Marlene. I wanted to understand their relationship, whatever shape it took, but the entries provided a frustratingly elliptical record of some of their meetings away from the bright lights. On 1 July, Joan wrote that she flew to Copenhagen and went to rehearsals at 10 a.m. followed by a performance at 7.30 in the evening. Then in tiny writing: 'Marlene asked me to zip her.' The next day, 'She came to watch.' Then on 3 July, 'Marlene brought champagne to dressing room.' On 5 July, 'Marlene sent flowers.' On 6 July, 'Dinner with Marlene.' On 7 July, 'Says I should work in black catsuit. Marlene bought me scarf.' These entries are accompanied by news of loving letters from Joan's live-in partner, Ulrico, in London. More about him later.

Then, on 13 July, 'Long walk with M.', followed by 'Marlene last night' on 15 July. In her memoir Joan recounts how Marlene repeatedly sent gifts to her dressing room:

After the first night, each evening when I returned to my dressing room there was a little gift from her and a glass of champagne (she didn't know that I didn't take alcohol – but I did get used to it later!). Later she bought me a lovely crystal glass which seemed to have a teardrop in it. Sadly it was later broken and lost for ever, but the memory clings. I do still have a scarf and note saying 'To match your blue eyes'; my eyes are green but the thought was nice.

We went one day to have lunch together at a fisherman's wharf and she enjoyed not being recognised – very cool are the Danes. One day I bought a very cheap Kodak camera, hoping to get someone to take a photo of her and me together, but I was too shy to ask. But anyway, I took one of her and she took one of me and then asked about the camera. I told her how cheap it was and where I had bought it – she said she would like one for, I think, her grand-daughter but she couldn't buy it herself because it would get to the press. So I bought it for her and

The only photograph that exists showing Joan (centre) and Marlene (right) close together, Copenhagen.

insisted she take it as a gift – feeling embarrassed that it seemed a poor comparison to the gifts she had given me.

Joan liked to show me her treasures, and one of her most prized possessions was a gift she said was from Marlene when they were in Denmark. It was a beautiful white feather fan made by J. Duvelleroy of Regent Street, London, the Rolls-Royce of fan makers. It has passed to me to keep it safe as time gradually withers its beauty. These days, its carefully made white and gold box is battered and falling apart, and when you open the fan, little feathers plume into the air. It is fragile but hanging on in there.

Joan must have been utterly bowled over by this unexpected adventure with a gorgeous global superstar. Maria spoke about how her mother had explosive passions; is that what she felt for Joan? She was certainly attracted to her. And it's not surprising. Here was a true rarity, a stunning, mature woman who was not only beautiful, elegant and clever but was as physically strong as any man. The actress and singer would have never come across anyone like this before. Like Marlene, Joan crushed gender stereotypes. It isn't stretching the bounds of possibility that sexual sparks were flying.

Or, more prosaically, they could have simply been intimate friends. Joan was 44 at the time, and her idol was twenty years older. Marlene admired true talent and was fiercely intellectual; she liked to spend time with gifted, witty and beautiful people, like Joan.

The details Joan related of their relationship were carefully pieced together. Her words and diary read like a sweet little love story, where these two extraordinary women went for walks and meals together, exchanged gifts, took snaps of each other and kept away from the world when they were not on stage.

And it wasn't a two-week wonder. Much later in their lives they were still in touch. Marlene sent Joan a postcard of herself during the time she was writing her autobiography, so probably in the late 1980s. It said, 'And how I remember you. Too bad our beautiful place is closed. I loved it there so much. I am ok – don't believe the papers. Writing my book which is a big bore. Love Marlene.'

Joan told me how Marlene would call her out of the blue in the wee hours of the morning. She said the phone would ring at 2 or 3 a.m. and there would be silence. Joan knew who it was and would ask, 'Is that you?' More silence, then an acknowledgement. Nothing much was said; Joan would hang on the silent line until her lonely caller had had enough companionship. This fits in with what Maria Riva wrote about how her mother lived in isolation in her Parisian flat for the last years of her life, but she would indulge herself by making endless phone calls and flirting with whomever was at the other end of the line. Joan said she intermittently received these calls right up to Marlene's death in 1992.

15

A QUEEN AND THE KING
ARE AMUSED

The strongwoman from the gutters of London had come a long way in a relatively short period of time. It was a transition of fairy-tale proportions, from rags to Hollywood royalty. But even the great Marlene Dietrich couldn't compete with the real thing. A few years before the two women met, Joan found herself performing for the most important audience in the world. She could hardly believe it when she was invited to Windsor Castle to entertain Queen Elizabeth. It must have been a surreal moment when she was approached to be one of a handful of specially selected stars to perform in the annual Christmas show of December 1958.

The invitation came out of the blue. Joan knew lots of influential people in the business, one of whom was a well-known performer called Peter Brough. At the time, he was a huge star with a popular radio show called *Educating Archie*. Brough was a ventriloquist, a bizarre act to feature on the wireless, but for some reason it appealed to the listening public. So much so that Brough and his dummy, Archie, were said to have attracted over 15 million listeners over three nights.

The programme from the Grand Christmas Ball at Windsor Castle, 1958.

Brough phoned Joan and asked if she was free to do the Royal Household Social Club's Grand Christmas Ball at Windsor Castle. There would be no fee but the honour it conveyed was beyond price. Of course, she jumped at the opportunity. It was only after she had said an enthusiastic 'yes' that Joan took a moment to think about what it all meant. Then she began to panic. Nothing in her life had prepared her for such a prestigious encounter. She felt completely out of her depth. She told Brough that she was clueless about protocol, but he reassured her that all she needed to do was her normal act. 'Be yourself and wear some white gloves if you have any.' This triggered another panic:

'I can't do my act in gloves,' I responded.

'No, darling, for when you are presented afterwards!'

So I had some lilac satin gloves which I took along, and an evening dress. On the way my car broke down and I had to leave it behind – was this an omen? I wondered.

In among Joan's stash of memorabilia is the carefully preserved programme for the evening and letters about the show. The event in the Waterloo Chamber at Windsor Castle was an annual tradition, a time when the royal family and the people who served them let their hair down and had a good time together. Although the room was vast and very grand, with its vaulted ceiling and huge chandeliers, this was an intimate occasion, very much a part of life at the castle.

The programme credits Peter Brough as the compère and shows that there were five acts. Joan was the only woman in the show and hers was the speciality performance. The rest of the cast were well-established mainstream comedians; the royal family liked to have a good laugh. This was guaranteed with five of the funniest men alive on the bill: Flanagan and Allen, Freddie Sales, Arthur Askey and Dick Emery. All huge stars at the time, chosen either at the request of the queen or with the sure knowledge that she would be entertained by them.

One of the most successful jokes of the evening came from Arthur Askey. Peter Brough announced him after each act but he never appeared. He finally came panting into the chamber, beamed at the queen and the Duke of Edinburgh and said, 'Sorry folks, when Peter Brough told me I was playing Windsor Castle I thought he meant the pub at Victoria Station.' One report said that Princess Margaret, the queen's sister, complained that Askey had made her laugh so much her mascara ran.

From Joan's description of the event, it was all very civilised. The cast were treated to a few drinks before being shown to some disappointingly basic changing rooms. Joan put on her best frock and was careful to do a natural-looking job of her make-up – there wasn't time for rehearsals so she wasn't sure what the lighting was like. She hadn't altered her act in any way for the occasion and began with her usual request for male helpers, only this time she was hoping for a royal volunteer:

'Good evening,' I said, 'I'd like the help of four gentlemen as a committee – please help!' No-one moved. I was rather worried because this was my usual act and I became not a little cross. 'I did ask for gentlemen,' I said and to my relief the Duke of Edinburgh stepped forward smiling and three others also came forward and so I was able to perform as usual. I bent a steel bar round my neck and handed it to two of the men, saying, 'Please straighten it out, I'll need it for my next show.' They couldn't. So I handed out 6-inch nails and said, 'In a moment I'll tell you what to do with them,' causing a ripple. I then explained that I was going to break one of them – the nails, not the men – so could they please bend the nails for me. I even gave the Duke my duster.

He struggled but couldn't manage it so to save face for him I held it up and said, 'Look – you've got a kink' (meaning, of course, the nail). Everyone laughed, including the Queen, and I proceeded to break it and hand it back to him. He dropped it. I finished with the telephone book, everyone applauded and then I was off.

A few newspapers reported that Joan had been chosen to perform for the queen; reading the cuttings, it is clear that she had carefully planned this joke as she spoke about how she would help the duke to bend a nail and get a kink. One of the features of her act were her witty, saucy quips. It was a cheeky joke and a bit risky to cast aspersions on the duke's sexuality but, as ever, the risk paid off and Joan got away with it:

Someone came to my dressing room when the show was over and said we had to line up. I changed into my cheap and cheerful

evening dress and put on the gloves. We lined up and the Duke
and Queen Mother came along to thank us for a lovely show –
the Queen Mother whispered to me, 'But you are so graceful,
my dear!' I towered above her and blushed! Peter Brough drove
me home. The show had gone well and apart from 'He has a
kink' I didn't disgrace myself. It is so easy to do that if you have
no-one to advise you! And I enjoyed the compliment from the
Queen Mother; it had always been my 'thing' to be graceful on
stage as everyone expected me to be big and ugly, and I wondered what my aunt would have thought.

There it was again; even at the moment of her greatest triumph,
those damning words about being big and ugly continued to eat
away at her. Not even the admiration of the royal family could
assuage her insecurity about her appearance.

Joan's act was well received. It was reported that the queen had
spoken to Joan and expressed concern about the strength needed
to bend bars and nails. The queen asked her if it hurt her hands.
Earlier, while on stage struggling to emulate Joan, the duke was

Joan was on her way to fame. One of her proudest moments in her exciting career was when she did a show at a staff party at Windsor Castle before the Queen and Prince Philip. The ease with which she bent stout nails amazed the Prince.

A magazine cartoon strip about Joan's encounter with the Duke of Edinburgh.

heard to say that it was 'tough going'. A letter from Peter Brough later confirmed that the queen had sent him a personal message saying how much she had enjoyed the cabaret. How sad that instead of embracing such a precious interaction with the royal family, Joan couldn't fully enjoy the moment. She was stalked by her cruel past.

This was not Joan's only encounter with royalty. At roughly the same time as meeting the British monarchy, she was booked to perform at the Moulin Rouge in Paris. She was puzzled to receive a mysterious invite from fellow performers who were on stage at the Lido. They were called the Bernard Brothers, an American double act who dressed in large, chequered frocks with big bows on their heads and brilliantly sent up current hit records by miming them. Joan was a friend of theirs and had often been to see them at their hotel, which was rather more luxurious than hers. But this invitation was to join them in their dressing room as 'someone' wanted to meet her.

The 'someone' turned out to be Elvis Presley, The King of Rock and Roll. I have tried and failed to think of a comparable contemporary figure who might illustrate to younger readers how huge a figure Elvis was in the mid-twentieth century. I know he is still 'big', but he has become part of the rich wallpaper that surrounds us every day. In the 1950s, Elvis was like a deity to the younger generation. He transformed music, he embraced Black culture and his performances were blatantly sexual. He created a new culture and laid the foundations for the likes of Mick Jagger, David Bowie and Michael Jackson.

When Joan told me that Elvis had asked to be introduced to her backstage at the Paris Lido, my mouth dropped open in awe. Imagine that, The King, the sexiest man alive, actually asking for an audience with you! My mind jumped to all kinds of scenarios but try as I might, Joan spoke of the encounter in the most circumspect way. It was frustrating, to say the least. In her memoir she describes 'loud voices' and 'a slight commotion' at the bar during one night of her act at the Moulin Rouge:

I just got on with my act and things settled down. Afterwards I asked what it was all about and was told that a famous American star had come in to see the show. The next day I was invited by George Pierce to go along after the show to the Lido, where he was appearing with the Bernard Brothers. They often invited me to their posh hotel for drinks or a coffee so of course I went, although it seemed a bit strange to go that night but it was nice to be asked.

George was busy ironing the famous check dresses and bows and the Bernards were making up in front of the mirrors. I had just sat down in a comfortable chair when an Assistant Stage Manager came to the door and said, 'He's here now, shall I bring him down?'

'Oh yes,' they replied, 'he wants to meet Joan.'

I secretly thought it must be a journalist or agent – when in walked Elvis Presley in full dress army uniform! They introduced me and he shook my hand and pressed it quite gently – I was thrilled! George opened a bottle of champagne and we all toasted each other. I did offer to go but they chorused, 'Stay, stay,' so I did and sat myself in a corner to watch and listen.

George Bernard joked with Elvis, asking, 'So which one did you have?' It seemed that a couple of days earlier Elvis had invited all of the Bluebell Girls back for a party at his hotel, the George V. He kept glancing over at me, but I was in awe of him. He was tall, slim and so handsome – I cherish the hour that he was there. He was taken into the cabaret to sit at the bar and watch the show.

Much later George told me that Elvis liked me and my act, but that night he had to get back to Friedberg or there might be trouble. It was sad that he died so young, but he was, and still is, a big star.

Oh, to have been a fly on the wall. As we know, Joan was a woman who embraced secrets and was good at keeping them, so what happened during that encounter with Elvis will never be known. I did try time and again to get her to 'remember' more, but to no avail. She said she didn't recall a word of the conversation. Really? If the most famous person on the planet had specially arranged to see you, would you forget every word? It's unlikely as Joan had a great memory for her own life experiences. In her memoir, she managed to recall names and places clearly after sixty years or more. Alas, we will never know.

Although Joan often found herself in the company of the rich and famous, she never forgot her roots; she was not impressed by wealth and wasn't a snob. She was the kind of woman who was happy to do what she could for those around her. She had a great social conscience which is no doubt why she found herself appearing at some weird and wonderful venues. One of them was Maidstone Jail in Kent.

This was four years before her appearance at Windsor Castle, December 1954. The charity event was put on for the inmates, some of the staff and their guests and was part of a series of Sunday shows organised by Rev. John Nicholls. The vicar must have had some great contacts in showbusiness as he managed to attract quite a line-up. It included the comedian Dick Emery, who was to go on and have a hugely successful career in television. He'll be remembered particularly for the show named after him which ran for eighteen years on the BBC up until 1981. In it he would take on the guise of different characters including a saucy old lady whose catch phrase was 'Oooo you are awful, but I like you.' Also appearing in the prison were the Tanner Sisters, Jimmy Wheeler and Grace Cole with her all-girl band, who travelled from Darlington for the show.

The prison had its own theatre space with all the accoutrements like curtains and special lighting. The one big difference would have been the bars that surrounded it. For the hundreds of inmates who attended, a show such as this must have been a reminder of the world beyond the cells. Add to that the presence of gorgeous girls in a land of grey-clad men and you can imagine what a great impact the event must have had.

From Joan's account it seemed to go well, with enough warders to ensure the crowd of 300 didn't get any fancy ideas. The inmates weren't allowed to take part when Joan got to the bit of her act where she asked for volunteers, so four prison officers got the short straw. There were great roars of pleasure from the audience when the men failed to beat Joan when it came to bending nails or winning a tug of war:

Jimmy Wheeler got the show off to a good start: sitting in the front two rows, with about three hundred prisoners behind them, were the Governor and his guests in their everyday clothes. Prisoners in those days wore 'prison grey'. Jimmy asked, 'Who let them in in their own clothes?' which got a big laugh.

When it came time for me to ask for my four volunteers the eager prisoners were not allowed on stage and I ended up with four prison officers who were all jeered when none could even put a kink in any of the nails. Of course I was cheered loudly when I then broke them, and even more loudly when I did the tug of war. As I was taking a bow or two at the end someone shouted, 'Tell us the secret!' so I went back on stage and whispered, 'The secret is the strength' – which got the applause of the evening. I was so happy it all went well.

Joan had one other reason for agreeing to do the show, which wasn't paid. Someone had asked her to be a courier and bring in some cigarettes for an unnamed variety artiste who was doing a ' stretch. It turned out he was helping backstage. She said he was so delighted with the fags that he acted as though she had given him gold. Cheekily he asked for one more favour – he wanted the remains of the large phone book Joan had torn into quarters. This wasn't to keep as a prized momento, though: he told Joan that the pages would come to good use as toilet paper.

Everyone involved was under strict instructions not to say anything to the press but that stricture was never going to be obeyed; not when you had a beautiful woman who could bend bars appearing before hundreds of prisoners who would like to do just that.

There would have been plenty of leaks to the media as it was also a great publicity stunt for everyone concerned. Joan said there were full reports in several newspapers. The *Daily Express* ran the story on the front page with the headline 'Strong Girl Cheered', another paper declared 'Joan Bends Iron Bars in Jail' (for the record, they were steel bars but that wouldn't have made such a good headline). The Giles cartoon in the *Express* showed two prisoners who had escaped and were desperately sheltering from the winter weather under a bush. They were looking very glum and the caption read, 'Thanks to your master escape plan we missed a jolly good concert in the warm.'

16

WINIFRED 'TOINETTE' MORAN, MUM

When I began writing this biography I knew that Joan's mum, Winifred, wasn't a pleasant woman; after all, she had deserted her four tiny children, including a newborn baby. Then again, there could be many mitigating circumstances for her behaviour, such as post-natal depression. I had hoped to find redeeming characteristics, but instead my research uncovered quite the contrary. Winifred was a monster.

I knew that as Joan became more famous, appearing on the radio and TV, regularly making the headlines in national newspapers, she had a battle on her hands to control a past that kept stalking her in the shape of her repugnant mother. Seemingly always there, lurking in the shadows ready to pounce with demands for money, clothes and unearned love. The more successful Joan was, the more pressure she came under from the woman who had abandoned her at the age of 3.

What I didn't realise was that Winifred had strong political views that were predominantly racist. She was known as an antisemite and had a criminal record to show for it. She was a woman of extremes. Joan would talk to me about her but there was always an unfamiliar hardness in her voice. I don't know if

Joan's mum, Winifred, who called herself Mrs Moran. She worked in London during the war as a driver.

she hated her biological mother, but she certainly felt powerful emotions when she tackled the subject. In fact, it was partly that anger that Joan believed fuelled her remarkable strength. I understood the tumultuous rage she felt to some extent, but it was only after discovering more about her mother that I fully grasped the depths of it.

Joan was very much a liberal by nature and practice so it must have pained her enormously that her own mother was an outspoken antisemite and an active supporter of the British fascist movement in the 1930s and 1940s. She was 'wedded' to the cause: for twenty-seven years she lived with Tommy Moran, a key figure in the British Union of Fascists. Although they weren't married, as Tommy already had a wife, she passed herself off as Mrs Moran. I originally thought that maybe she went along with the movement to show solidarity with her 'husband'. But then I tracked down a series of newspaper reports of hearings in Derby Magistrate's

Tommy Moran and Winifred.

Court in 1948 where Winifred was accused of behaviour that could lead to a breach of the peace.

This incident came when feelings were running high after two British army sergeants were murdered in what was then known as Mandatory Palestine. The hangings were carried out by an extremist Zionist group called the Irgun, who wanted British troops out of the region and the establishment of an Israeli state. The murders triggered violent reprisals in Britain. It led to a resurgence of fascism, and Winifred shared the outrage about what had happened. The court heard that she was speaking one evening at a gathering in the marketplace in central Derby. Nearby, there was another meeting underway organised by the League of Jewish

Ex-Servicemen, and they were using a loudspeaker. This infuriated Winifred, who began verbally abusing them, saying they were 'dirty Jews' and members of the Irgun. The police intervened and arrested her. She was convicted, fined £5 and bound over to keep the peace for twelve months. It transpired that she had a police record and had already been bound over to keep the peace in the previous year after she attacked someone. This was not a simpering housewife feigning political interest to support her husband. Both were highly active.

In the hearings, she had given her name as Winifred Toinette Moran. This explained why searches kept bringing up a 'Toni Moran' who was known for speaking at fascist meetings and travelling from Derby across the north of England, particularly in Manchester. She was a fierce antisemite. Relatively recent online postings about Winifred said she would insult Jews in Yiddish. One contributor said Winifred's language was bad enough to make a fishwife blush. This may just be gossip, but it does fit with the picture painted of Winifred in the court hearings.

She appealed against the conviction, but the court upheld the original verdict a month later on 29 June 1948. The deputy recorder said:

> It is quite clear from your record since August 1947, that you get very indignant about political matters. It led to you assaulting somebody in 1947 and I am satisfied that it was your hysterical indignation that led you to committing these offences. If this indignation boils up within you when you go to or conduct political meetings you are going to be a menace to the public of Derby.

He went further to say that he believed Mrs Moran uttered her abuse when she was in a state bordering on hysteria.

Joan would have been about 27 at the time. Although she was estranged from her mother, she was in touch with her sister Peggy, so it is likely she would have known about the events in Derby.

Peggy was a kind woman with a desire to reunite the family, tracking down her siblings and keeping lines of communication open. This worked well for the three girls, who developed warm relationships. Their brother, Peter, was adopted by an East End family. He eventually tracked down the family and demanded to see Joan when she was performing at The Savoy. The meeting went badly; Joan said he was a 'wide boy' who was associated with the Kray twins. She never saw him again and heard in later years that he had emigrated to Australia.

Joan's propensity to hoard documents helped enormously with the task of getting a feel for her mother. Digging around the archive, I found a bundle of letters written by Winifred. In light of her repulsive political views, they reveal a surprisingly pathetic, self-pitying character who would stoop to any level in order to get what she wanted. The worst of it was that she knew where to find Joan, keeping an eye on where she lived and where she was performing. Once she knew Joan's address, she got on with the business of bleeding her successful second child for as much as she could. She would appear at the flat in Belsize Park and shout outside the door, kicking at it and making wild accusations at all hours. Joan told me that in the early days she did give in to her mother's requests for money, often in the shape of loans that would never be repaid. From what Joan said, she invariably managed not to see Winifred; she tried to restrict contact by ensuring any communication was via the postal service. But as the demands continued, Joan decided enough was enough and stopped the handouts. This triggered some carefully constructed begging letters which show that Winifred used every trick in the book to pull on her daughter's heart strings. And when that didn't work she resorted to blackmail, attempting to publicly shame her in the national press.

Winifred appears to have gone through life thinking she had been cheated and the evidence suggests that she did have a rough time of it. As mentioned earlier in this book, she met Thomas Alfred Taylor at the age of 18 and was soon pregnant. This led to a quick registry office wedding and a world of pain, as Thomas proved to be a useless breadwinner and an even worse husband. He would show up at the house, stay long enough to make Winifred pregnant and then disappear again. His contributions to the household purse were meagre and his wife had to turn to her own mother for handouts. As we know, it led to the desertion of four small children. Winifred refused to take the blame for this and in her mind, there was a clear culprit. In one of her letters written to Joan in 1963, almost forty years later, she gives vent to her feelings towards her husband: 'I brought you, Joan, into this world alone, that thing Thomas Alfred Taylor left me as a young girl to bear the birth of you on the Bellingham Estate – Catford and I was alone except for Peggy. He is responsible for our broken lives.' Winifred was quick to accuse others of being responsible for her woes. The fact that Joan's was a difficult birth was often held up as a reason for her to feel deeply indebted to her mother.

Early on, Winifred did reclaim one of her young offspring from relatives, taking Peggy – the eldest and by all accounts the best behaved – and settling in Manchester, where her wider family lived. From the few pictures that exist, it is possible to see she was rather stout and plain. She was seen as quite a character. According to John Cash, Peggy's son, she was an accomplished pianist and had a creative streak. He relates how she made a living working the markets in East Lancashire: she would set up a pitch, stand on a box and sell strings of pearls, which were very much in fashion at the time. Winifred would shout at the passers-by to get a crowd around her and then she would bark out her sales patter extolling the merits of her high-quality necklaces. She would bite the pearls, clamping them between her teeth to prove that they were the real thing. Of course, they were fake. Winifred was an expert at proving the old adage 'there's a fool born every minute', and she was excellent at spotting them. There's an interesting parallel with how Joan also pitched on the street to gather a crowd of punters so she could persuade them to dig into their pockets.

According to one of her letters, Winifred began the relationship with Tommy Moran in 1936, taking his name and pretending that they were married from then on. This is the same year as the infamous Battle of Cable Street where thousands of Oswald Mosley's Blackshirts attempted to march through the East End of London, an area home to large Jewish and Irish communities. The marchers were confronted with impassioned anti-fascist demonstrators; some reports said the numbers ran into the tens of thousands. The route was blockaded and hundreds of police, some mounted, took up the middle position to try to keep control of a potentially explosive situation.

You can find original newsreel footage online. The event was surprisingly well documented for the time, with cameras in raised positions to get a good vantage point. Having seen pictures of Tommy, who was a bulldog of a man, it is possible to spot someone who looks just like him in the black and white footage. As a leading member of the British Union of Fascists, he would have been keen to take centre stage. The figure was caught on camera as he slugged it out with another man from the crowd. He threw a few punches and then ran for the safety of his compatriots. According to historians, he became known to fascists as the hero of the Battle of Cable Street for his actions that day.

Moran, a former miner, had abandoned the Labour Party in favour of a much more extreme doctrine. He was a close associate of Mosley; records show that his job was to spread the word about fascism and recruit new members in Wales and the north of England. The BUF, which supported Hitler and Mussolini, was loathed by the majority of Britons. It became a proscribed organisation once war with Germany broke out.

Moran was arrested and interned during the Second World War, but he is said to have continued his fascistic activities from the inside of a prison camp as warders turned a blind eye. Winifred lived with him before and after his incarceration; they were together until his death in 1963. It is hard to verify Moran's political journey after the war but there are a number of reports that he split with Mosley, disillusioned by his leader's dictator-like behaviour. Neofascist groups today claim Moran was known by the arch-fascist Benito Mussolini. There is even a bizarre suggestion that Mussolini sent a pre-written message to Moran's funeral saying, 'He was a fine man.' According to some reports, Moran reconciled with Mosley before he died. True or not, it appears Moran lives on as a fascist hero. What is known through Winifred, however, is that he ended up in a common grave in Kensal Green Cemetery.

Joan never spoke about Moran much and it appears she had very little to do with him. She would have abhorred the BUF and all it stood for. This makes the repeated demands for money to help him and her estranged mother even more bizarre.

In a letter dated 17 March 1953, Winifred berated Joan for not being in touch, once again reminding her that she went through hell to give birth to her. She tried to make good the fact that she deserted her children by saying her mother-in-law had agreed to feed and clothe the eldest girls. She said she wished she had gone into the workhouse as they could have been together. And then the begging started in earnest:

> I don't want to seem a scrounger, but Joan, as you take the same size shoe as me, if you ever have any you do not want, think of me will you, you don't know what a godsend they would be. Tommy's wages are so poor and I am in a part time job at a builder's merchants … I cut out all your photographs that I see in the press and I stick them in an album. Life must be wonderful for you, travelling everywhere as you do.

This was ostensibly a thank-you letter for a cheque that Joan had sent, so this wasn't the first nor the last letter of its kind. About a year later, Winifred complained about her daughter not getting in touch and threatened to 'do something we all shall be sorry for if I don't get some help'. Then she threatened to come to the theatre where Joan was performing.

In a letter dated 21 January 1955, Winifred went into graphic detail about Moran's poor health, describing at excruciating length how 'his bowel had been transferred outside his body' while his back strengthened and how it leaked excrement. She didn't elaborate as to what he was suffering from, but he clearly couldn't continue working as a hospital porter at this time. She moaned about how unfair it was that she and Tommy struggled to survive when immigrants got large payouts:

Whist [*sic*] he is at home I have to have the fire on all day and extra gas and loads of washing, yet foreigners can go and get £4 or £5 [...] Again, surely after the snub, I have had from you with no reply to my begging letters (for Tommy's sake) you must know how it is and no matter what you may think you must know in your heart I wouldn't ask if I wasn't desparate [*sic*]. You ARE my flesh and blood, no matter how you try to shelve it, so can you please help me. I would hate to think that any of my children came to me and I refused them anything even although it may only be a loaf or a meal. Mother

Tommy and Winifred left Derby, where they were both known as troublemakers and had trouble finding work. They headed to London and moved to a crumbling building in Maida Vale over a printer's premises. Tommy did get work as a hospital porter and Winifred got a job as a bookkeeper, ironically for a local Jewish tailor who had obviously been impressed by her ability to add up two columns of figures simultaneously and knew nothing of her strong antisemitic views.

It appears that they both stepped back from high-profile politics and sank into the safety of the shadows of London. Their social life was centred on the local pub, where both became regular fixtures. Tommy had a group of like-minded acolytes and Winifred's skills as a pub pianist kept them in free drinks, but her life was a constant struggle to make ends meet. She was always on the scrounge.

Joan continued to dodge her mother, and this led to an angry confrontation outside Joan's flat in the summer of 1955. Reviewing the letters that still exist, it is possible to piece together a picture of two women who were at war. Tempers had flared and it is even possible that someone got thumped. The drama began when Winifred turned up at her daughter's door at 10 a.m. one Sunday. It was 17 July, the day that a gushing and glamorous feature about Joan had appeared in the *Sunday Dispatch* – 'typical newspaper sensationalism', Joan later said. When Winifred began shouting and 'banging loudly' on the door, Joan told her to go away. But Winifred started kicking the door and making enough noise to awaken the neighbours. Joan recounts her version of events in her memoir:

> I was in bed and so was Bert; she was bellowing 'I know you're in there!' Bert thought it was a man, her voice was low and loud, so he went to try and stop her as the people next door were all hanging out of their windows.
>
> 'Oh, I see you've got a man in there!' she shouted, so I went to the door where Bert was holding out and when she saw me she increased her efforts to get into the flat.
>
> 'Sure,' I said, 'I've got a man. I'm over 21 and I don't want to know you.'
>
> She looked at me with such hatred that I never wanted to see her again. The next day Bert took me to a solicitor. She used to write to me, asking me for money, and to my shame I did send her some nearly every time she wrote, but I never did see her again. Peggy said that our mother didn't understand why I didn't want to see her again and had said, 'After all, she is my flesh and blood and I had a very hard time when she was born – a very large baby.'

Winifred claimed that her daughter struck her, something Joan denied. Both women came away from the encounter furious and determined to take further action. The timing of this fracas couldn't have been worse for Joan. She was writing a lucrative series of articles for the *Sunday Dispatch* (later to become the *Sunday Express*). She'd agreed to tell the story of her life and how she came to be the 'Strongest Woman in the World' after being approached by the news editor, Christian Petersen, at the end of May in 1955. He offered to pay an impressive £400 for four features. He said a ghostwriter would be employed but Joan said she had written a

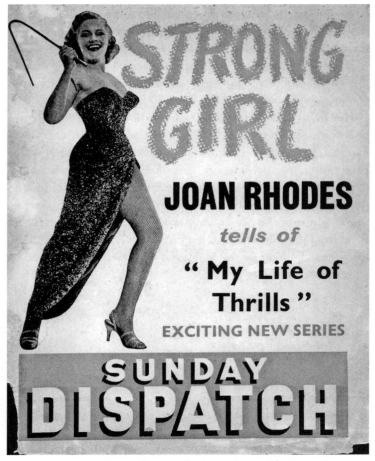

A promotional poster for Joan's features in the Sunday Dispatch.

lot of what appeared; clearly, she wasn't that embarrassed by the sensationalism of the pieces.

The letters show that Joan took her grievances to lawyers called Spector and Spector, Tottenham Court Road, London. She instructed them to write to her mother and get her to cease and desist from harassing her by making repeated phone calls and going to her flat. The subsequent letter they sent to Winifred said that their client was reluctant to take further action, but she would do so if necessary. Joan paid a princely sum of 2 guineas (£2 2s) for this communication, which ultimately didn't work. Annoying as her mother was, it would have cost a lot to get a restraining order, so it looks as though the legal action stopped with this warning shot. Meanwhile, the correspondence shows that Winifred was cooking up her own kind of revenge for being snubbed.

Her focus was on the *Sunday Dispatch* and the pieces it was publishing about her daughter. In her rage – she was known for having a fierce temper – she decided she wanted to publicly shame Joan and expose her as a liar. It is likely that during the doorstep confrontation she would have given voice to her intention to show Joan up as a fake. Four days after the incident Winifred wrote to the editor of the *Sunday Dispatch*. As she was approaching an authority figure she changed her physical writing style, adding in lots of grandiose hoops and loops, as if to show that he was dealing with a person of note:

Letter to the editor of the *Sunday Dispatch*
July 21st 1955
RE <u>MRS Joan Rhodes</u>
Dear Sir,
Further to my telephone request to speak to you personally I would if you can spare me a little of your time like to state a few facts in connection with The Life Story of <u>Mrs Joan Rhodes</u>.

I believe you have accepted this story in good faith, but in view of the fact that I, her mother <u>can</u> prove that the first instalment is a tissue of lies, I cannot imagine you as the Editor of a good paper allowing it to continue without confirming the truth of Joan's story.

I know you can put forward the fact that 'as she uses the name of Rhodes' (her husband's name), that her story does not affect me and mine.

But as one of your regular readers who accept life stories as the truth I think it grossly unfair to print the future instalments if proof to the contrary is given to you.

I was asked by your Sub-Editor (on the phone) if I was attempting Blackmail.

This is a question which even the law would not dare to suggest to a decent woman and I am sure <u>you</u> would not dare to suggest such a thing to a reader.

I tried to see my daughter before troubling you, but I was assaulted.

I am terribly hurt and distressed, and I am sure if you can see me you would respect my confidence and see my point.

I am advised to take a summons out against my daughter for assault, and if I do I shall take relatives along to the court which will prove her story to be a lot of Balderdash and unfit for the readers of a National paper who are 'looked to' for truth.

Mrs Moran

The paper's answer to this attack on Joan was to send her the letter and leave it to her to deal with it. The editor appeared to agree with the sub-editor who accused Winifred of being a blackmailer. Her claims were dismissed, and she failed to scupper the writing deal. The threats of legal action came to nothing.

In Joan's memoir she tried to be dismissive about the woman. But it must have been unnerving to have Winifred snapping at her heels and never knowing when she was going to appear. She even pestered other celebrities, trying to get them to intercede. Joan was particularly mortified when Winifred accosted her friend Leonard Sachs, who was hugely famous for compering the TV programme *The Good Old Days* over thirty years:

I don't know much about my mother, although when I was doing well people would tell me that she would stop them in the street to say that since I'd become well known I was ignoring her. Leonard Sachs said she stopped him several times – and once a man phoned me from a pub and said my mother was crying, and would I speak to her. 'Certainly not,' I replied, 'you don't know the full story,' and put the phone down.

Joan never saw her mother again. There is one last letter from Winifred in the archive, dated 31 July 1963. In it she appears to be in a desperate state as Tommy had died and she said he was due to be buried in a common grave in Kensal Green the next day. She had no one to go with her to the funeral other than a neighbour:

> My Dear Joan, For God's sake how can you be so hard and cruel, tell me what have I been responsible for that you can treat your own mother like this. Is your heart so unforgiving that you can remember a bit of temper and a row at a time like this. I forgot that you hit me and the moment my dear pal died I turned to my own daughter. I brought you, Joan, into this world alone, that thing Thomas Alfred Taylor left me as a young girl to bear the birth of you on the Bellingham Estate – [in] Catford and I was alone except for Peggy.

Then she goes on to map out how poor she was, entitled to no benefits as she wasn't married to Tommy; his pension went to his legal wife. It is an extremely sad letter, but it runs in the same way as most of the others, designed to manipulate the reader by engendering pity and then asking for financial help. It didn't work. By now Joan was impervious to the begging letters.

Winifred died in 1979. She had been living on her own since Tommy's death and latterly in sheltered accommodation in Maida Vale. She maintained the lie about her marital status right up to the bitter end, and her death was registered in the name of Winifred F.L. Moran rather than her legal name, Taylor. Joan told me she didn't want to go to the funeral, but Peggy persuaded her to relent. As it turned out, they were the only two mourners there.

As for Joan's absent biological father, there was no trace of him until quite recently, when John Cash tracked him down and found that he had a son who was born not long after Joan. Thomas Alfred had a second family, dodging between the two while Winifred struggled with her growing number of offspring. There is no evidence that he ever tried to contact his four children from his marriage. Winifred clearly did know where he was or how to find him, as she had recorded in her desk diary that he died on 11 June 1961.

17

THE POWER OF ANGER

Ironically, Winifred wasn't wide of the mark when she said there were untruths in the series of newspaper articles Joan wrote about herself in 1955. Studying them I can spot lots of discrepancies. It is possible, even highly likely, that she did remember things differently as the years passed. We all embroider our own truths, either by choice or because of fading memory. How many of us have been convinced we precisely recalled an incident only to find out that, in reality, it was the memory of a photograph or someone else's version of the occasion? It is easily done.

The contents of Joan's story meant a lot to her; she saw it as her legacy, and she didn't want people to be sad when they read about her after she had died. She wanted to continue to spread joy and laughter. For her, the show had to go on long after she had bent her last bar and she was eager to continue pleasing her audiences either side of death. She'd rehearsed and reworked her heroic tales many times. When she was older, she spent most days scribbling away at her anecdotes. She'd get me to read them, and her nephew, John, edited them for her memoir. When he corrected her, though, the sparks would fly. I wasn't as brave as him and simply told Joan how fabulous her words were. It was what she wanted to hear, and I would be given an extra Hobnob biscuit for my flattery.

Joan throws her weight, and a man, around at a gym.

Everyone was happy. Joan was not open to suggestions of tinkering with her manuscript.

The greatest aspect of writing your own history is you can pick and choose the bits that suit you best, depending on what image you wish to construct. This is all very well, until an annoying biographer comes along after you have died and trawls through the facts, thereby untangling some of the carefully woven myths. No one, least of all Joan, likes being contradicted when they are in no position to fight back.

For example, in the first feature in the *Sunday Dispatch* she said that at 14, she ran away to join the circus, painting a classic romantic picture of how she became an acrobat for Grey's Circus. Yet later in life, she would vehemently deny this was the case. She would insist that the origins of her act were the result of working with buskers on the streets of London. She maintained that the only circus she appeared in was the Medrano in Paris, after her career had taken off. As for being an acrobat, this was something she never mentioned to me. She did describe herself in this way to Dame Laura Knight, but as far as I could tell that was the end of this assertion. It suited Joan better to have come from the gutters of London; as a history it was much more dramatic and dangerous. And, better still, it was closer to the truth.

The articles dealt with lots of her stories, including the one about King Farouk wanting her to help break his beds and a champion bullfighter who wrote her poems which he then passed on to Ava Gardner, pretending he had written them for her. She told the story of how she got her place in a freak show. All juicy stuff accompanied by lots of glamorous sexy shots of Joan. Perfect column inches for a popular Sunday newspaper.

But there were oddities in the copy that puzzled me. She painted a disturbing picture of what an odd child she had been. She said in one instalment that she lived with her sister Blackie at the Red Cow pub in Smithfield, run by her 'kindly' aunt and uncle. The truth was that her sister never lived there, nor did Joan see her aunt as a kind woman. Joan said that she was showered with gifts, which also doesn't add up with the image of her grudging Aunt Lily in her memoir.

Joan described how she was given a pretty doll on her 10th birthday. She wrote that it was the first doll she had ever held and couldn't understand why anyone would give her such a beautiful thing when they could have kept it for themselves. When some boys teased her about playing 'mumma' she ripped it apart, smashing the porcelain head into a thousand pieces. In this version of 'Joan' she really was a handful, sullen and distrusting, manifestly unhappy and at odds with the world. Angry to the point of violence at the tender age of 10. Not an appealing image.

She related how she heard one of her aunts comment that it was a shame to waste such lovely blonde hair on an unsmiling face; that does fit in with her later assertions that she was labelled as big and ugly. In the article, Joan related the time when she had been given a new pair of shoes and she threw them on the fire as she thought people would stare at her if she wore anything too new. Aunt Lily slapped her on the face but all that did was ignite Joan's anger and defiance: 'I stood with my eyes blazing and said, "Hit me, hit me, you can't hurt me."'

She wrote how one Christmas, Aunt Lily came into the dining room carrying the pudding that had been set ablaze with brandy. Little Joan believed this was a deliberately cruel act designed to torment her by wafting in front of her a delicious dessert she would not be able to eat because it had been burnt. She said she looked down and saw she had twisted her fork with her fingers, as though it was as bendable as a hairpin.

These were strange stories for a star to share with the millions of people who read the articles. Joan was a great self-publicist, so these pieces were written to endear herself to her public and broaden her fanbase. She would have wanted to show how a girl from the roughest background could make good in a world where the odds were set against her. She wanted to be seen as a champion of the underdog, destitute runaway to glittering starlet. So why would she write about how unpleasant she was as a child? In the anecdotes of her childhood, she came over as an extremely troubled girl, full of rage and hatred – certainly not a sympathetic character whom the public could embrace and adore. It's almost as though she mis-calculated the impact of the anecdotes she was sharing. They were so brutal that they must have been true. Today, it's what could be called an overshare.

At the time of writing the articles, Joan would have been just 34, and so the early events of her life would have been fairly fresh in her mind. Perhaps Joan had not learnt how to dissemble in print at that stage. It is possible that a lot of what she wrote was more accurate than the later tales she told that had a lifetime to mature and become embroidered.

There is one section of the first article where she said she had asked a doctor about her incredible strength. His view was that it was her subconscious that was behind this phenomenon:

A doctor told me recently that my strength is just a sort of sublimated naughty temper. It is true that I have always been passionately determined, and was a very sullen aggressive little girl, who would never cry and never give in. You know how sometimes when you are pushing at something and it won't move you suddenly get silently angry and the next thing is that you have pushed the thing halfway across the room? Well they say my strength is like that, as I was constantly fighting for my life.

In these few extracts Joan reveals so much more about herself than perhaps she intended. The question that dogged her life and still clings to her memory is, where did that strength come from? I have no doubt that her ability to bend bars, lift two grown men at a time and so on were real but then again, I couldn't help but repeatedly wonder how this super-strength came to exist. How could a slender woman with no pronounced musculature be so strong that even the most powerful men could not match her? I asked Joan about this many times, always trying not to annoy her as she must have been sick to death of the subject. She had obviously wrestled with the same question over the years, and she stuck to what the doctor had told her; she believed it was down to her deep anger.

Stories of people lifting extremely heavy objects to rescue others are legion. Joan had her own tale of lifting a car when she came to the assistance of Jill Day, a well-known pop star at the time, and Jon Pertwee, best known for his role as Doctor Who:

Often I am asked what is the strongest feat I have ever performed, and on thinking about it, I should say that it was on the night that Jill Day's car got stuck, on the way back from doing a show at an American Air Force camp in Oxfordshire, during a terrible snowstorm.

We had all ploughed across country to reach this airfield camp, and when the performance was finished we were all glad to start for home. I was driving my little Morris, which was skidding all over the icy roads, with snow deluging down the windscreen.

My headlamps picked out a man, sitting on a black hump at the roadside among the snow and waving wildly. I stopped and found it was Jon Pertwee, who had also been performing at the camp. Jon had stopped to try to help. Jill Day was shivering inside her pianist's car. They had run off the road and were deeply embedded in the ditch and entangled with fence-wire. Jon and I tugged at the wire to try and clear it away, and pushed at the car, which wouldn't budge. Jon is by no means a weak man.

Suddenly I became angry. It had been a rotten evening anyway, with cold, over-crowded changing rooms and a wrong atmosphere about everything, and now here I was getting chilled and soaked to the skin. I remember shouting: 'Stand aside!' Jill Day told me afterwards that I shrieked it, and Jon Pertwee jumped aside as if he'd been shot at.

I tore away at the fence wire, jerking it free of the car like rotten string, and then braced my heels and shoved! The car, with Jill Day still inside it, came out of that ditch so quickly that I fell flat on my face. Jill's pianist scrambled into the driving seat and drove away without a word of thanks, and I followed him in a furious temper, thinking that this was a rotten way to show gratitude, but about six miles up the road I found he had halted at a tavern and was waiting for me.

He said: 'I'm sorry I drove off like that, Joan, but frankly I was a bit terrified – your eyes were blazing, and the way the car came out of that ditch, well – it just didn't seem human!'

I laughed rather weakly and said: 'Perhaps it wasn't.'

In another of the articles Joan wrote for the *Sunday Dispatch*, she explained how she came to the painful conclusion she was abnormal, a freak, and there was nothing she could do but own that fact. She told how she was looking for work, doing auditions, and she had been successfully chosen by two top West End shows. But it didn't feel right:

I should have been happy. But one cannot escape one's destiny, and I knew that although I was apparently beautiful and blonde-haired enough to be accepted as a West End showgirl in two theatres during one morning of trying for a job, yet I still carried my strange embarrassing secret of my ungirlish strength. It was like a throttle jammed wide open inside myself. Given any task the required strength, whether bending a steel nail or – as I was later to frighten myself discovering – the task of heaving a wrecked car out of a ditch in emergency and the strength came surging through me as it must have done, all through history to saints or madmen or beserk warriors.

Perhaps it was no more than a kind of focused bad temper but it was there and it was inescapable. Without it I might have been a fairly happy nobody – an ordinary girl with enough attractions for me to love. But with such strength I was a freak. Yes it had to be faced. I was a freak.

Is there such a thing as superhuman strength, other than among the mythical heroes of comic books? It's a tricky question that has no definitive answer. There has been limited scientific research into the subject. One man who has made human physiology his life's work is Vladimir Zatsiorsky, a professor of kinesiology in America. He has done extensive research on the biomechanics of weightlift-ing, and his findings are often quoted. He divides strength into two categories, the 'absolute' and the 'maximal': the former refers to the force that our muscles theoretically can apply and the latter is the power we can summon through conscious exertion.

Prof. Zatsiorsky found that you or I can utilise about 60 per cent of our body strength in normal circumstances. In contrast, an ath-lete, such as a wrestler or weightlifter, could get as much or more than 80 per cent force after being trained how to access it on con-scious command.

We know Joan was a protégée when she was just a young teen-ager at the Mayfair gym run by Mickey Wood. She said she was keen to learn judo. Boxers are coached to focus their power into their fists to give maximum force when it is required. Wrestlers learn how to lift weights and how to pick up other people, often many times their size. These are techniques that can be learnt, and they were certainly skills that were apparent in Joan's act. Another aspect of super-strength is the ability to cope with the pain that your body feels when you are pushing your powers to the limit. From the few studies available, it would seem that one of the key mechanisms required is the ability of the brain to suspend pain through analgesia. Basically, switching off the feeling of pain and

The lethal-looking tools of Joan's trade.

then accessing the extra reserves of strength we rarely use – literally working through the pain barrier. If Joan had that training, and it is likely that she did, then in theory it was physically possible for her to have a kind of super-strength.

Is it also possible that a deep-seated internal anger played a key part in Joan's strength? I decided this was a question for a top psychiatrist, so I enlisted the help of Ian Palmer, a retired professor of military psychiatry who just happens to be my husband. He also was the one who introduced me to Joan and knew her well.

Ian acknowledged that, in his view, humans could perform acts of enormous strength in a crisis, but he felt that these occasions were very rare. In Joan's case, he believed she was channelling a deep-seated anger when she performed. He felt the anger must have come from violent incidents in her childhood:

> In psychoanalytical terms, if aggressive things happen to you when you're a child (or at other times across the lifespan) it is not uncommon for people to 'introject' (swallow or take in) this aggression and turn it round passing it onto other people. This is termed 'identification with the aggressor.' With inconsistent and dysfunctional families there is enough anger and aggression to go around for everyone to take their share. In common military parlance, shit rolls downhill, you just pass it on. This is not necessarily focused and liable to leave traces in employment histories and relationship difficulties.
>
> Another way of thinking psychologically about anger, is when it is related to grief. It is seldom recognised but it's an integral part of the grieving process. So in the case of an unreliable, inconsistent and possibly violent mother, the loss of 'the good mother' which lives in our fantasies can lead to anger and possibly violence but in this situation it is there to protect the vulnerable inner child. So, it is protective rather than destructive. I think that I can identify this form of anger in Joan's behaviours over the years from what I have read to date.

Obviously, Joan had a physical frame and level of fitness which were commensurate with her professional performances which looked effortless but must have belied mastering certain techniques in order to maximise the focus of her strength. This clearly requires the presence of mind and suggest to me that a deep-seated anger could, with training, perhaps be called upon at will as a way of focusing her strength in one place for a specific activity and a given length of time. Akin to the punching in boxing and kung fu.

Clearly Joan was able to train herself to turn her anger into a positive and remunerative activity rather than lashing out indiscriminately. If she had anger management problems she would have found herself in trouble with the law, probably have a trail of failed relationships and a much stormier professional career than she did.

Having extensively explored what details there are about Joan's childhood, it is clear where the deep-rooted anger came from. Reading her own account of her younger self it is possible to see the rage that burnt inside. Were her actions an indicator of what was to come? Ian Palmer thinks they were:

> This behaviour may be seen as a temper tantrum but from what I have read it is more likely to come from an inner distress. It is always easy to focus on anger and aggressive outbursts in a negative way but I sincerely believe that something occurs before the anger is released. In terms of childhood, acts of aggression usually follow perceptions of hurt and are almost reflex physical outbursts of distress.

Joan was remarkable because she turned her feelings of distress into something positive; she did not lash out at the world nor was there an ounce of self-pity in her. She really was a prime example of how to confront difficulties and turn them into assets. And that was something she wanted to share with others who found themselves facing hard times. She had a great sense of positivity despite all she went through as a child, and she wanted to encourage others to feel the same.

But it is likely that the ructions caused by her confess-all articles in the *Sunday Dispatch* gave rise to a new caution in her mind. After all, the people she was writing about were still very much alive and kicking. If any of them wanted to come forward and contradict her or call her a liar they could easily do so, as her mother demonstrated. The articles would have been read by millions of people, not just in the UK but around the world as they were widely syndicated. The cuttings I have, for instance, are from South Africa. It is possible that when Joan wrote about her childhood, she hadn't thought through the fact that her family, Winifred and Aunt Lily in particular, would be reading it and might not be happy to agree to her version of events.

While on the one hand she was pleased with the publicity and the large payments, she was also worried about what the repercussions might be. This mood of uncertainty overshadowed her next decisions. The news editor of the *Sunday Dispatch* wrote to her later that year and began talking about book rights. Then five days later, her agent, Solly, who now worked for Lew and Leslie Grade, wrote that the question of film rights was being discussed with £250 for a six-month option, with a further payment of £2,250 if the option was taken up. That added up to a handsome sum and must have been incredibly tempting to Joan. But her fears must have niggled away at the back of her mind.

She already knew what her mother was capable of and perhaps, on reflection, there were exceptions to the old adage that all publicity was good publicity. With such a volatile family, Joan would have realised that pursuing her story in this way might be counterproductive. She would have no control over what family members said. A major omission from her articles was the fact that she was married, widely known among her relatives but something she made into a closely guarded secret in public. She would have worried that her fans wouldn't be understanding about her leaving her husband, especially as he was a Second World War veteran. Nor would it reflect well on her to be 'living in sin', first with Bert and then Ulrico. And who knew what other tales might be dug up?

As it turned out, the family kept their silence after Winifred's blackmail attempt. But Joan had learnt a painful lesson – she was happy to wash dirty linen in public, but only if she was the one with the scrubbing brush. Like her decision not to go to Hollywood, mention of the book and film projects stopped abruptly at this point. She appears to have ignored the offer to publish a book about her and make a film based on her life. As she was at the height of her career in the 1950s and 1960s, her judgement will have been that it was too risky. As it was, she had plenty of work to occupy her time. Bookings were flooding in, both at home and abroad, for stage shows and TV appearances. Her act continued to appeal in those early days of television.

She spoke about writing her own book in later years; it was something she would mention in the numerous media interviews that she did. By the late 1960s and 1970s, 'living in sin' was no longer something to be ashamed about and she would have been less worried about exposure. Time is no respecter of beauty and physical ability; age would soon catch up with Joan and she would have to abandon her persona as a svelte strongwoman. But while she had the world's attention, she was determined to make the most of an act she had developed and honed over decades.

18

LOVES OF JOAN'S LIFE

The 1950s and 1960s were Joan's golden age. Her act was famous around the world and her diary was packed. She was recognised wherever she went, both at home and abroad. She travelled to more than thirty-five countries, where she was in demand on stage and television. To give an idea of how busy she was, her 1955 diary was filled to capacity with lengthy engagements abroad: she worked in Brussels, Cannes, Copenhagen and Reykjavík, as well as doing shorter cabaret appearances in Paris and Lisbon and continuing to perform in the British theatres and clubs where she had already appeared over the years. Into this busy schedule, she managed to squeeze attending, at Dame Laura's invitation, the private viewing of the Royal Academy Summer Exhibition to see her portrait on view, as well as telling her life story to the *Sunday Dispatch*. She also made a return visit to New York for the *Ed Sullivan Show* on 13 November, this time performing her whole act with great success.

Despite such a heavy workload Joan still had the energy for a hectic personal life, and she would invite a chosen few to her home for gatherings. She was happiest in what she called her secret garden. The French doors from her living room opened directly onto it, a large, old white chair served as a throne and she would spend hours entertaining if she had visitors or chatting to the birds and squirrels that inhabited the merry chaos. It was basically an overgrown patch jammed with lots of unruly shrubs, sculptures, a tinkling fountain, old tables and chairs and ancient bits and pieces of crockery and glass. She also strategically placed shards of broken mirrors around the site to add some God-given sparkle. It sounds like a mess, but it was heaven, so peaceful and endlessly entertaining.

Her flat was just as she wanted it to be, but the same could not be said for her love life.

Joan had met Bert during the war, when she was in her early twenties and at the end of a brief and unhappy marriage. Bert was an important part of her set-up. As she was abroad so often, he kept things ticking over nicely in Belsize Park. If she needed anything he would parcel it up and send it to her. Sometimes she would ask for fresh supplies of phone books, and if Joan didn't have the right clothing, Bert would send her the coat or whatever she needed. He must have become accustomed to being virtually invisible. Because of the wartime identity card legislation under the National Registration Act of 1939, he did not officially exist; he was under the radar and wanted to keep it that way. But it meant he couldn't get a passport to travel, and he wasn't entitled

Joan and Bert, 1945.

to any government benefits. This all changed when the act was repealed in 1952, and Bert successfully applied for a passport. He joined Joan on her travels at least once, when he went to Majorca, but it seems that his place was firmly in the home. The roles of this couple were clearly defined: Joan was the breadwinner, very much in the limelight and out in the wider world, whereas Bert had no income other than doing odd jobs for people. He was a handyman, a word that captured him well.

The acerbic wit and charm that had originally attracted Joan was no longer in evidence by the 1950s; Bert preferred to be silent. The love she felt had died and had turned into a feeling of frustration and detachment. One of Joan's throwaway comments in her memoir is revealing, as she wrote about hopping on and off planes:

> I had to pay quite a lot for excess baggage, taking nails, steel bars and telephone books. I would only take four books with me and then find something similar in the country I was in – sometimes airline or train timetable books or catalogues, whatever I could find. Once or twice I had to phone London and Bert would put some phone books on a plane for which I was suitably grateful. Bert was a good friend during this period – but not, alas, a lover! I felt very unloved, just a novelty which men wanted to compete with. Ah, me!

This was a time when men were expected to be the ones bringing home the cash while their wives stayed at home to sort out the supper and so on. The role reversal must have been hard for Bert. He was a proud, intelligent man who spent months and months alone in the flat as his partner lived the high life with some of the most prominent people in the world.

The initial attraction was well and truly dead by now, and they were no longer lovers. Joan used to tell me that she wasn't that bothered about sex; it wasn't one of her big drivers. What she wanted was love, someone to share her career triumphs and interests as well as her bed. What it boiled down to was that they were both terribly lonely and found no respite from that when they were together. This situation was made more difficult by the fact that Bert was not well.

Like most people at the time, Joan would have been fairly dismissive of 'depression'. It wasn't regarded as a serious illness – more of an indulgence or laziness, especially in men. In those post-war times, people were expected to quietly carry on with their lives. There was no room for what was seen as weakness. The fact that depression could destroy someone's life by eating away at them from the inside out was generally not recognised. Thankfully we know differently today, and public perceptions of the condition have become much more informed. If Bert did have full-blown depression that would explain his change of character, his social isolation and introversion. With Joan he maintained a painful silence, which really irritated her:

> We spent sixteen years together but in the end he no longer found me attractive – I had become his slave and sometimes he wouldn't even answer when I spoke to him. He didn't work and became a full-time layabout, but was always there when I came home on a Saturday night. One day I got cross with him and said, 'Why do you stay?' And he left.

Joan said she did not expect him to react in this way. There was no further conversation; he just went. It was possible that Bert had intended to leave 37A anyway, perhaps his bags were already packed, but his immediate departure was a shock to Joan. He did have somewhere to go, though. For some time, a mutual friend called Jane Stuckey, who lived a few doors away, had been popping in to the flat on a regular basis, ostensibly 'keeping an eye on him' when Joan was away, which was often. She would bring him meals and longed for company. Feeling as low as he did, Bert would have been vulnerable and open to any overtures that made his world feel a bit better. They were probably lovers, and the bonus was that

Jane was around all the time and was happy to embody the traditional female role.

When Joan spoke to me about this betrayal, she dismissed what happened as just one of those things. There was no sign of anger towards Bert or Jane, and in fact she remained friends with them. It is likely that Jane had done her a great service by removing a burden from her shoulders. Joan had a good heart, and she wouldn't have wanted to throw a sick Bert out on the street. It makes sense that she would have wanted him to be safe and comfortable. Having him move a few doors down to live with Jane was an excellent outcome.

All the while, Joan would have put on a brave face in public, as we know she was great at smiling through adversity, but it must have hurt like hell to find herself single in her mid-thirties. Famous and successful, but unloved. Then again, she was not a woman to let the vagaries of life get the better of her for long. Her natural reaction was to fight back – she wanted love, so she went out and found it. And as it turned out she didn't have to look too far afield.

A matter of weeks after Bert moved out, Joan was invited to a party at Jane's flat, the same place where her former lover had set up shop. It is perhaps a reflection of how much this new arrangement suited Joan that she decided to go. For all of her putting on a brave face, it is possible to detect a degree of rancour in what she wrote about these events. When she saw her ex sitting next to a girl, Joan went out of her way to show him that she really didn't care. She had a few stiff drinks and looked around the room for the most handsome man and proceeded to chat him up and ask him to dance. And just to make sure Bert felt terrible, she kissed this tall, dark stranger. Like many women who have been abandoned for another, she wanted the man who had dumped her to bitterly regret what he had done. Ironically, the recipient of Joan's impulsive behaviour turned out to be the love of her life:

> He was foreign and didn't speak English, so I tried my Spanish
> on him and mimed dancing. We danced and it was nice to have

his arms around me. I suddenly noticed Bert staring at me, so I kissed the man on the cheek and he responded with passion. I flirted – I'd never done that before – then realised I was getting hot and wanted to leave. He hung on to me but I went out through the door, with him following. He asked me my name – 'Josie,' I said and fled.

A few days later a little note was dropped through my letterbox. It had a drawing of a heart on it and read, 'Here is my heart – have it. Ulrico.' I ignored it. A few more days passed and I was walking along Fitzjohns Avenue when I came face to face with him. He smiled and said, 'Josie,' and spoke in French [Joan spoke better French than Italian at the time] and explained that he lived in the house behind him. He was an artist and was having his first exhibition in London at the New Vision Gallery – Denis Bowen was the owner – and would I like to see his paintings?

We went into the house, climbed several flights of stairs and almost entered a small room which was filled with large abstract paintings. I liked them very much, but I couldn't see how he also managed to sleep in the room and the smell of the paint reminded me of my art school modelling. I promised to meet him the next day for coffee.

Overnight I thought and came to a conclusion. As long as he didn't 'come on strong' I could let him use one of my large, almost empty rooms as a studio – but only in daytime. He must keep his room in Fitzjohns Avenue for sleeping, etc. He came to see the room and was suitably delighted and before I knew it he was painting away.

The gorgeous and talented Ulrico Schettini was soon invited to cross the threshold to number 37A. Looking at the photographs of him you can certainly see why Joan was smitten. He was the very embodiment of a tall, dark and handsome stranger with his thick, black hair and beard. The way Joan tells the story, the pair were chaste for a time. He would honour her edict that he would go back to his own place at night but return each day to work away at his mainly abstract creations. Ulrico was preparing for his first solo exhibition which was due to open in December 1958, and now he had a wonderfully large studio space to work. It must have been a heady time for both of them, the sexual tension palpable. They were so close but not quite close enough.

A local paper, the *West London Star*, did a report on Ulrico's exhibition and used Joan's presence there to open it as a peg for the story:

> Joan Rhodes, the strong girl who usually spends time tearing up telephone directories and bending six-inch nails in half, had a strange task on Monday. She opened an art exhibition at the New Vision Centre, Seymour Place, Paddington.
>
> It was the first one-man exhibition in England of Ulrico Schettini, from Italy.
>
> In the exhibition's programme he thanks Miss Rhodes for her help in making the exhibition possible. So it looks as if the strong girl is becoming a patron of the arts.
>
> Schettini has done most of his work in Rome. It is in the modern idiom. I find his work intriguing. At first sight it is a bewildering blur. But as you look at the picture it begins to take a shape. Pictures and patterns appear.

From what Joan says, their relationship developed quickly. The chemistry between them was always going to lead to the bedroom:

> Ulrico one day said he couldn't keep his room any more and as he'd always kept to my rules I said he could move into the studio. We were friends, not lovers. Then a potter friend of his was getting married and we went along. I was plied with drink, which I wasn't used to, and when we came home 'that was it' and we were lovers. After Bert he was fun: flowers and choco-lates and cuddles – and he cooked wonderful Italian food. Yes, he was Italian, but soon was speaking passable English. Each day I would give him a phrase to say which he had to repeat as many

times as he could. (One of those phrases was 'Don't take liberties with me'!)

And so we went on for the next twelve years, going to Italy many times. He was always loving and amusing and would sing in a very loud voice. After Bert it was such a contrast – he had always been quiet and sometimes didn't speak to me for days. Of course I was still working away, but I would rush home whenever I could and we had a lot of fun together. We liked to visit exhibitions by other painters and one in particular I remember was by Max Ernst, whose work I liked although we had never met. He (Max) signed my catalogue and, to my astonishment, wrote 'to the strongest girl in the world – Max'. I had no idea that he had heard of me!

Joan and Ulrico on holiday, early 1960s.

In the stash of photographs of the couple, there is plenty of evidence of how deeply in love they were. The seemingly endless beach shots are in black and white, but you can still feel the sun's warmth and smell the sea breeze. They were so happy. Ulrico was perfect for Joan. He may have been eleven years younger than her, but he was the more mature of the two. He was well read and cultured, classically trained in the arts. Joan's nephew, John, knew him and says he was a charming man. Unlike Bert, he was the life and soul of a party. He would chatter on in his newly acquired English or play the guitar and serenade the group.

When Joan met Ulrico, he was a promising but penniless artist. He was born in Cosenza, Italy, in 1932. He went to law school for a brief time but dropped out to follow his creative muse. He studied art in Pesaro, Paris and Rome. Then, in 1958, he came to London. His work was heralded as fiercely modernist and abstract. He was, and is, an extremely talented artist. His early works stand the test of time. Pieces from the 1950s and 1960s are coming up at art auctions more frequently in the twenty-first century and their value is going up.

Joan used to make a great joke with audiences that no one wanted to marry her and that she'd never been asked, always 'forgetting' to mention that she had been married. With Ulrico, things were different. He was determined to marry her; he wanted a homelife with all the joys that would bring, especially children. He asked her repeatedly over the upwards of twelve years they were together, but she would always prevaricate. Looking at the pictures and hearing joyous stories about their time together, it is so sad that their relationship did not last. It looked as though Joan almost had it all, but she couldn't take that final leap of faith and let someone else share the task of running her life. When they were first together, Ulrico had very little to offer in terms of financial stability, and love would not feed a brood of little Schettinis. Joan was the breadwinner, just as she had been with Bert. She held the purse strings and the whole set-up relied on her continuing to be successful and well paid. Joan was very much in charge of her destiny and that was the way she liked it. For that she paid a considerable price.

When she spoke to me about Ulrico it was always with warmth and a wistful look in her eyes. There was an unspoken sadness about what might have been. As we know, Joan would wrap herself in secrets, like a protective cloak. It seems likely that she was not completely honest with him. John believes that she never fully told him about the dreadful early life she had suffered. This would have made it difficult for Ulrico to understand her reticence to marry and have children. It's possible that she might not have been able to have a baby after her abortion many years before. When you know

Joan and Ulrico happy at home, early 1960s.

what she went through, it is easy enough to understand why the thought of having a family of her own would terrify her.

The media interest in her love life was consistent. One summer when Joan had been working in Paris, Baden–Baden and San Remo, the *Daily Mail* caught up with her and asked her about Ulrico; somehow they had got to know that he was desperate to marry her. The article they ran had the inevitable glamour shot of Joan and was headlined 'Artist proposes to strong girl':

> Blonde, shapely, strong-girl Joan Rhodes flexed her gleaming muscles, cracked a six-inch nail for fun and said: 'I've got six weeks in which to accept a proposal of marriage'. The man who made it, and wants to have the strongest wife in Britain, is handsome, bearded Italian abstract painter Ulrico Schettini, 28, now in London. 'If I say "Yes," it will be because Ulrico is so sensitive and makes me feel almost fragile.'

Joan had no intention of saying yes; she was simply using interest in her romance for publicity. No matter how many times poor Ulrico popped the question in the years they were together, she would always procrastinate. Eventually the failure to resolve the question of marriage and children took its toll. Ulrico craved a family of his own; Joan was the woman he loved, and he did not understand why she refused to 'settle down' with him.

As the years passed, it became clear to him that Joan would never accept the role of wife and mother. In 1966, not long after he had a hugely successful exhibition in Hull, he decided to stop painting and destroyed many of his early works – an act of artistic vandalism that came from sadness and despair at Joan's refusal to commit to him. He found a new career path as a lecturer at art colleges both in Britain and America. A few years later, he changed his name from Schettini to Montefiore and moved back to Italy.

The end came in July 1973 when he and his brother returned from Italy and visited Joan when she was doing a stint at the Pier Theatre in Shanklin on the Isle of Wight. There was a showdown of some kind, maybe another ultimatum from Ulrico, but Joan believed he had been unfaithful.

In her memoir Joan explained what happened from her point of view:

> He came back a different person – the beginning of the end. I was working on the Isle of Wight and he and his brother came to visit and I could feel the chill. He had met a girl at my sister's, a married woman with two children, and that was that, I asked him to leave. It didn't last with her for more than a few months, so he packed his bags and went back to Italy and I believe he has done well there. I did miss him at first.

I tracked Ulrico down; at the time of writing this book he was 89 years old, living in Milan and still working. He was as charming as I had been led to believe. But all the events I wanted to talk about had happened a long, long time ago. He couldn't help with detail but there was no doubt that he continued to love Joan, or Josie as she was known to close friends back in the day. He'd kept in touch, saying he had written to her regularly for the rest of her life. He visited 37A not long before her death, when she was very ill. After that, he wrote to her every day. In his emails to me about Joan, there is a palpable warmth that has spanned the decades:

> Inevitably, I think of Joan Rhodes in a particular way and, over time, I have idealized her personality and memory.
>
> From Josie I received a great inner wealth, day after day; she also taught me to deeply understand and love Great Britain, its people, the cities, the wonderful countryside, the often very poetic villages.
>
> Now they tell me that Great Britain is no longer what I knew and loved; it seems impossible to me and my heart suffers from nostalgia.
>
> We stayed together. I was a few years younger than her [11 years] but never experienced difficulties of any kind; she was

a continuous joke full of life and with a great sense of humour. An authentic thing; perhaps she was experiencing a childhood she had missed and making up for a difficult youth. She never spoke of her parents; she only said that she and the other two sisters, Peggy and Blackie, were abandoned at a very tender age.

Joan Rhodes was an international headliner and, for her work, travelled constantly. Me, an artist at the beginning of my professional career. But we were a real couple. Josie never died; she lives inside me because she remains an important part of who I am.

This confirms that she was determined to be secretive about her past. If he had known, he may have understood why she insisted on her autonomy and didn't want the wife and mother roles that so many craved.

She summed it up in her own way:

I've had some very happy years and some, of course, not so happy (mostly with men); my girlfriends have been loyal but they have nearly all gone now. But I've always been a loner and never wanted a family – a lesson I learnt when I was very young, and I had no friends when I was a child so I learned to live without them and to always rely on myself and be very wary of trusting people. I expect that this made it difficult for people to get to know me (especially men!) but the few who have suc-ceeded have turned out to be true friends. I've been lucky really; some of my friends, like me, get older and fatter, but to me they don't change, they are real friends.

19

A NEW WORLD

In Britain, Joan was a household name. She was earning easily enough to support her lifestyle in Belsize Park. The arrival of a new lover meant things were very different in her home life. She now had a man who was driven; the contrast to Bert couldn't have been more different. Like Joan, Ulrico was determined to make his mark on the world. Ulrico laboured tirelessly on his pieces, but Joan said he was also able to leave work behind when he left the studio and let his hair down. They regularly had close friends around and must have vied for attention as they both took delight in entertaining. Her beloved, chaotic flat was filling up with Ulrico's work, which was often on a large scale. He was prolific and was recognised by the wider art world as an emerging talent. His pieces were often experimental and radiated an abstract power which is still palpable today. But, like most young artists through the ages, there were very few buyers despite the admiration.

It must have been frustrating for Ulrico to be a kept man, but his presence in Joan's life fed her happiness. He encouraged her to follow her long-held ambition to become a painter. Under his guidance, Joan gave vent to the artistic talent that had bubbled away all her life. It was the first time anyone had encouraged her, and she loved it. She would paint canvases of places she knew, numerous owls, clowns and self-portraits. I've got some of her works which are pleasing on the eye with their naïve and individual style.

Joan guarded her privacy. She was very choosy when it came to her social life. She had her favourites like Quentin Crisp, but she strictly limited the number of those allowed to get close to her. Having developed a distrust of the popular press, she generally kept her door shut to journalists. Despite this, many column inches were written about her in the bestselling papers of the day. Oddly enough, I think it was a piece in the local press that seemed to me to sum up best how she was seen in the context of that time. Marjorie Wright from the *Willesden Chronicle* was granted an audience in 1959, invited to cross the threshold and enter the hallowed sanctuary of 37A.

I can imagine the scene. Marjorie would have been treated to Joan's best smiles and charm as her host wafted around the colourful flat jampacked with memorabilia and souvenirs. There would have been tea in china cups and biscuits. Joan would have been at her wittiest, given to outbursts of theatrical songs and cheeky quips. Marjorie was, like me, charmed by her extraordinary interviewee. I think she summed Joan up rather well:

> There's an air of independence and determination about this girl, who has fought her way up by sheer dogged persistence backed by great physical strength. [She] has a lot of hobbies. She paints gay, colourful scenes of places she visits, plays a guitar, reads a lot – anything from science fiction to Freud – plays snooker, is a water skier, likes interior decorating. She's the sort of person who must be doing something all the time, but when she does rest you can see that she relaxes properly. She has an air of vitality, of controlled strength, of optimism. 'I believe that if you want to do anything badly enough you can do it,' she told me.

But inevitably, there were clouds on the horizon.

Ever since she picked him up, literally, in the Empire Billiards Club in Soho, Solly Black was everything a good agent should be. He believed in Joan. He knew how to look after his acts even if he could be hard on them. When Joan complained about her digs or pay, he would brush off the moaning. Joan would send him all her cuttings, hoping to squeeze more money out of him for her next bookings, but, like most agents, he was astute at burying these requests. Once, when she tackled him about her wages, he sent back a cutting which read, 'Young red-headed Solly Schwartz stood in the middle of Madison Square Garden and stood his ground.' Joan had to laugh, she knew she wouldn't be able to budge him. He made a good, steady income out of her act but his investment in her was not just as an agent. Yes, Joan was good for business, but he also took a paternal interest in her. He wanted to ensure that she didn't fritter away the money she made like many of her compatriots. He encouraged her to make financial plans as he knew harder times would come.

An example of Solly's concern was when he heard of an opportunity to invest in a property in Brixton, south London, that provided digs for performers. It looked like a good earner, so he put it her way. Solly hadn't minced his words with Joan; he had told her point-blank that her novelty and popularity would not last, that her bookings would dry up. It was an unpleasant but real prospect. It was with these dire warnings in mind that Joan took over the lease of Monroe House. It must have felt strange after her early years in rough digs to find herself as a landlady. Sadly, the venture turned sour, and it became more of a nightmare than a handy pension plan:

Monroe House was a Variety and Cabaret 'digs'; any artiste from abroad was given the address and most of them stayed there if they were working in London. There were thirteen letting rooms, all with stoves and wash basins in them, a big yard or garden where acrobats or jugglers could practice, and enough room outside to park a car.

Before I could think we had an agreement and I was a landlady! In one room was an elderly lady called Mrs Zampa and she had worked on the telephone exchange before retiring. Her son had an act and that is how she came to be living in the house. After a while Lily, the cleaner, decided that she wanted to leave and Mrs Zampa said she would like to take over the job

It seemed like a good idea so I said OK, as I now had lots of work, all over the world. There was always something going on. She told me she had hidden two Russian circus performers who were defecting or absconding in the cellar and that a couple of KGB men had come from the Russian Embassy asking for them. She told them they'd never stayed in the house and since she hadn't registered them in the book they were not found. Then the lease was up for renewal and I got a letter from a Jewish charity to say that they had granted the lease to the Monroes who were refugees from Hitler's Germany and Mrs Munroe had no right to pass it on to me. They paid me £600 to move out as soon as possible and to leave the beds and furniture. I moved out and Monroe House was no more.

The truth was that Monroe House was more trouble than it was worth. The place 'washed its face' but made little money, and certainly not enough to live on. It wasn't the little earner that Solly and Joan had hoped.

Joan's world was shaken to its core when Solly died suddenly in 1959. He had been such an important part of her life, and with his demise Joan had lost a close ally and father figure. This was one rare occasion where Joan didn't put on a brave smile.

Joan might have lost a key figure in her life, but she still had to earn a living and here she was extremely fortunate. Solly's move into the mighty Grade Organisation meant that she was on the books of one of the greatest powerhouses in the entertainment industry. Lew and Leslie Grade dominated their world. They had fingers in many media pies and were looking to a future in television and films. That was where the big hitters in the variety business were heading as the bright lights of the stage were fading as audiences were dwindling and venues were closing. Joan had been in at the beginning of television back in the 1940s, but at the time she couldn't have known that it was a harbinger of change that would have a dramatic impact on her life.

It was fortuitous that Joan's act easily transferred from variety stage shows to the television screen. In the early days, when the BBC was the only TV broadcaster, it adhered to a high moral agenda established by the first director general, Lord Reith. He was long gone, having left the role in 1938, but his powerful influence remained. The BBC had a clear purpose according to Reith, summed up in three words: inform, educate and entertain. For an act to be accepted by the corporation it had to be suitable for family viewing. Joan's patter in the past could be quite saucy but it was easy for her to alter the content.

Joan loved working abroad; as audiences in the UK changed, she began to feel that she wasn't as appreciated by the home market. For several years her diary showed that she would be booked up in clubs and theatres across Europe for long periods. Although the world was changing for Joan, the Grade Organisation kept her busy. She was booked by ABC Television to take part in a series called *You'd Never Believe It*. Joan was in the edition called 'It's Tough to Be a Girl'. The publicity shots are rather odd, showing her holding a chair out horizontally with her arms fully outstretched. The filming was done at Teddington and while she was there, Joan told the team that she wanted to change the direction of her career by getting into acting. They recommended that she write to the assistant casting director with Iris Productions. She sent a letter and some of her best publicity shots to Tony Arnell, who was very young at the time, just starting out in a hugely successful career. He later did the casting for *The Saint* in 1967–68 and *Dempsey and Makepeace* in 1986–87, among many, many others.

His response was disappointing but perceptive. He said he would keep the pictures on file but didn't hold out much hope for Joan's ability to switch from a speciality star to an actor. He was blunt: 'The difficulty, I feel, is for people to take you seriously as an actress, although Carey tells me you originally trained as this.'

It's not clear where he got the idea that Joan was a trained actor; perhaps the mysterious 'Carey' had said this was the case, but it didn't really matter as her punt came to nothing. What was important about this exchange was that it reflected how tough it was to break into acting, even if you were already treading the boards and famous around the world.

Not that this rebuff stopped her; as we know, Joan was not one to give up. In 1962, she was booked to appear in a training film for British Transport Films. To my delight the original is now in the hands of the British Film Institute, who have lovingly had it digitally remastered. You can find it in the BFI archive in all its detailed glory. The piece was called *Manhandling* and was part of a series put together by Edgar Anstey, a founding father of the British documentary movement. It was made to encourage transport workers to take more care with lifting and moving heavy objects. Joan's presence during the first few minutes was designed to get the men's attention, which it certainly must have done. She was

A still from Manhandling, *a staff instructional for British Transport Films, 1962.*

dressed in a black leotard covered by a short jacket cinched tightly in at the waist. Her long legs were clad in her signature fishnets, and she was mincing around in tall black stilettoes.

The film started with a tight head-and-shoulders shot of Joan wearing a porter's hat and a cheeky smile, her long blonde hair tied back in a ponytail. As she sang 'It's not what you do it's the way that you do it', she was accompanied by Ronald Gaston, who was known as a stuntman, on guitar. She lifted sacks and moved a large barrel to show how to do it safely. When this was made, Joan was in her forty-first year, but she could easily have passed for someone in her late twenties. The piece captured Joan's jolly public persona – there was something about her vitality and cheek that made her a joy to watch.

That same year, Joan made an appearance in a programme filmed at Leeds City Varieties. *The Good Old Days* was the BBC's attempt to revive music hall on television; it was a massive hit and ran for thirty years. The audience got into the mood by dressing in period Victorian and Edwardian costume as they were transported back to a time when speciality artistes were all the rage. Each act was summoned by a character positioned behind a desk at the side of the stage. He was called the Chairman, played by Joan's friend, the actor Leonard Sachs. At the end of the show the cast and audience would all sing 'Down at the Old Bull and Bush'. Joan would have loved it, but she would also have been painfully aware that this was the first time she had appeared on British television for two years.

The world of variety performers was a relatively small one. Everyone knew everyone else, and they looked after their own. A few of them, the luckier and more talented ones, would survive for decades, but the majority would have a moment in the limelight before disappearing into the shadows again. The friendships Joan made on her way up in showbusiness were precious to her, but they were also to prove useful when she realised that she would have to reinvent herself to survive. One prime example of this was the comedian and presenter Larry Grayson.

Joan first came across Larry when she was performing in a club in Leeds. It wasn't a propitious start. As she was going through her paces, Joan and her audience were distracted by loud laughter coming from one of the bars. She was furious and concluded that there was another act performing at the same time as her, not an acceptable situation. When she complained to the manager, she was told that it was only Larry Grayson holding forth at the bar and that he was a laugh a minute and you didn't need a ticket. She went to see for herself and was immediately captured by his gentle, camp style as he delivered witty anecdotes. She found herself sharing the uproarious laughter he provoked.

When Larry eventually stopped to draw breath, Joan was introduced to him and so began a firm friendship on and off the stage. Joan knew talent when she saw it. In 1962, the pair did a cabaret tour in the Midlands, basing themselves in Coventry and appearing at a new venue each night. The tour ended in Larry's beloved hometown of Nuneaton. The chemistry the pair had went down well with audiences. People loved Larry's exaggerated camp humour; he would send himself up and bitch about imaginary friends of his such as Slack Alice, Apricot Lil and Everard. He was never openly crude or vulgar, using the British love of naughty innuendos to charm his fans. Joan and Larry were a perfect stage pairing; they were not the fiercely competitive type of performers so they didn't upstage each other, and he could easily make Joan laugh so they had a great rapport. The audiences were delighted at being in on the jokes.

Larry went on to be a much-loved star on British television, fronting several long-running shows. Although he never spoke about being gay, neither did he feel the need to hide his sexuality, even early on when homosexuality was illegal. Like Quentin Crisp he stood his ground, brave enough to do camp stand-up in working men's clubs. Like Quentin, he would have come in for a lot of abuse, both verbal and physical. He started out doing drag and all-male reviews but developed his own form of stand-up where he would be outrageously effeminate without swearing or being obviously smutty. Most famously he would suddenly stop in the middle of a chatty anecdote and shout 'Shut that door,' or he'd run his finger disapprovingly over the surface of the back of the bentwood chair he'd dragged on stage and complain saying 'Look at the muck on 'ere.' Larry is widely regarded as one of the first overtly gay entertainers to be accepted by the growing TV audiences.

Even typing the words 'homosexuality was illegal' stops me in my tracks. It is almost impossible to believe that the law still existed in my lifetime. Identifiably gay men like Larry ran the risk of being arrested and prosecuted right up to 1967. It was only then that the Sexual Offences Act was repealed. Prior to that, under the Criminal Law Amendment Act of 1885, men found guilty of 'gross indecency' could be tried and sent to jail. The most notorious case was against the author and great wit Oscar Wilde, who was given the maximum sentence of two years' hard labour for this offence in 1895. Wilde was destroyed by his prison term, his staggering talent as a writer was crushed by this dreadful law. A bright light snuffed out by homophobia. Thankfully Larry dodged this law. He was adored for his observational material and his queeny bitchiness. He related anecdotes involving ordinary people, sending them up mercilessly, and audiences lapped it up. A lot of the early material came from his family home. They were the only ones in their street to have a telephone so neighbours would come in to make calls and he would then transform their gossip and tales of everyday life into his patter.

The pair remained friends for the rest of their lives, Joan always speaking fondly of Larry as a kind and gentle soul. As he rose to the top, he kept her interests at heart. With the passing years, Joan's act was becoming less popular so she was desperately looking for work as an actor. In September 1972, Larry invited her to appear as a guest on his prime-time TV show called *Shut That Door*. She had a lengthy slot, where the two of them sat and chatted about old times. It was a perfect showcase to remind everyone of her existence and advertise her availability for acting work. Joan was painfully aware that her world had changed, just as Solly had said it would.

By the 1970s, Solly's warnings about the limitations of her act had become a reality, but Joan was ready for the challenge. She had listened to Solly, and she came to an accommodation with this inevitable change. According to Ulrico, 'she was accepting of the gradual slowdown in her personal work. She knew how to keep her femininity, her splendour.'

20

TELLY AND SILVER SCREEN

By this time, Joan was putting more and more of her bound-
less energy into her acting career. She told interviewers that the
strongwoman act was history, although it continued to dog her
steps for the rest of her life because that was how people remembered her. The broadcast media had always been a friend to Joan;
she had appeared on television and films from her very early days
as a performer. The camera liked her, and she was rather fond of
it. But fickle fate was always in the wings. One of her favourite
stories was about the really big one that got away: her chance to be
an iconic figure in a Bond film.

In 1963, she got a letter from Harry Saltzman, the Canadian
film producer who worked with Albert 'Cubby' Broccoli on the
Bond films. From the way the letter is written, it is clear he knew
Joan personally. He told her to phone an agent called Bill Watts,
who duly set up a meeting with Cubby in Park Lane. She was
instructed to look glamorous and wear a clinging costume to show
off her figure. The big man was impressed with what he saw, and a
few days later Joan got a follow-up call to ask how she felt about
appearing nude on a couch. She said she was happy to do this so
long as she didn't have to jump about. It seemed that Joan had
got the much-coveted job of a Bond girl, appearing in *Goldfinger*
(1964). She was to play Jill Masterson, who ended up gorgeously

dead sprawled on a couch painted head to foot in gold. In the film the character died from asphyxiation because her skin could not breathe through the paint. It is one of the abiding iconic images of the Bond films. But fate had other plans for Joan. The filming was to take place in two weeks, and she was booked to do a stint in Portugal:

> I phoned the venue in Portugal and they asked me how many days it would be for. Of course I didn't know so they reminded me that I'd signed a contract for four weeks and they'd done a lot of publicity so apart from illness there was no way out. I phoned the Park Lane office and told someone there that I couldn't get free to do it and the next thing I knew, Shirley Eaton got the job. So the next time *Goldfinger* is repeated you will know that the girl in the gold paint should have been me! That's Show Business!! She was so much better than I could have ever been – and it's the luck of the draw.

Shirley Eaton was an accomplished actress sixteen years younger than Joan. You can see why Eaton was chosen to take Joan's place, as the two women looked remarkably alike.

Joan's next foray into film came in 1972 with *Burke & Hare*. The director was Vernon Sewell, who Joan worked with on her first noticeable film appearance in 1956. Sewell was making his last picture, a dark comedic take on the true horror story of William Burke and William Hare. The pair, who had worked as navvies on the Union Canal, were graverobbers who began a killing spree in 1828 in Edinburgh to cash in on the shortage of fresh cadavers for dissection used in teaching anatomy. In this case they were being paid handsomely by the famous surgeon and lecturer Dr Robert Knox, who wasn't fastidious about the provenance of the bodies. Sixteen murders were attributed to Burke and Hare. Hardly the stuff of great humour, but it was a story that fascinated the public.

Joan said she relished playing one of their early victims Hairy Mary, portrayed as a drunken old bag. The role couldn't be further from playing a Bond girl but she had come to terms with the changes in her appearance brought on by age. Ever the pragmatist, Joan decided to use these alterations to further her acting career. In her first scene, Joan wrestles with a landlord trying to throw her out of a rough public house. She waves a bottle of booze which she then chucks through one of the pub's windows. The police get involved and she is about to be taken off to be incarcerated when the wicked William Burke, played by Derren Nesbitt, steps in. He has been watching and plotting how to get hold of Mary so he can murder her and sell her body. He bribes the police officers and takes her home.

Joan didn't have any lines as such, but she managed to do lots of drunken shouting and carrying on to make the most of the part. Dressed in billowing rags, she is made up to look raddled and plain and had a tousled wig plonked on her head. In the next scene she is bundled onto a bed and suffocated when Burke puts his hands over her mouth as Hare holds her down.

This was followed by a role in a much more star-studded affair. *The Pink Panther Strikes Again*, the fifth in the series, was released in 1976 and directed by Blake Edwards, the husband of Julie Andrews. This time Joan hit comedy gold. She only had a few lines, but they had a lasting impact. Joan, who was in her mid-fifties, played a puritanical old bag called Daphne, alongside a friend called Fiona, played by Damaris Hayman. This time the make-up was much kinder, but she was looking her age in a billowing cape and long loose dress.

The pair come upon Chief Inspector Clouseau, played by Peter Sellers, after he has just rescued Charles Dreyfus, played by Herbert Lom, from a lake. Sellers straddles him and tries to give him the kiss of life. Daphne is appalled at what she sees as homosexual promiscuity and shouts 'Dirty old men!' after belting Sellers over the head with her handbag. She drags Fiona off in a huff. The scene became famous and even now appears in show reels of the funniest moments from Sellers's time in the *Pink Panther* film series. Joan told me that she wasn't impressed by Sellers off set; as she had found with other comedic performers, he was quite a different person away from the cameras. Blake Edwards said later that Sellers was in a bad way during filming, both physically and mentally. I suspect he wouldn't have had much time for an extra.

Joan's career on the big screen came to an end with a brief appearance in the most prestigious production she had been involved in yet, the 1980 film *The Elephant Man*, starring John Hurt as the eponymous character. Joan played the cook at the London Hospital where Joseph Merrick, the Elephant Man, was a permanent resident. She serves Sir Anthony Hopkins, playing the British surgeon Sir Frederick Treves, with a bowl of gruel. The encounter is over in a blink of an eye but there is time to see how our girl, who was about to hit 60, had broadened out to fill her cook's costume.

Her career in television programmes and TV films was much more successful and long-lived. In 1974, the BBC commissioned a set of twenty-six plays based on passages from Winston Churchill's *History of the English-Speaking Peoples*. It was a huge undertaking, with each play lasting forty minutes. The first episode was broadcast on 30 December, with Joan cast as a wicked monarch. She played the part of Cartimandua, a duplicitous first-century Celtic queen who sided with the Romans and betrayed the resistance leader Caractacus. I would have loved to see her in queen mode, but it looks as though the programmes did not survive.

A popular television comedy series which ran from 1973 to 1977 was *Beryl's Lot*, produced in Leeds by Yorkshire Television. Starring Carmel McSharry, it was the story of a Battersea milkman's wife approaching middle age who decides to broaden her horizons by taking evening classes, a storyline inspired by the similar real life of contemporary writer Margaret Powell. Episode ten of the second series (in 1975) was entitled 'The Devil to Pay' and Joan was initially cast to play a character named Meg. When the episode was broadcast, however, the part of Meg was performed by the actress Antonia Pemberton. Joan's fee did little to counter her disappointment.

Fortuitously, another television booking, by Vision International, quickly followed. This time Joan was to play herself and the recording was to take place in Bremen, Germany, for ARD TV. She was to take part in *Am laufenden Band*, a German version of *The Generation Game*, in which four pairs of family members of different generations compete in performing various tasks which are first demonstrated by a guest practitioner. Joan gave her victims two tasks each to perform: a nail to bend and a telephone directory to tear in half.

She was introduced by the show host, Rudi Carrell, and came on wearing a floor-length black gown. She also had on elbow-length, gauntlet-like gloves in grey. Having handed a six-inch nail to each contestant, she then bent one, without the use of her trademark yellow duster and relying on the gloves to cushion the palms of her hands from the point and head of the nail. The contestants, as expected, failed to bend theirs, although one, like the Duke of Edinburgh before him, did achieve a slight kink. Joan then retrieved all the nails and bent them in quick succession, before peeling off her gloves to attack a telephone directory.

Although the performance was as professional as ever, it was obvious that the gloves had been no substitute for the yellow duster and the palm of her right hand had suffered accordingly. Tearing the directory, too, gave her some difficulty. She covered it beautifully, making it appear to be intentional and all a part of the act, but this was not how she wanted to be seen to perform. For the viewers and the contestants, however, it was all great fun. The participants were given telephone directories which they proceeded to tear in half, a few pages at a time, making an ever-increasing mess to ever-increasing laughter. Eventually one of the contestants was declared the winner and the mangled remains of his directory were presented to a laughing Joan before she swept off, throwing them over her shoulder as she went.

A few bookings for the Mighty Mannequin were still coming in and she felt honour-bound to accept them, although it is also noticeable that most venues were asking for new photographs rather than those from earlier years. Such requests were imperiously ignored. So far as Joan was concerned, there was no way she was going to waste money on new publicity photographs for the act which she had been trying to escape from for some considerable time. Nor was she about to have new costumes made. Improvisation was the answer, just as it had been at the very start of her career. Help was on hand from an unexpected quarter: the fashion industry came to the rescue.

Although the micro miniskirts of the sixties were still very much in evidence, designers decided that the time had come for clothes that covered up; hence the arrival of the floaty maxi dress. Flared trousers also made an appearance. To show off these new shapes and make them quirkier, the clothes were made in striking fabrics. Bling was in. There were also kaftans and loose-fitting styles based on Victorian dress being produced by firms like Laura Ashley. This move away from figure-hugging frocks was perfect for Joan, and she embraced it both at home and when she was working.

It was sometimes a real struggle for Joan to move on. Her appearance might have altered, but there were many who didn't want to let go of the svelte strongwoman. For instance, she received a letter in August 1976 from comedian Derek Roy, which read, 'Can you play a date with me on October 2nd at a Conservative Club in Ipswich? When quoting, do bear in mind that it will be cash on the night.' Derek Roy's heyday was in the late 1940s and early 1950s on BBC Radio, his material penned by writers of the calibre of Spike Milligan; one of his shows had provided Galton and Simpson with their first break. He also hosted a talent show, *Variety Bandbox*, boosting the early careers of numerous well-known performers. Described as 'well liked, well known and very vulgar,' by the mid-1970s his time was past. For Joan the reply was simple, as the thought of reverting to 'cash-in-hand' performance was anathema.

By now Joan had bought the lease of 37A, which in the end was a great move as Belsize Park properties rocketed in value, though at that point she found that demands for rent were replaced with expensive service charges from the freeholder. She needed to keep earning as much as she could. Selling her paintings didn't really help, as the money she made only just about covered the cost of materials. Work did come in, though demand for her slightly over-the-top characterisations was limited. She played a Gypsy lady in a 1983 episode of *Duty Free* (a sitcom starring Keith Barron, Gwen Taylor, Joanna Van Gysegham and Neil Stacey) and a bag-lady in an episode of *The Bill* in 1988; both had evolved from her portrayal of Hannah, a dust-woman in *Victorian Scandals* of 1976. The year 1987 brought an appearance on Rory Bremner's first television series, *Now Something Else*, following one on *Game for a Laugh*. The latter resulted in a long-standing friendship with presenter Matthew Kelly; Joan was as always quick to recognise someone who shared her humour and outlook, regardless of any age difference.

A surviving contract from 1986–87 reveals that Joan took part in filming an advert for Castella cigars (Imperial Tobacco) but no other evidence exists. In 1989, Joan took part in a programme produced by Central Independent Television about one of her dearest friends, whom she missed terribly. It was called *Contrasts: Dame Laura Knight*. Add in a one-off appearance at the Metropole in Brighton in 1988 as the Fairy Godmother and it appears that these years were a period of hard work for minimal reward.

A welcome letter from Her Majesty's Inspector of Taxes arrived in 1981. As already stated, Joan was scrupulous with her tax returns and as a result, the Inland Revenue was well aware of her correct date of birth (even if the Passport Office and Driver & Vehicle Licensing Centre were not) and, as she had now reached her

60th birthday, she was informed of her entitlement to a state pension. There was the small matter of outstanding contributions for 1980–81 to be settled first, but the unwelcome reminder of her age was tempered by the prospect, for really the first time in her life, of a regular, guaranteed income.

Joan was not going to let a few setbacks stop her pursuing a career in acting. She still had plenty of contacts in the business and she was happy to use them. She landed a good part in the TV series about the highwayman Dick Turpin, starring Richard O'Sullivan, who was a great heart-throb. The production was made for London Weekend Television and broadcast on a Saturday evening, and Joan starred as Big Nell, the landlady of the Cock and Bull, a rough tavern frequented by Turpin and lots of extras dressed in period rags. In all, she appeared in eight episodes that were first aired between 1979 and 1980. She had lots of airtime and plenty of

Joan as Big Nell in the London Weekend Television show Dick Turpin. *(Picture from her personal archive; original picture from LWT)*

lines, which she delivered with gusto. She was dressed as the arche-typal wench, in a grubby-looking long frock with sad frills and a plunging neckline which got alarmingly lower when she began to stomp about the set. Her accessories were a mop cap and a clay pipe, not a sequin in sight.

Watching her episodes now, it is clear that Joan was having the time of her life. She took great pleasure in shouting orders at her underlings and generally throwing her weight around. You can tell that she had happily immersed herself in the role, which must be one reason why she puts in such good performances. When she starts shouting, the viewer feels rather intimidated and ready to obey! You certainly wouldn't want to come to blows with a lady like Big Nell. There is one episode where she liter-ally throws a few men over her head and then pushes a huge refectory table to trap them against a wall. In fact, the whole piece is about her being arrested and Turpin fighting to save her. Considering what a softy Joan was, she slips into the role of scary old woman very well.

Joan hoped this was a new beginning, the dawning of a fresh era in her long career. This was supported by the renewed interest the media showed in her. There were the inevitable publicity shots of her holding Richard under her arm. Once again, features were being written about her and she was in demand for big spreads. The magazine *Titbits* did a feature on her. She was interviewed by Douglas Marlborough, and she appeared to be refreshingly realistic about how she had altered since her days as an Amazonian beauty:

It's alright to have a 22-inch waist when you're young, but why worry as you get older? I enjoy life, eating and drinking. I don't want to be a star, I just want to play character parts that will help me to live. I've played all sorts of little bits, but I find it difficult getting over my strong woman image. When people are casting they either remember me as rather glamorous or they think I'm past it.

THE TOUGH TIMES ARE OVER FOR THE STRONGEST WOMAN IN THE WORLD

It was the golden age of Joan Rhodes; an era which won her world-wide acclaim for her strongarm acts.
But times—and tastes—change and Joan found herself out in the cold. She's back this week on *Looks Familiar*, recalling some of the stars of yesteryear.

by PATSY HUXTER

A TV Times feature on Joan, 1974.

Her words were for show; the truth was rather different. For many, getting old is an unpleasant journey, especially when you have spent your life in front of an audience who endlessly praise you for being slim and beautiful. But Joan was a pragmatist and a determined optimist. She made the most of it.

The headline to the piece read 'Why Joan is Coming On Strong Again,' part of which turned out to be the title of the book she eventually completed almost thirty years later. Less flattering was a piece that appeared in the *Daily Express* by Adella Lithman, who wrote that Joan was 'about Diana Dors's age now, jolly fat, and delighted with her new career as an actress, playing Big Nell, the innkeeper's wife in the Dick Turpin series.' I winced when I read the phrase 'jolly fat'. Joan might have been a bit happier about her comparison to the British star Diana Dors, who was ten years younger than her.

The series is still widely available; it was re-released in 2003 and you can buy it on DVD, so it was simple enough to track down.

It's actually lots of fun. People who bought it recently gave it full marks but perhaps a lot of that was down to nostalgia – for a certain age group it was a much-looked-forward-to TV programme on Saturday evenings. Joan would be thrilled to know that she is still popping up on screens more than forty years on.

When I began researching this part of Joan's life, I thought her exploits with a handsome highwayman were the end of her television acting career. I was bowled over to find her in the credits of *Clinton: His Struggle with Dirt*, a TV special broadcast in 1998. I was even more overjoyed to find that the writer, director and producer of this piece was the hugely talented satirist Armando Iannucci. It was a mockumentary set thirty years in the future, examining the longer-term impact of US president Bill Clinton's sex scandal with White House intern Monica Lewinsky. The story of their affair had broken in January 1998.

Joan played Clare Short, who was Secretary of State for International Development when Tony Blair was Prime Minister. Joan did a convincing job in terms of looking like her subject, but her accent was missing the Brummie twang. The programme portrays Blair dashing over to the White House to support Clinton but then rushing off to be sick when he hears the details of what Clinton got up to with Lewinsky. Short was very close to Blair in the early days of his government so in this send-up, her impersonator, Joan, talks about him throwing up and being distressed. She does it incredibly well and gets plenty of screen time in the four clips that were used. Joan is sitting as an interviewee would in a documentary, in an anonymous room, tucked into a chair and talking to someone just left of camera. I wonder if it was Iannucci? He obviously rated her highly to choose her for such an important part.

What strikes me as odd is that she never mentioned this to me, and yet it was so recent. John knew vaguely about it but he said she never really thought of it as a highlight. I wonder if Joan didn't realise exactly who this talented Scottish director was.

21

JOAN'S BESTIE:
QUENTIN CRISP

Quentin Crisp was one of the most important people in Joan's life, and they were very close for more than fifty years. He was one of her best friends and 37A Belsize Park Gardens was an important safe house for him. According to Joan, he was truly off-duty in her large garden flat; he would sit politely on her chaise longue and relax. He felt he did not need to perform – she was not an audience; she was family. He might call himself the 'Stately Homo of England' but with Joan he wasn't grand; he was simply Quentin. It was as though, in those times together, they had found their own version of a close family which both had been missing in their lives.

This was not the witty, sharp-tongued raconteur who quipped his way through life while hiding his true self. In that flat, he abandoned the public persona who had to constantly entertain and became a peaceful and kind friend who sat back and let the world drift by. This worked both ways. Joan adored his company as he made her feel safe.

They were very much part of the Soho café society. These were not glamorous or fashionable coffee shops – more like numerous greasy spoons – but they did allow those who frequented them to hang around gossiping and chatting for hours for the price of a drink and sometimes something to eat. A favourite was the Bar-B-Q in Chelsea. Quentin would have his pale grey coffee, Joan her builder's tea, and then they would sometimes order the cheapest food on the menu, like an egg on toast.

Quentin was obsessed with the cinema, and he would regularly invite Joan to join him in what he called 'the one and nines', the cheap seats at the back of the stalls. The cinema they often frequented was on the same road as his room, Beaufort Street. He particularly adored Bette Davis and Joan Crawford and would sit there with his eyes glued to the screen, living the action. Joan said he didn't like to go alone because he was once accosted by a man in the cinema. No one would approach him with Joan in attendance.

Sometimes she was invited to his room, which later became notorious for being filthy because he boasted about how he never cleaned it. It became one of his most famous quotes that lives on to this day: 'There is no need to do any housework at all. After the first four years the dirt doesn't get any worse.' In his defence, Joan said the dust wasn't really that bad.

One of Joan's joys was to cook him Sunday lunch. He only had a limited diet when she first got to know him. He told her he lived on Complan, a powdered food supplement which is still on the market today. Quentin would buy it in bulk from the chemists and mix scoops of the powder with milk or warm water to create a soup or a drink. Joan didn't think this was enough to keep him healthy and would question him about looking after himself, but he insisted that he had all the vitamins he needed. He also confessed to her that he relied on Complan and the occasional beans or egg on toast in a café because he couldn't cook. She immediately decided she could redress the nutritional balance, and so began their Sunday lunch sessions at 37A:

> It was Scrabble and my cooking which cemented our friendship. He would phone up and say, 'Do you fancy a game?'
>
> 'Yes,' I nearly always replied, 'Come to lunch on Sunday.'

I'd build a big fire (I didn't have central heating) and heat the large living room, we'd have a game and then eat – and afterwards play into the night.

Quentin seemed to enjoy playing me. At times we were well matched though he had a better knowledge of words than I did, but I was very crafty and hogged all the best squares, like getting my J, Q, X or Z onto a triple score square. He never groaned but would say something like, 'Today you've achieved greatness, Miss Rhodes. Shall we play another?' and then, of course, he would win.

We would sit on the large sofa in front of a roaring fire and then he'd drink a whisky and I some tea and off he would go to the Tube for Chelsea. He told me he was never accosted on the Tube although a lot of staring went on which he didn't care to notice! Quentin would arrive promptly at 1 p.m. and mostly leave about 10 p.m. He was always relaxed and entertaining – as he would have said, 'We chat about this and that, not ever that though.'

Mostly we didn't talk about our lives but rather about the topic of the day, and he never gossiped or said anything about his youth – what's more I never asked him – he was on the whole a very private person until he hit America. There I think he was exploited until his dying day.

Joan was a Scrabble fiend; she was highly competitive and crafty. She had a crib sheet of two-letter words which she said had often clinched a game in her favour. She showed it to me, making me promise not to tell anyone, but I don't think she would mind me revealing her Scrabble secret now. She certainly helped me improve my game. Often, when I visited her in the last years of her life, she would be sitting at her refectory table facing her pretty garden in deep concentration as she played against herself.

Joan was proud that Quentin liked to visit her for a meal and company. She was a keen cook, making all the usual Sunday lunch favourites like roast beef and vegetables. In the winter

she would cook him soups, which she said he relished. Quentin
was very slightly built and didn't eat very much on a daily basis,
but Joan said he always cleared his plate no matter how large
the portions. He always had good manners and would excuse
himself from the table saying he had to go to the little boys'
room or 'be a gent'. She said she never had the nerve to ask him
to do the dishes, which was just as well as her kitchen was so
small that both of them would have had trouble washing plates
in it simultaneously.

Their time together was inevitably limited by Joan's frequent
trips away, but what they did have sounded idyllic. They would
spend hours in Joan's precious garden in the summer, hitting the
Scrabble board under the shade of a cheap sun umbrella. She would
make fresh lemonade and a meal which would include produce
she'd grown herself including lettuces, tomatoes and apples. Like
any performer, she kept a strict eye on her diet, so there would be
steak but never chips.

Quentin would discuss his worries with her and she would
come up with helpful suggestions, one of which became a key
part of his future performances. He had agreed to do a talk on his
life and times at the New End Theatre in Hampstead. It was a tiny
fringe venue with only eighty seats but Quentin was in a bit of a
tizz as he had not done a formal one-man show before and they
wanted him on stage for two hours. He was horrified at the idea of
having to fill so much time.

She reassured him that he was the perfect person for such a
show, as he liked to talk and people liked to listen to him. As for the
length of the show, she suggested that he involved the audience by
getting them to ask questions:

I said why not send around a box during the interval and people
could write their questions and when you draw them out if
there's one you don't like you could always make one up. 'A
great idea,' he said, clapping his hands. He stayed with me the
night before his appearance which had good advance publicity.

I wonder if anyone will come, he pondered. We arrived quite early and there was a queue for tickets, you had to be a club member but could buy as many seats for guests as you liked. We went to the upstairs bar where Quentin, shaken, downed a whisky. Then we went down behind the reception desk as people rushed into the theatre. There was an overflow. The stage was small, no curtains but a desk with a chair and a jug of water. A bell rang and out walked Quentin. Very smart in a lilac shirt and a lilac silk handkerchief flowing from his breast pocket. The applause was deafening. He smiled his jolly smile raised his hand and sat in the chair and poured himself a glass of water.

'So,' he said, 'you've come to hear a straight talk from a bent speaker,' and then continued for at least forty minutes. He explained about the box for questions.

During the interval Joan went to the bar and was amazed to see Quentin sitting there, whisky in hand, still chatting away surrounded by admirers. He was in his element:

The bell went and I made my way down. The audience hushed and Quentin walked through the front of house door onto the stage. The box had been placed on the table. He picked it up opened it and drew out a question. 'Oh yes,' he said, 'I do dye my own hair,' putting his hand on his head which had the famous rat at the front (I never asked him why he did it that way I just accepted it, it was Quentin) and so the evening went on, it was a great success.

Quentin's hair was always a focus of attention. It was often styled into a bouffant, where it was swept up and combed into a large swirl above his forehead; the shape resembled a small rodent, hence the nickname 'the rat'. He liked to dye it different colours, initially using henna to turn it red but later going for more dramatic colours like purple. He told Joan that he wanted to grow old disgracefully.

Picking up Quentin Crisp at the launch of his book The Naked Civil Servant, *at Schmidt's restaurant, Fitzrovia, 1968.*

There is a lovely publicity shot of Joan with Quentin sitting on her shoulder waving his new book around. This was at the launch of *The Naked Civil Servant*, the hugely successful autobiography that was to secure him a place in history. The lunch was in 1968 at Schmidt's restaurant in Fitzrovia, London, a famous German eatery frequented by literary giants such as T.S. Eliot. Guests paid 10*s* for the food but the wine was courtesy of the author.

It was a dark day for Joan when Quentin fell in love with New York. During trips there, he found that he was much more accepted; people didn't spit on him and beat him up for the way he looked. There was a greater degree of acceptance.

He sent her a letter in March 1979 from the Middletowne Hotel on East 48th Street where he made it clear he intended to cross the pond for good. He confirmed that he had been unwell, with his fingers swelling up and his 'feet going wrong':

I think there is something in the air of New York takes a lot of absorbing. If you look down into the street from the fiftieth floor of a building, you can see a thin grey blanket of something lying across the street below you. Mr Gill said breathing in this city was like smoking two packets of cigarettes a day. No wonder I succumbed.

All the same, happiness is here. Everyone is so kind – so hospitable; you need never buy anything; it is all given to you. If only you could get here, you would be in heaven. You could run a café with one hand and dance in the streets with the other.

Quentin said he was going to find a way to live permanently in New York, something he achieved in 1981. This left a big hole in Joan's life, but the pair continued to chat regularly on the phone and correspond until Quentin's death in 1999 at the age of 90. When Quentin returned on visits to England, mainly for work, he would often stay at 37A. Joan kept more than a hundred of his letters, which are intimate, often self-deprecating and always amusing. I have included a few excerpts that reflect the close friendship between the pair. He invariably started his letters 'My dear Miss Rhodes':

46 East 3rd Street
4 December 1981
As you see, dear Miss Rhodes, I now have an address and a telephone number. The telephone service here is much more efficient than in England, you have your telephone within two days of applying for it. Bell Telephones are business-like (greedy).

I live in what is disparagingly called the Lower East Side. My landlord said to me, 'I have put a rubber ring round your front door key to make it instantly recognisable. You may need to use it in a hurry.' I live in the same street as Hells Angels but secretly I am relying on their unconditional support.

12 April 1982

I am finding it almost impossible to proceed with this one last book. As you know, I've never liked the chore of writing books and now fear that I may have become too old to organise my thoughts.

11 April 1992

If I am never made to give up my room here I am sitting pretty – I have just been given $600 a month. I explained to the Authorities I am not a full-time American but they brushed this detail aside with a slightly irritated gesture. I also receive a small old age pension from Mrs Thatcher (or her stand-in) so I might be able to live forever without ever getting out of bed – which, as you know, was my aim from birth.

Quentin was never afraid of speaking his mind, even if it did get him into trouble and meant he was going against popular opinion. One of his targets was Diana, Princess of Wales:

15 February 1998

For the record, I did say that Miss Diana was trash. I can't think how dying made her into a saint. Her behaviour was disgraceful, traipsing around Paris with an Arab! Whatever next?!! She was Lady Diana before she was a princess. She knew the racket. Royal marriages have nothing to do with love. They are political mergers. All she had to do was to stand beside her husband and wave and smile, and for that she would never have another financial worry as long as she lived. What more did she want?

Joan's collection of letters reveals a man who was struggling with getting old and infirm. He said he looked revolting and that ageing was 'not for sissies'. He appeared to be depressed by the whole process. In April 1999, he wrote to her about his enlarged heart that meant he couldn't walk more than a few yards before being seized with terrible chest pains. He also spoke about dreading coming on tour to England in the autumn and wrote that his agent forced him to make the arduous journey despite his poor health:

12 April 1999
I've been appallingly busy and now I have to go to Cleveland, Chicago and finally to England. I pleaded with the policeman [his agent] NOT to send me there but he was adamant … I am dreading the whole trip and will try to telephone you and cry when I get there.
Yours miserably,
Quentin

Joan was planning to see him after his shows in the north of England; he called her, wanting to know what the venues were like. She said they were respectable and he sent her a sweet little thank-you note. That was the last time she heard from him. Quentin died of a heart attack shortly afterwards in November 1999, just one month before his 91st birthday. He was in Manchester on the eve of the nationwide revival of his one-man show.

In her memoir Joan summed up her dear friend:

Quentin was never anyone but himself but I miss his gay – in the original sense of the word – company. I was sorry to hear how he suffered the last few years of his life – he just wanted to be left in peace and not exhibited like a circus freak.

Joan enjoyed writing poetry and would often run her work past Quentin. She called the poems 'Odes by Rhodes', and this was her tribute to him:

Quentin Crisp
He sped brightly across the town
Looking neither up nor down.
'Bloody poof,' the stranger said
'Come home with me and share my bed.'

On his face a look of pain
Then they jostled him again!
'How have I offended you?'
Then they'd punch him black and blue.
He crawled away and wondered why
Oh, why was he born and when he would die?
But that was long ago- long past
Then fame came and he is loved at last.
A man who came out of time
Sped brightly
And won this heart of mine!

22

TEA AND TIMES

From the beginning, Joan was driven by her determination to survive no matter what. The warning she had from her agent and friend, Solly Black, may have seemed premature back at the start of the 1960s, but she took it seriously. She knew that he was right about her variety act losing its appeal. Tastes were changing, and so was her body. The truth was that you could try and control the march of time when it came to the physique and appearance, but you would never win this battle, even though Joan gave it her best shot.

She worked out each day; her favourite exercise was walking, especially on Hampstead Heath, which was virtually on her doorstep. She followed her own carefully concocted diet which included raw meat and eggs. All this helped prolong her stage life as a strongwoman. But the years of stress on her body were taking their toll. She'd used every ounce of her strength on a daily basis for decades. She told me she would get sore knees where she used to bend the bars; her teeth had become looser as she'd used them to pick up everything from tables to an ironmonger's anvil – she got to know her dentist very well. Among her mountain of bits and bobs in her flat were numerous dental moulds of her teeth where work had needed to be done. Perhaps more pressing for Joan was the constant battle to keep off the pounds.

Joan lifting an anvil with her teeth; she hated every minute of this photo shoot, which she did for a bet.

That's not to say bookings evaporated completely; Joan was still in demand at some stage shows and cabarets. She had appeared at the ultra-posh Savoy Hotel in central London on numerous occasions over the years. It had always been for one-off bookings but, as this was a celebration of the end of the 1960s, the hotel had decided to put on a special show called 'London Pride' (not to be confused with the fabulously outrageous annual LGBTQ+ event now held every year). This was a glitzy, old-style variety show running for three weeks over Christmas and the new year.

The headliner was the much-loved veteran comedian Tommy Trinder. He was one of Britain's best-loved entertainers in the twentieth century, the kind of stand-up who wasn't afraid to challenge the current social fashions, a bit like Ricky Gervais. During the Second World War his blunt, down-to-earth working-class patter helped keep spirits up in such dark times. He was known for his catchphrases such as 'You lucky people' and 'If it's laughter you're after, Trinder's the name.' He had a number of television shows and appeared in films. Trinder was a big favourite of the queen, who gave him a CBE in 1975. He was a classic cheeky chappy who was a master of ad-libbing, double entendre and observational comedy. Fellow entertainer and music hall historian Roy Hudd credited him with being an 'alternative comic' before the phrase was even thought of.

Joan had worked with him many times, including the show for the queen at Windsor Castle. She had his measure. Trinder was known as something of a womaniser but according to Joan he never tried his luck with her: 'I was well aware of Tommy's reputation with women, but he was always wary of me. I think it was the strongwoman image which, although it may have been a turn-on for some men, was definitely not for him.'

Looking at footage of Trinder you can see that he had a slender build, so it wouldn't surprise me if he was just a bit too scared of Joan's enormous strength to hit on her for fear she would hit on him – hard! That didn't stop him standing by her during the New Year's Eve show at the Savoy when the audience got out of control despite the plush setting. As Joan went through her routine, the situation was getting nastier, with food being hurled at the stage. Give him his due, Tinder was on hand to try and calm things down even if he couldn't help making a joke of it:

> Anyway, we were good friends and on New Year's Eve the audience were getting rough and throwing bread rolls onto the stage. I heard Tommy's voice off-stage: 'I hope they don't hit the poor cow – I wouldn't like to see her in a temper!' He was kindness itself and later I was photographed at the Dorchester holding

him upside down and we laughed about the Savoy. I still have the photograph. So many stars were not so helpful.

A clear glimpse into Joan's changing world came with her anecdote about having to get a special costume made only a few days before the show got underway. It was a gorgeous sequined black and pink basque. What she didn't focus on was why she needed to rush to a seamstress. The answer comes when you look at a publicity shot of her for the Savoy. It was obvious that she had put on weight and changed shape. Her old costumes simply did not fit. She must have been mortified and probably angry after her hard work to keep her all-important figure.

The growing gaps in her bookings diary were a great worry to Joan. She knew she had to diversify. She was busily plugging away at getting her acting career off the ground and, as we saw with the film and TV roles, she had a degree of success but it wasn't enough to keep the bills paid. She had tried being a landlady but that hadn't worked as a form of career switch. It turned out to be a lot of hard work and headaches for little return. Joan was always open to new opportunities so when she spotted an exciting project in north London, she grabbed it with both hands. Little did she know that it would become an integral part of the next thirty years of her life.

A lease was available for a greasy-spoon-type café in Crouch End. Other than one disastrous day at the Mount Pleasant café when she was 14, Joan had no professional experience in catering for the thirsty and hungry. That minor detail didn't get in her way – she reasoned that anyone could make a cuppa and a sandwich or a piece of buttered toast. After all, she had spent many hours in places like this one; she was an experienced customer so she was very familiar with what needed to be done.

She called the café Josie's, using one of her many nicknames. It was a great find, and although it was never a huge financial success it was a perfect way of bringing in enough to keep her fed and clothed. They say location is everything and, in this case, it was perfect for the kind of establishment Joan had in mind. It was close to the high street, on Crouch Hill, and across the road from the Mountview Academy of Theatre Arts. Joan judged correctly that students were always hungry and thirsty, especially if the price was right. She had stumbled on a winning venture.

Josie's was run absolutely on Joan's terms, which meant no early starts for her and she would shut up shop when she'd had enough. She wasn't interested in getting up at the crack of dawn to deal with the breakfast trade and got someone else to do that. As she was still doing theatre and cabaret work, she needed her evenings clear. I've got a copy of the hand-decorated menu that was in the window. It mysteriously announces the hours are '10 a.m.–3 p.m. Monday–Friday APPROX!' There was a minimum charge of £1 between 12 and 2 p.m. On offer was a cup of tea for 35p, a 'decent coffee' 50p, as well as cheese or poached eggs on toast, a mere £1.20. But what caught my eye was at the bottom of the sheet. Joan had written 'We are small and slightly arty – you can ignore that if you wish. Why not share a table, meet a friend, have a chat. See you!!'

When I was imagining Joan in her café, I realised that, in creating this dramatic space, Joan had provided herself with her own stage. It was like a theatrical venture where she was director, producer, writer and star all in one go. She was even the girl selling sweets and snacks. The place was decorated with sexy publicity shots of Joan in her heyday and pictures of those she had worked with like Marlene Dietrich and other big stars. There was a hand-carved wooden owl swinging above the entrance; Joan was known for her love of owls, and in her time away from Josie's, she would paint them and then sell the work in her café. Every space was crammed with trinkets and curios from home. It was an echo of 37A but so much more. She was selling to the punters, putting on a show and pulling in the crowds as she had done all her life. It sounds reminiscent of her early days working pitches on the streets, only this was much more stable: these encounters were taking place on home ground, on her own terms where she could do whatever she liked.

Josie's oozed her personality. She would even put her latest 'Odes by Rhodes' in the window to entertain passers-by.

It was perfect; she had a guaranteed captive audience for her daily performances. The young, impressionable drama students were hungry not just for egg on toast; they came for tales of greasepaint and bright lights, a glimpse of what fate might have in store for them. Joan had her own props on hand and lots of opportunity to wow with her tales of great adventures in the entertainment world. And no one was there to boss her around or curb her exuberance. She would wear floaty frocks that disguised the cruelty of age and her blonde hair was always carefully groomed, with just the right amount of make-up on her eyes and lips. This was her little kingdom and it was just as she liked it. That must be why it lasted for so long: Josie's existed for more than three decades.

A witness to these colourful café days is the actress and charity ambassador Vicky 'Sparkles' Ogden, known for her appearances as a barmaid at the Rovers Return in *Coronation Street* in the 1980s. She was a student at Mountview and a tenant in the flat above the café which came with the lease. Vicky became a close friend of Joan's, and she explained to me how she helped defray some of the rental costs by doing café work for her landlady. She would get up at 7.15 a.m., an ungodly hour for a drama student. But Vicky appears to have been happy to play her part. She would get the show on the road by turning on the all-important water heater for endless cups of tea and coffee. She would pop to the local bakery to fetch the day's order of bread and buns and would put the goodies on display. She opened the door to customers after 9 a.m. before handing over to someone else and rushing to class.

Vicky says Josie's was a hugely popular watering-hole, comfortable and cheap. Invariably it was packed with students between lessons and at lunchtime. They came like flies to a honeypot; they felt the place was touched by the world of showbiz magic with its resident star in the shape of Joan and her stories of her life at the top.

They would have been particularly bowled over in the early days as high-profile work was still coming in for Joan – she most definitely had not given up her day job. Although the number of bookings was shrinking, she was still in demand. She did several cabarets and recorded a spot at London Weekend Television for the *Kenny Everett Show*. An unusual request came through for her to appear as a strongwoman for the Festival of London Stores. This might not sound like much, but it was a labour of love. One of the capital's trendiest shops, Aquascutum in Regent Street, had decided to outshine its rivals by putting on a circus-themed show. Part of it was an exhibition of circus works by Dame Laura Knight, including the portrait she did of Joan. As we know, the pair were firm friends, Joan idolising Laura and over the years seeing her and her husband, Harold, regularly for long lunches at the Arts Club.

One of the press officers involved, Ken Thomson (also a friend of Joan), wanted her to appear in her strongwoman guise wandering around the shop doing her amazing feats. She was more than happy to take part and would have done anything to support Dame Laura, who was then in her nineties. The store couldn't resist cashing in on Joan's ability to bend nails. It came up with the gimmick that any customer who could break a six-inch nail before Joan would have their bill halved. The press release read: 'In fact, any customer who is the first on any day to break a 6-inch nail provided by Miss Rhodes, before her, will receive back half the amount he has spent in the store – "HALF-THE-BILL-FOR-HALF-THE-NAIL", as it were.' There were plenty of takers but no winners.

Dame Laura died exactly a month after the show at the age of 92. It was a devastating loss, and Joan told me she never stopped missing her idol.

A much more demanding, and dangerous, booking came through at about this time. Out of the blue, Joan got a call from the manager of comedian Frankie Howerd, asking her to be part of a Christmas show for the troops in Northern Ireland. This was quite a request when you consider that the province was a highly risky place to go to at the time; it was in the midst of the Troubles, and it was basically a warzone with regular bombings and shootings. The British forces were hated by all sides, and it was a particularly tough military posting on home ground. But Joan had never worried about this kind of minor detail. She was certainly ready to hop on the plane and appear with Howerd, who was ultra-famous at the time. I don't think Joan gave much consideration to conflict; she was too busy surviving. But this was not the case for the star of the show.

Before the trip, the cast were invited to Frankie's house so they could all get to know each other. When Joan arrived at his home in Edwardes Square, near Notting Hill Gate, she was a bit worried when the great man answered the door with an angry glare on his face. She thought she had done something wrong but was reassured by others that he always looked like that. She was excited about meeting Frankie but was horribly disappointed with what she found:

I'd so much looked forward to meeting him – he was such a big name and I was told that he was a comic dream. Well, to me he was a nightmare and moaned most of the time.

We flew to Belfast – Frankie seemed very nervous to me and there had been reports about bombs, but he soon raised a laugh with his 'Oh God, what have I let myself in for now?' After one of the shows we were invited to the Officers' Mess for the usual drinks and an officer made his speech about how much they had all enjoyed the show. Smiling faces all round and then: 'Joan Rhodes, would you step up to the podium?'

What on Earth had I done wrong, I asked myself. A soldier was hiding something behind his back as I stepped up. He handed it to me and I was aware of Frankie's face looking very upset as I saw what they were giving to me. I was presented with a rubber bullet inscribed 'To Joan Rhodes from 45 Edo – keep it up!'

'Oooh,' said Frankie, 'Why didn't they give me one?' He was quite petulant and didn't speak to me again.

Have you ever seen a rubber bullet? I was greatly surprised. It still adorns my trophy shelf.

We had to move hotels a couple of times because Frankie thought the IRA might be angry because we were helping to keep up the morale of the soldiers. Although he was a pain to work with it was nonetheless a very happy and well received show, soon over and soon forgotten I suppose. I think Frankie was probably brave as he was so nervous, but his performance was brilliant. Afterwards there was a great party in the Officers' Mess with Frankie getting all the laughs he craved, but no rubber bullet!

Back in Crouch End, Joan got on with the business of making egg or beans on toast, tea and what she called 'really good coffee'. She refused to do chips or anything fried or tricky to cook. This suited her clientele perfectly. I suspect she was mostly too busy entertaining her customers to concentrate all that hard on what she was serving up.

Some of Joan's celebrity friends would pop in from time to time, especially Quentin who had his usual 'pale grey coffee'. But the arrival of recording studios across the road in 1984 brought in a new brand of superstar. The facility was built in a vast upper room in the old religious building and was known as The Church. Annie

In Joan's Crouch End café with world-famous musical performer Annie Lennox.

Lennox and Dave Stewart, who had just formed Eurythmics, were behind the venture which was a great success and attracted some of the biggest names in the business from all over the world. It turned out the pair liked nothing better than a cuppa and beans on toast, and they became regular visitors to Josie's. Joan wasn't easily starstruck and treated them just like any other punters. I think it was because of this that she became good friends with Annie, who was another feisty woman with brains and talent. There are a number of pictures of the pair where they are arm in arm, relaxed and sharing a joke no doubt.

When I was researching this part of Joan's life, I found there was an intriguing urban legend around one of the famous visitors to the studios that is still doing the rounds today. I was overjoyed when I realised that I had stumbled across another version of the merry tale, but for my 'legend' I had proof – the testimony of someone who was there.

The original story goes something like this: Bob Dylan came over from America to work with Dave Stewart at The Church. But he got lost, the way artistic types might when they couldn't read quickly scribbled notes on where they were going. He gave the cabbie who picked him up at Heathrow the right number but the incorrect road in Crouch End and had no idea he was knocking on the wrong door (I resisted any pun here). The woman who answered, Angie, didn't recognise him and it just so happened that her husband was also called Dave, but he was a plumber and had popped out for a few minutes. When Bob said he had come to see Dave she thought he meant her husband and let him come in to wait. It also transpired that Dave the plumber was a massive Dylan fan. So, when he got home, he was dumbstruck to find the great musician/poet sitting quietly on his sofa sipping tea and watching a game show called *Blockbusters*. Legend has it that the three of them chatted and listened to music all afternoon.

There are a number of different versions of this tale, the best being a comedy drama for Sky Arts in its series *Urban Myths*, first broadcast in 2017 with Eddie Marsan as an utterly convincing bewildered megastar. The programme makers were at pains to point out that the piece was based on a myth and might or might not be true. But they weren't going to let that stop them telling a good story.

I was talking about this to Joan's friend Vicky, and she came up with a new sequence of events for a similar sighting, only this version had even more sparkle and she was a first-hand witness:

> One day I was dashing in to give Joan some news about a job I had just got and as I rushed into the café with all the joys of spring and the anticipation of her excitement at my news, I noticed that there was only 1 table full of 4 people in the corner tucking into their poached eggs and cup of tea. Annie Lenox [*sic*], Dave Stewart, Mick Jagger and BOB DYLAN were sat there. Joan was standing at the counter looking a little tense. As I was stopped in my tracks and completely taken aback by this group of SUPER STARS I stammered and said 'I'll come back later'. Joan said cheerio and I fell back out of the door. Completely out of breath!!
>
> When I returned an hour later, I wanted to know all about the visit from rock legends. She told me they loved their poached eggs and they paid!!!! I was in awe.

It's easy to think of Dylan tucking into egg on toast in a rough-and-ready Crouch End café, but Mick Jagger? Now that would have been quite a photo opportunity.

By the mid 1990s, when Joan was in her seventies, she was struggling. The cost of living had risen steeply and her income failed to keep up. Her stage career had been over for some time and her focus was the café. Although it didn't bring in much money, Joan was an expert at being frugal; she never forgot the lessons she learnt as a homeless teenager on the streets of London. She used her natural optimism to keep her little show on the road, but even that wasn't enough to prevent the inevitable. Her health was deteriorating and the world was becoming more difficult to navigate, especially in the field of catering. New food and safety regulations had come in that made her rather shambolic way of catering technically illegal. She didn't have the right facilities and the cost of the alterations needed was well beyond her means. At this point Joan was having to count every penny. The local council enforcement officers were unwelcome visitors but, in true Joan fashion, she used her cunning to find a way to dodge around the rules.

Her solution was simple: she just stopped selling food and drink. As Josie's was already packed with items for sale, she decided to go the whole way and turn it into a bric-a-brac shop. Her stock came from 37A and adventures rummaging through any skips she found en route to and from Crouch End – basically it was a bit like a charity shop where she was the sole beneficiary. On the quiet she did provide a cuppa and no doubt a snack for the loyal regulars who continued to pop in and demand that she entertained them.

The last straw came when there was confusion about the rent she had been paying. She would send a cheque to a local address and they had always been cashed. But this all unravelled one day when she received a letter from someone calling themselves the landlord. She had never heard the name before and to her horror the formal missive claimed she owed more than two years' worth of rent at a vastly increased figure. It's not clear what was behind this, but Joan went into battle. Setting out her case, she demanded to know why she had not heard from this man before and where her payments had been going if not to the landlord. This half-sorted out the problem and he appeared to abandon the so-called debt. What he did do, though, was hike up the rent which had been the same for ten years. This was a crushing blow and there was no way of wriggling out of this increase; the rent had remained incredibly reasonable for most of Joan's time at the café. The man was within his rights. All this was compounded by a break-in at her flat, the second in a matter of months. For once Joan had to admit defeat. She got friends to help her gather her vast collection of bits and bobs and move it home.

It was more than just the end of an era. It was the penultimate act in the drama of Joan's life.

23

HEALTH

Other than her gynaecological troubles, Joan was blessed with good health for most of her life. An exception to this came when she was working in Israel in the early 1970s. She was in a flat changing her clothes one day when she noticed a peeping Tom. Furious, she got on a table to try to grab him through a high window, but she fell and broke her arm – a terrible blow for someone who relied on her arms for work. Fortunately, it healed well and quickly but she said she had never felt so alone as she did at that time as no one came to help her. But a broken bone was nothing compared with what awaited her in 1988.

One Sunday, Joan was exercising in her garden, skipping, when she noticed that there was something odd about her left breast; it just didn't feel right. When she examined it, she found a lump on the side, the size of a quail's egg. It was the kind of discovery that strikes terror into every woman's heart. Alarm bells rang and the next episode of Joan's life went at alarmingly high speed.

Joan went to her doctor the following day. The GP shared her concern and made an urgent call to the Royal Marsden Hospital in Chelsea, the world-class centre for cancer treatment. You can tell when something is medically very serious as the wheels of the NHS start to move incredibly quickly. In Joan's case she was booked in for an appointment for the next morning. They did a mammogram and took a biopsy of the lump. She was admitted to the Royal Marsden on the Thursday and told to bring everything she needed to stay for several nights.

Joan was taken to a ward and settled into a bed where she waited anxiously for someone to tell her what was going on. Knowing Joan, it is easy to believe that her fears would have been masked with smiling, joking and singing to the staff and other patients. Keeping the show going was her way of dealing with a crisis. A doctor came, examined her and said they planned to remove the cancerous lump. Joan said this was the first time the c-word had been used. But she was a clever woman and she would have already gone through every scenario in her head. She knew that she had a cancerous tumour in her left breast.

The worst part for her would have been the lack of control she had; there was virtually nothing she could do about the situation she was in and she had to leave her survival in the hands of the medics. That would have been as tough as hearing that she had cancer. She was warned that because of where the lump was, she might have to have a mastectomy. This was a potential disaster for someone whose cleavage was part of her act, even if she was long past being called upon to wear a plunging neckline. Before she signed the consent form Joan did try her best to influence what happened when she was under. She asked if the surgeon would try and save her breast but also that he went in through the left side, thereby causing the least possible damage to her cleavage. In all the drama, she had a rare moment of feeling a bit better when the surgeon said he knew her work and would do his best. A shaft of light, a tiny reminder of her heyday, in her darkest hour:

I went through the usual pre-op business and Friday, the next morning, I was operated on – I went down singing after the pre-med. When I awoke, I was fully bandaged and felt my chest to see if it was all there – it was, flattened, but there were still two lumps. I shouted for a cup of tea which a lovely male nurse brought me. He took charge of me and my dressings. I had many visitors. I was in hospital about two weeks and had various treatments. When the bandages came off I was quite surprised; one of my breasts was half sized and I had a large wound in my armpit – lymph glands removed I was told, but I felt good! I had to attend the hospital and took tablets (Tamoxifen). Visits at first every month, then three months and then six months, a year and finally I was told I was all clear and I am. I realise how lucky I was that it all happened so quickly.

Her all-clear from cancer was great news and it lasted for more than twenty years. With true Joan aplomb she made a speedy recovery. Her friends, including Annie Lennox, had visited her in hospital and kept a close eye on her once she got home. She learnt to live with the change in her shape; she adapted just as she had always done. But the inevitability of the body's innate frailty was catching up with her.

To Joan's frustration, the cancer had got in the way of her struggle to keep the pennies coming in. The good news was that Josie's was still functioning at this stage. It was always busy and full of interesting clientele, but the flip side was that it wasn't much use as a serious breadwinner. At 50p for a cuppa, her prices were ridiculously out of date. The sale of bits and bobs and artwork helped boost her income, but not enough to allow her to relax.

By now, Joan was represented by Barry Spencer and Associates (who became Penny Harrison (BSA) Ltd). They worked hard to find bookings for her as she had such a limited acting repertoire, and the strongwoman routine was consigned to history. Looking at her publicity shots from the time, Joan clearly had fun getting dressed up as a scruffy old hag and shouting drunkenly. She'd distort her face and use her larger body to intimidate the rest of the cast. She was scarily good at it. In truth it was her favourite, and only, characterisation. Her joy in the role came across in the handful of performances she was asked to do. The trouble was that demand for this type of character was limited.

Sadly, Joan's attempts to establish herself as a 'mature' star of the small screen failed and her hopes and dreams fizzled out. It was hard enough to make your mark as an actor even when you were young and gorgeous. Like so many before her, Joan could not beat the clock. She was not alone – the ageing star is a familiar trope – but that didn't make it any easier. She began to work on her memoir in earnest, safe in the knowledge that many of those she would write about were dead and gone. It was a gamble she was happy to take.

Then, on 19 December 1999, there was another medical emergency. Joan's sister Blackie, who was in the habit of phoning her flat every morning, didn't get an answer. Made anxious by the unusual silence, she called Vicky and another close friend from Mountview, Trevor Hopkins, an award-winning TV producer.

Vicky was another daily caller and she had also got no reply despite repeated attempts. She contacted Trevor who went around to 37A. There was no answer at the door but when he looked through the letterbox, he saw Joan on the floor. He called the police who came and broke down the door. Joan was barely conscious; it transpired that she had collapsed the night before on her way to the toilet. By the time help got to her in the shape of paramedics and an ambulance, her hands and feet were blue. They had their work cut out restoring her body temperature but once she was admitted to the Royal Free Hospital, her condition stabilised.

Once again Joan cheated death and made a remarkable recovery; the stroke hadn't left any really noticeable lasting damage. Vicky was on hand to help when she came home to 37A and was staggered by how quickly her dear friend pulled through:

> She was a bit weak for a while and took it easy. Her mouth drooped a little at the beginning when she was in hospital then it corrected itself. Afterwards she was a bit slower and didn't do as much walking but that was all. We put it down to her constitution and strength of character.

According to Joan, one of the reasons for her full recovery was the fact that she was used to hardship. She would point out that she had been living for decades without central heating in her large flat. In her mind, surviving the chill made her able to fight off coughs and colds. But as the twentieth century ended and the twenty-first got underway, Joan, at the age of 79, was less able to deal with physical trials and tribulations. As well as having a stroke she had developed diabetes. Fortunately, her nephew, John, and his wife Pam became regular visitors around this time, and they set about making life more comfortable for her. One of the first things John did was organise some central heating: 37A was to be overhauled and made fit for the new millennium with toasty radiators. Who better to do the job than a registered local plumber appropriately named Alan van der Loo? Meanwhile, John set to work on the dangerous electrics that hadn't been touched since Bert had cobbled something together more than fifty years before.

When the new millennium arrived, Joan was still in the hands of the NHS after her stroke. She went from the main building of the Royal Free Hospital to a unit for the elderly called Queen Mary's House. She wasn't happy with what she found there in the shape of the sick and immobile, echoes of what she might become, while most of them were actually younger than her. The thought of being trapped there would have been a powerful incentive to get better as quickly as possible and she was home by February.

Joan was supported by family and friends who helped with shopping and the maintenance of 37A, but evidence of declining health was all too apparent. A neighbour, Pip Rau, had been hoping to get to know Joan for years as she'd always been intrigued by the exotic creature who lived right next door. Now Joan was at home so much she made her move, and they became firm friends. Pip would drive Joan to the supermarket once a week and generally do her bidding. Like so many of us, she fell under the spell, as did Pip's team of friendly builders who were renovating Pip's huge house. Joan was quick to find the jolly gang jobs to do; the years hadn't diminished her love of having handsome young men at her beck and call.

One of the remarkable aspects of Joan was her appeal to people of all ages and backgrounds. Her positivity and power were infectious, and her presence continued to light up a room. She still had her fan base and into this happy muddle came 25-year-old Christine Handy. She was a resting actress who worked as a carer as she waited for her performing skills to be called upon. Initially, she was part of the support team brought in to help Joan resettle at home after discharge from hospital. This was only supposed to last for a few weeks but when Joan asked Christine to continue her weekly visits, she was overjoyed. Like me, she found that her heart had been captured and the sixty-year age gap was irrelevant. I'm not sure how much cleaning was done but that didn't matter when there was lots of fun to be had:

I often think we found each other at a time we both needed each other. It was a beautifully symbiotic friendship. I know it's easy to romanticise things with the passing of time, but I truly believe I fell in love with Joan from that very first time I met her. Head over heels!

Joan sparkled and crackled as she told her stories. Never ever, ever, had I ever met anyone like her and from that moment my life changed. I believe there are moments for each of us where the universe tingles, dances and sings loudly and this is how I remember that day. Remembering back, I still tingle. Joan was magnetic!

I couldn't talk about my visits to Joan without mentioning the singing. During my visits we would sing our heads off at full volume! Josie (one day Joan told me, I want you to call me Josie, so from then on, Josie it was!) would teach me fabulously raucous songs, 'Abie, Abie, Abie my boy! Vhat are you v'aiting for now?' or 'I want to be a lady and peroxide me 'air!' to name but a few. I would mix in a few songs from my own repertoire … if I stopped singing Josie would call out, 'Why have you stopped singing!' I love that Joan loved my singing! I loved it when we sung together.

Each time I arrived for my weekly cleaning visit Josie would say, go and put your pinny on. I remember the day Joan unearthed my pinny from somewhere in the depths of her hordes of things! A 1940s style, wrap around with brown, yellow, orange flowers. She was so happy to give this to me and wearing it became one of the many traditions of my visits.

Joan loved seeing me dress up in her fabulous clothes and telling me the stories behind them … 'I wore this one to Lady Docker's son's engagement party.' Or 'I wore this at opening night of Ulrico's exhibition!' … a story for every outfit. I would skip about in giddy excitement at wearing something so utterly glamorous and I think Josie relished my excitement. I think we would spark and bounce off each other in this way. Though we were so far apart in age, our friendship often felt like we were girlish school friends. Joan had a deliciously playful, joyful nature. I am now the very proud owner of many of these beautiful items of clothing and celebrate every opportunity to wear them and tell people all about the amazing woman and stories behind them.

As Joan's health declined the logistics of simply leaving her flat were complicated by her lack of mobility and weight. The steep concrete stairs up to the front garden path became a daunting challenge. She did get out a bit, making a few public appearances such as a speaking engagement for the Concert Artistes Association and one for the Max Miller Appreciation Society. She was particularly delighted to be given a lifetime achievement award by the Oscar Heidenstam Foundation. She would use these opportunities to read her poetry, which someone likened to the work of William Topaz McGonagall, the Scotsman described as the worst poet in British literature. It was a rather harsh criticism that would have made Joan laugh on the outside but fume on the inside.

This is where I came into Joan's life, quite by chance. John was not happy with the care she was getting so he got onto her local medical team and pushed for more to be done. He and Pam had noticed a worrying deterioration in their aunt's health. It just so happened that my husband, Ian, was working as a locum at the local Hampstead surgery and went to see Joan because of John's very vocal concerns.

Ian was bowled over by her, so much so that he asked if he could put me in touch as I was working on a new book about strong women in the broadest sense. I had just finished my book *Queen Coal*, about the women in the 1984–45 miners' strike, and was thoroughly sick of women being written out of history. I think my BBC credentials as a correspondent and presenter for more than twenty years must have sparked her interest in wanting to meet me, even if illness had put paid to my broadcast career. Despite the lupus and bouts of life-threatening flares, I was the author of three books. I had also gone back to school and got a BA in Fine Art from Chelsea, so Joan and I had even more in common. Not only were we both artists but, as her health deteriorated, I was in a good place to understand how tough that was and how best to ensure getting what was needed from the NHS. I knew that squeaky wheels were called for.

She certainly needed medical care, but she also required the oxygen of an appreciative audience. It was the best 'pick-me-up' she could have, as good as if not better than the stacks and stacks of medicine boxes that had joined the bits and bobs that were crammed onto every shelf and surface.

I wrote a formal letter to 37A and had an immediate reply that was just as formal inviting me to lunch. As Christine said, entering her bemusing lair was a one-way journey. By the end of our meal, I was smitten and on board to help with her memoir, mainly by listening to her read her latest chapter and help find a publisher.

After toying with various titles such as 'Men I Have Picked Up', Joan chose to call it *Coming On Strong*. She would work for hours writing the manuscript by hand and then sending the product to John in Derbyshire to type up. He's such a precise man, accuracy means a lot to him, so he would tinker with some of the facts or phrases that he decided were incorrect. This would trigger many explosions when she noticed what he had done. It was her story, and she wasn't happy with anyone altering her narrative. Other than that, the process was successful and resulted in a manuscript that she was happy with. There was interest from a publisher, Virago

Press. But there was one huge stumbling block: they wanted to put the project in the hands of a ghostwriter and there was no way this was acceptable to Joan.

Eventually she decided to self-publish using a company that specialised in the field, Serendipity. This turned out to be a huge mistake. She paid them thousands from her savings and despite selling many books, she never got any money back.

Once again Joan found herself hitting the headlines, but this time for all the wrong reasons. The local paper, the *Ham and High*, reported on her plight in October 2008 under the headline:

Strongwoman, 80, is ripped off by publisher

[...] In 2006 she decided to write a book on her incredible life and handed over £8,400 of her life savings to publishers Serendipity, but never saw a penny for the 3,000 copies which she believes they sold. The company pocketed thousands – and has done the same to more than 100 other people up and down the country.

She finally learned they had gone into voluntary liquidation this month. 'I was supposed to get royalties in December last year and then July this year,' said Ms Rhodes, who is in her 80s.

'I used to phone them all the time asking why I hadn't got any money and they kept telling me the man dealing with it was on holiday or wasn't in. They kept saying they would get him to get back to me, but it never happened. Then they started saying the cheque was in the post, but it never was, or that it must have been lost and they would send me another one, which never came.'

She now only has two copies of her book and can't get hold of any more because of the company's collapse. Likewise, she is unlikely to get anything from the liquidation proceedings.

'I didn't know if I would be able to write a book, so I was really pleased with it,' she said. 'The launch was lovely too and I sold 79 copies there, but Serendipity insisted on keeping the money. I enjoyed my work very much and people kept saying to me to write it all down. It was going to be the thing to earn me enough money to see me through the rest of my life. I think the stress of all this is what has damaged my health. I wish I'd never been involved with them.'

RMT Accountants and Business Advisors in Newcastle are dealing with the liquidation of Serendipity which operated under the company Ardrope Limited.

The company is said to owe £197,000, much of which belongs to authors – mostly pensioners – who were never paid the royalties they were promised.

To say that Joan was devastated is an understatement: she'd been talking about writing her book for most of her life and now the dream was a nightmare. She'd lost money she could ill afford but worst of all, she wasn't well enough to go through the process of publishing all over again.

It was awful to see her beaten after a life of triumphs against adversity, although she did her best to keep the trademark smile on her face. The publishing nightmare was such a shame, as her friends and colleagues loved the book. The praise was led by the late lamented Roy Hudd. Not only was he a great satirist and performer but he was also a leading expert on the history of music halls and their acts. The pair became good friends in their later years. He wrote the foreword for Joan's book and described her as being unique: 'Joan is a shining example of what can be done if you set your mind to it and ignore setbacks, personal disappointments and the loneliness of the long-distance speciality act.'

In the years I had the privilege to be Joan's close friend I would pop in to see her a number of times each week. We would have tea or what she called 'posh coffee' which came in a sachet and went frothy when you poured boiling water on it in a mug. It was my job to bring the Hobnob biscuits and put the kettle on as she found it increasingly difficult to move around. Her joints had become sorer and her legs were badly swollen with oedema.

Early on in our friendship, she was well enough for me to take her out for brief jaunts to local pubs. I found it tricky to wrestle with her and the wheelchair, but it was worth it to find ourselves sitting outside one of Hampstead's glorious pubs next to the Heath. I would happily listen to her reminiscing as we sipped gin and tonics. But that didn't last long. Eventually the only way Joan could get beyond her own four walls was to have an ambulance come with a couple of young and strong staff. She wanted me to go with her to medical appointments and this worked out well when Joan had been stuck waiting for hours to be seen. As a journalist I knew how to get help and action, especially when I felt she had been forgotten. No matter what pain she was in Joan was always smiling, ever the optimist. Her ebullience would infect the overcrowded waiting rooms and by the time the doctor was ready to see her she would be singing 'The Lambeth Walk' to an appreciative but broken collection of fellow patients.

We had a few hairy ambulance journeys with the siren blaring. A dramatic ride in one of those vehicles always looks exciting on the telly but, believe me, you want to avoid it if you can. I think the folks driving were trained at Brands Hatch racing track. By the time we reached the hospital we were both green around the gills. I was with her when the doctor told her that the breast cancer had come back. He thought I was her daughter and Joan appeared to be comfortable with that as she didn't correct him. He said that surgery to remove the tumour was out of the question. I asked about chemotherapy which he said was possible, but he didn't recommend it as Joan was so sick. I didn't want to lose her, so I argued for the therapy; how selfish of me. The doctor wasn't going to budge, though.

Inevitably, the day came for the final trip in an ambulance; it was a month or so after her 89th birthday. That year she had broken with her strict tradition of having a party; she just didn't have the health to entertain her usual crowd. This time I didn't notice the young paramedic's driving; I was too focused on my dear friend who was bundled up on a stretcher, clearly in pain and lots of discomfort. As we drove away from 37A, Joan gave a royal wave from her prone position. I think she knew she would never see her beloved flat again. She didn't say so, it was just one of those things that we both knew intuitively. I choked back tears and did my best to emulate her courage as I held her hand and tried to babble about nothing to distract her.

She was admitted to University College Hospital on the Euston Road. They put her in the five-storey block that overlooks north London in the distance. To be honest I can't remember which floor she was on; it's all a bit of blur. Once she'd been settled in her bed, I sat with her for a while, and she motioned for me to come close and give her a hug. My so-far supressed tears got the better of me; my brave face was banished, my determined smile exhausted. It seems odd now I look back to that time in May 2010. Joan was comforting me when it should have been the other way round. She stroked my hair as you would stroke a child's and kept telling me that it was all right. I visited her every day, bringing in ridiculous trash magazines which she would never read. On one occasion Joan wanted to show me the cancerous tumour that was eating her alive. If I am honest, I recoiled at first, but it was a small thing to do for her, to acknowledge her killer and make peace with it.

The tumour was at the top of her left breast; it was the size of a peach. She wanted me to touch it. I complied. The lump was red and angry looking. It was very hot to the touch and easy to see as it appeared to be trying to burst through her mottled skin. This wicked growth seemed to have an independence. The memory of meeting it as it killed my dearest friend haunts me still.

Ian and my girls, Tallulah and Aurora, would join me for some of the visits to support me both emotionally and physically. Annoyingly, my own health problems got in the way. I was having a nasty lupus flare at the time. I wasn't very well, with swollen and painful joints, so my mobility was impaired. On 30 May, we arrived as usual but were intercepted by a young nurse with a face that spoke a thousand words. All she said was, 'I'm so sorry, you've just missed her; she passed a few minutes ago.'

They were words I had dreaded but I was also prepared to hear them. We were allowed to see her; she'd been moved to a side room the week before. She was still warm when I kissed her forehead. The ward team were brilliant; they just left us there for as long as we needed to say our farewells. I think we were all in shock.

As we left, I was overcome with a powerful desire to go to Primrose Hill, one of Joan's favourite places. Now I am not one to have mystical moments – I tend to be grounded in fact – but what occurred next was so strange that I couldn't be sure there wasn't something spiritual going on.

I got to the top of the hill with difficulty as my joints were on fire. Once there I looked out at the hospital in the distance where Joan lay dead and cried for the first time. The air had been quite still but suddenly I found myself in the embrace of a warm, kind breeze that was heavily laden with spring blossom. Pink and white petals enveloped me as though I was at the heart of a benign mini-tornado. The colourful cloud enveloped me, ran up my body and then dispersed in all directions, exploding gently onto the landscape around me.

Aurora said later it was as though the breeze had hugged me before sending the blossom in a hundred different directions. Other people on the hill stopped and watched, puzzled by the strange force of nature.

Am I mad to think that was Joan's spirit, free at last from her worn-out body? Saying one final farewell to me? Yes, probably – but that is what it felt like. I found it a great comfort: just the possibility that, somehow, she had cheated death, found a way to dodge around it in her time-honoured way of refusing to accept what fate had in store for her. Her indomitable nature was ready for the next instalment of her remarkable story.

EPILOGUE

When I began writing this book, I had no idea what I was getting myself embroiled in. The process has taken me on a hugely personal journey filled with joy and pain. I have learnt so much more about my dear friend Joan Rhodes. I will always love her, but after studying her closely for a year or so I know her so much better. I accepted she had her own versions of 'the truth' but some of the revelations were a bit of a shock. Foolishly, I felt hurt that she hadn't been honest with me about being married. Then again, I know if burying the truth was what it took to survive, then so be it.

After she died, the task of sorting through the mountain of 'stuff' in her flat was bravely undertaken by John and Pam. I recall Joan worrying endlessly about what would happen to her lifetime of treasures. She would be comforted to know that they are now spread far and wide among family, friends and fans. In the year after her death, the cunning Cash plan was to invite those who were close to Joan to visit 37A and take what they wanted. There are pieces from the flat scattered about my house, so she is never far from my thoughts. I even have a little box of her ashes. I treasure my piece of Joan. One of my prize possessions is the green sequined costume that I had mended by the team at *The Repair Shop* programme on BBC1 in 2019. As I said at the start of this book, I was surprised and delighted to find that the very young production team on the show were so curious about Joan. They would sit me down outside the barn where they filmed and ask questions about this powerful female role model. They would even get angry that she had been forgotten and it was that display of emotion that persuaded me it was time to get her inspirational story out there.

I always thought of Joan as a woman of great fortitude but having studied her so closely I now see her in a broader context. She was a role model, especially for other women. I see her as a 'functional feminist'. She wasn't radical; she didn't go on marches or 'burn her bra'. She was the living, breathing epitome of a woman dealing with life as she wished, in a world controlled by men. If you had to pin down her politics, they would be liberal, despite her brief flirtation with communism in the 1940s.

As I researched and wrote this book, I regularly visited the internet. To my joy I discovered Joan is still very much with us. All these years after her death in 2010, you can find thousands of pages, images and videos of her online and their number is growing all the time. She would have loved the idea of being immortal. Even in death, Joan has the ability to captivate her audience, young and old alike.

Joan would want to have the last word, not that I think she will ever be silenced. I believe her magic will continue to inspire and captivate future generations. If anyone asked her age Joan used to say she was somewhere 'between eighty and death'. She managed to sum herself up brilliantly in this poem, which she would merrily recite to anyone within earshot:

I shall wear green and gold when I am old
And paint my nails and colour my hair
And not notice when people stare.
I might (just might) take to drink
And chat to myself as I totter along;
Sing rude words to any old song.
If I get thin I'll pad my hips,
Wear blue eye shadow and bright red lips.

270

When you get old people don't notice you,
I'll push in at the head of any old queue.
There's a lot of things I know I'll miss;
Come on young man – give me a kiss;
Ah – men!
Amen

SELECT BIBLIOGRAPHY

Baker, Richard Anthony, *Old Time Variety* (Barnsley: Pen & Sword, 2011)

Crisp, Quentin, *The Naked Civil Servant* (London: Jonathan Cape, 1968)

Knight, Laura, *The Magic of a Line* (London: William Kimber, 1965)

Orwell, George, *Down and Out in Paris and London* (London: Victor Gollancz, 1933)

Rhodes, Joan, *Coming on Strong* (Darlington: Serendipity, 2007)

Sargaison, E. Miriam, *Growing Old in Common Lodgings* (London: The Nuffield Provincial Hospitals Trust, 1954)

Wise, Jeff, *Extreme Fear: The Science of Your Mind in Danger* (New York: Palgrave Macmillan, 2010)

ILLUSTRATION CREDITS

All images are courtesy of Joan Rhodes's personal archive unless otherwise stated. Though every care has been taken to trace or contact all copyright holders, the publishers would be pleased to rectify at the earliest opportunity any errors or omissions brought to their attention.

INDEX